Re-Thinking Eating Disor

In *Re-Thinking Eating Disorders: Language, Emotion, and the Brain*, Barbara Pearlman integrates ideas from psychoanalysis, developmental psychology and cutting-edge neuroscience to produce a model of neural emotional processing which may underpin the development of an eating disorder.

Based on clinical observations over 30 years, this book explores how state change from symbolic to concrete thinking may be a key event that precedes an eating disorder episode. The book introduces this theory, and offers clinicians working with these challenging clients an entirely new model for treatment: internal language enhancement therapy (ILET). This easily teachable therapy is explored throughout the book with case studies and detailed descriptions of therapeutic techniques.

Re-Thinking Eating Disorders will appeal to students and practitioners working with this clinical group who are seeking an up-to-date and integrative approach to therapy.

Barbara Pearlman, Consultant Clinical Psychologist, is an Honorary Fellow at the Centre for Clinical Neuropsychology Research, University of Exeter. In 2010, she was awarded a PhD for her theoretical work on the neurobiology of how emotions and language are processed in eating disorders, which led to the creation of a new treatment: internal language enhancement therapy.

Re-Thinking Eating Disorders

Language, Emotion, and the Brain

Barbara Pearlman

Routledge
Taylor & Francis Group

LONDON AND NEW YORK

First published 2018
by Routledge
2 Park Square, Milton Park, Abingdon, Oxon OX14 4RN

and by Routledge
711 Third Avenue, New York, NY 10017

Routledge is an imprint of the Taylor & Francis Group, an informa business

© 2019 Barbara Pearlman

British Library Cataloguing-in-Publication Data
A catalogue record for this book is available from the British Library

Library of Congress Cataloging-in-Publication Data
A catalog record for this book has been requested

ISBN: 978-1-138-61650-9 (hbk)
ISBN: 978-1-78220-540-1 (pbk)
ISBN: 978-0-42946-083-8 (ebk)

Typeset in Times
by Apex CoVantage, LLC

MIX
Paper from
responsible sources
FSC FSC™ C013985

Printed in the United Kingdom
by Henry Ling Limited

I would like to dedicate this book to the memory of Professor Phil Richardson, who was my first supervisor at Essex University and the Tavistock Clinic. I remain grateful to him for creating an atmosphere of academic curiosity that allowed me to follow my interests and instinct into the field of neuroscience and for his belief in, and support of, my ideas.

Contents

Acknowledgements

This book could not have come into existence without the generous support and help of many people, but none more so than my husband Joe, who has steadfastly believed in my work and the importance of taking it forward, not to mention offering his research skills to locate papers and to come to my rescue when my computing skills gave up the ghost. From critical appraisal to cups of tea and sympathy when the going got tough, his loving support and contribution knew no bounds.

I would like to thank Professor Bob Hinshelwood for his invaluable and erudite supervision of the thesis upon which this book is based, and whose superego presence was perfectly calibrated. I would also like to thank Professor Rachel Bryant-Waugh for her support and generous help in the sections dealing with eating disorders. I thank Dr Ian Frampton for his enthusiastic championing of my ideas and his crucial supervision of the neuroscientific content of my work, also Dr Catherine Loveday for her very clear-minded and helpful guidance on how to approach the design of clinical trials and to Heather Schuman for her invaluable advice on the detail of cognitive–behavioural therapy (CBT) treatment. A particular thank you goes to Mrs Mary Twyman for her excellent and much appreciated psychoanalytic supervision of my work and her steadfast support.

Foreword

I met Barbara in 2010 in London, an introduction facilitated by a mutual colleague who was eager to put us in touch with each other. His excitement about making this contact was soon borne out, as it has been my pleasure and great fortune to have become acquainted with her. I have come to respect, admire and thoroughly enjoy all aspects of my relationship with Barbara, personally and professionally. Her keen clinical insights have provided stimulus for shaping new ways of dealing with the daunting challenges of providing treatment for patients with eating disorders. Barbara has been an invited speaker at the Eating Disorders, Compulsions and Addictions Service, which I direct, at The William Alanson White Institute for Psychotherapy and Psychoanalysis in New York City for many years now, and she has contributed a chapter to one of my edited books. She also happens to be a great cook and raconteur.

In writing this book, Barbara Pearlman has made a brilliant contribution to research and theory on patients with eating disorders or disordered eating by integrating her clinical thinking with the realm of neuroscience. With distinct creativity, she explores how the brain processes emotional information, using data on developmental neuropsychology and on the use and development of language, and she has proposed that by following the logic of how the brain functions, we can increase the power of therapy to effect change. Her clinical acumen focuses on identifying the exact triggers that provoke state changes from symbolic thinking to concrete thinking. These state changes ultimately lead to concrete, maladaptive attempts to contain overwhelming affects via eating disorder symptoms (i.e., restriction of food, bulimia, or disordered eating). Keeping the idea of detoxifying anxiety at the forefront, Pearlman recognises the need to accurately pinpoint the thought that allows the patient and therapist to work on the specific moment that leads to the patient's inability to regulate her emotional state. With this in mind, she emphasises how the pragmatics of interaction with the patient transforms and processes emotional data in a system she calls internal language enhancement therapy (ILET).

We live in a world obsessed with physical appearance, cultural imperatives to be thin, and few, if any, can escape the social pressure to conform to an unrealistic ideal of beauty. Understanding that nature and nurture go hand in hand, the delineations between the biological, psychological and social forces underlying eating disorders are no longer viable distinctions. Culture and experience infuse the genetic vulnerabilities of patients with eating issues and each patient brings her own rich constellation of biology, psychology and culture into treatment, as does each therapist. Culture, as one piece of the biopsychosocial perfect storm in which the patient with an eating disorder finds herself, offers many forms of visual objectification, providing such patients much opportunity to feel scrutinised, objectified, and cut off from their bodies. When bodies are experienced as aesthetic wrappers of the self while simultaneously being thought of as central signifiers of identity, one is more vulnerable to expressing pain via an eating disorder. Add to the mix the psychosocial and gendered pressures interwoven in complex developmental and attachment histories and it is in these contexts that more physiologically informed difficulties in self- and affect regulation emerge, all of which play a role in how eating is felt and symbolised. Effective treatment requires a balance between these myriad factors, as no part of our bodies or our brains can fully function in the absence of crucial links which constitute embodied self-awareness and the capacity for connection to others.

However, no matter what theoretical orientation or school of thought one ascribes to, most clinicians would agree that when one is in the throes of an eating disorder, one is trapped in the prison of one's own mind–body or body–mind. It is through the linking of symptoms with their emotional and interpersonal meanings within the context of the therapy relationship that allows patients with eating disorders to find their way out.

Pearlman admirably joins the ranks of contemporary thinkers at the forefront of exploring this dilemma for patients with eating disorders. Her focus is on the mind's ability to change its thinking and access the meaning of what makes one anxious. And her particular innovation is on how specific attention to linguistic shifts creates symbolic access and capacity – and with that, more adaptive coping – than the eating disorder patient's familiar need to 'do' something to the body to manage intense affective distress. The body may speak clearly to those who know how to listen, but words themselves can have both concrete and symbolic resonances that can shift in meaning in the mind of the patient. The mind–body split or body–mind split (meaning top down organisation, mind to body, or bottom up organisation, body to mind) is always being enacted in the eating disorder patient's life.

How do we therapists get 'in' between these patients' relationship to food or behaviours? This is often a central challenge in this work. On a gut level, a patient suffering from an eating disorder does not feel that others can imagine what she feels on the inside. Therefore, part of the treatment is helping the patient make the connection between 'not-body' as a temporary body state and something that is 'not-me' as a self-state. Body states are non-verbal experiences and may not be known through the mind with words. The body 'articulates' the unspoken. But Pearlman suggests we can do more with the words of our patients with eating disorders by recognising that the brain either processes emotions symbolically or concretely and helping patients to identify their shift from the symbolic realm to the realm of the concrete, and with it into the body based language of symptoms.

And here is where our schools of thought differ and then converge. As an inter-personal/relational psychoanalyst, I am trained to look for the blind spots, the gaps in the continuity and coherence of a patient's life story, looking for how symptoms and bodies say what is not being said with words, while also holding that both words and the reliability of relationships with others have lost their meaning. Pearlman emphasises the concreteness of the words and examines the change of state in the brain from symbolic to concrete in language itself. In stopping the action in the brain, has she found a way in? She illuminates for us a possible way to further our understanding of how affect regulation disrupts our thinking, and she offers clinical strategies to directly address these symbolic-to-concrete shifts with our eating disorder patients. We are only at the beginning of appreciating the neurobiological underpinnings of eating disorders, but Pearlman has made use of that data in the realm of language processing to offer us all new ways 'in'.

Eating disorders confront clinicians with profound difficulties as they attempt to help their patients make links between mind and body, self and other, and the concrete and symbolic. In melding research and theory from disparate theoretical disciplines of neuroscience, psychoanalysis, developmental psychology and linguistics, Pearlman's approach is groundbreaking and timely. This is a comprehensive book, not to be read in one sitting but to be savoured and digested in its richness many times over.

Jean Petrucelli, PhD
Director and Co-Founder of the Eating Disorders,
Compulsions & Addictions Service at
The William Alanson White Institute, New York City
Editor of Body-States: Interpersonal/Relational
Perspectives on the Treatment of Eating Disorders

Preface

The problem in the field of eating disorders is that there has been little interest in researching and creating a unified theory to explain the development of this group of illnesses. Research has mainly involved trying to discover 'what works' to reduce the symptoms. As a result, the most widely used 'gold standard' cognitive–behavioural therapy (CBT) approach to treatment is based on a 'maintenance model' that, at best, produces only a 50% 'cure' rate.

The approaches to treatment that are informed by psychoanalytic theory lack good outcome research, and the neuroscientific approach to basic research and treatment is in its infancy. Surprisingly, the well accepted neuroscientific research into emotional processing has not previously been applied to eating disorder research.

This book aims to fill the theoretical gap by integrating and underpinning psychoanalytic ideas, the development of the self and attachment, with well accepted research into alexithymia, right hemisphere function, and emotional processing from the field of neuroscience.

Clinical observation over 30 years has led to the creation of the hypothesis that state change from symbolic thinking to a concrete mode of thought precedes an eating disorder episode. This state change, it is hypothesised, is a consequence of the patient being challenged to process complex and negative emotional information that overwhelms the fragile emotional processing functions. This results in the lack of access to the symbolic emotional processing pathway and the utilisation of the corporeal pathway with access only to concrete language.

The result is a proposal for a discontinuous model of neural emotional processing which, it is suggested, underpins the pathology of eating disorders.

Based on this research, a novel treatment approach has been formulated.

Chapter 1

Introduction

This book came into being as a result of the concluding statement of a meeting, on the past and future of psychoanalysis, held at the Freud Museum. It was declared that the future of psychoanalysis lay in neuroscience but that it would take at least two generations for a workable therapy to come about. This is a sad reflection of how the different disciplines in mental health tend to keep to their separate worlds, as in the field of eating disorders one such therapy has been created.

Those of us who trained in the 1970s and 1980s often worked in hospitals and departments that encouraged cross-fertilisation between the organic, behavioural and psychoanalytic schools of thought. Creative therapies were integral to our work and I hope I have continued this proud tradition in creating a new way of thinking about and treating eating disorders: internal language enhancement therapy (ILET). ILET introduces a new way of approaching eating disorders. It is based on a discontinuous model of neural emotional processing in eating disorders', which more simply means that the brain *either* processes emotions symbolically *or* concretely – but not both at the same time. In other words, we can either think about the meaning of things and what they may represent and test our understanding against reality and what we have learnt in the past, or we only understand the literal meaning. For example, 'I have too much on my plate this week and I cannot manage to do it all' is symbolic; we are not talking about actual plates but feeling overwhelmed by our schedule. 'There is too much food on my plate and I cannot eat it' is its concrete counterpart; here we are talking about food and plates and stomachs and what we cannot take in to our bodies – the symbolism has been lost.

This new therapy is based on understanding how the brain processes emotional information, developmental neuropsychology and the development of language. It employs theory and techniques from psychoanalysis integrated with those of CBT. This approach to treating eating disorders is an amalgam of widely differing theoretical approaches that generally remain separate. But, as in many fields of study, when we synthesise information from different disciplines, it can result in innovative ways of understanding and approaching a problem.

I have spent my professional life as a clinical psychologist and group psychotherapist working in the field of eating disorders and, in 2010, was awarded a

PhD for theoretical research into how the brain processes emotion, from both the neurobiological and psychoanalytic perspectives, in eating disorders. For 30 years I have had the privilege of working with my patients, who have kindly given me their trust and permission to use their stories to illustrate this new approach as well as agreeing to participate in clinical research.

The neurobiology of the brain is very complex and is a field that is growing but is, as yet, still imperfectly known. However, there is increasing interest in, and research into, the neurobiological underpinnings of eating disorders (Frank, 2015; Garrett et al., 2014; Juarascio, et al. 2015; McAdams & Smith, 2015) and we now understand that neurological deficits have a direct effect on the expression of eating disorder symptoms (Fotopoulou & Tsakiris, 2017; Martinez et al., 2014). This book suggests that our understanding of these deficits should influence how treatments are designed. The neural networks described in ILET are necessarily schematic but are based on well accepted research in emotional processing.

It has been a widely held truism that 'an eating disorder can never be cured' – a statement that has caused much distress to eating disorder sufferers. This work describes a new way of thinking about and treating eating disorders that presents the possibility of allowing an eating disorder to fade.

As we go through the book, patients will be denominated as she, as this reflects the 10:1 ratio of female to male sufferers – although this may be an underestimation of the prevalence of male sufferers. There is no theoretical reason why male sufferers would not respond to the ILET treatment in a similar way to their female counterparts. There is an increase in the diagnosis of eating disorders among young men and that is of concern. This can be partially explained by an increasing awareness by clinicians who hold the possibility of seeing eating disorders in young men, as well as this group feeling more able to come forward for help. To add to this, high profile men have bravely spoken in public about their struggles, making it easier to admit to having an eating disorder.

Anyone who has experienced an eating disorder or who has cared for someone who has one, be that a family member or a professional, knows how confusing and difficult this illness is to understand and treat. Something happens to communication – instead of the usual 'chit-chat' of family life, a preoccupation with food and bodies becomes overwhelming for the sufferer and dominates her thoughts. Why is this?

When families are faced with a daughter (or, less frequently, a son) who becomes consumed in this way, by definition the young person is unable to think about the many other areas of her life. This creates the situation where parents may naturally step into this void and begin to think for their child, as they might have done when she was younger. This then can create a vicious circle where the young person relinquishes more and more control over the real decisions she needs to make and face, while the parents are increasingly drawn in to compensate. This may look as if the eating disorder patient is trying to control the only thing left that she can – her body – and the parents are trying to control and dominate their child. But if we consider that the eating disorder sufferer just cannot think meaningfully about her emotional life and is caught up in the concrete world of the body, then her parents' actions can be understood as desperately trying to help their child by taking over the thinking tasks and are then frightened to let go lest their child cannot maintain her health and even her life. That is why it is usual to support the family as well as the sufferer, as the anxiety in the family needs to be lessened to allow a supportive space for the sufferer to grow into.

It can also happen that when there is an ill member of the family, the family system coheres around the ill member to protect her. This might mean that difficulties at the parental level may have to be put aside and that may, in turn, add to the pressures within the family. Siblings may feel unable to put their needs forward when parents are preoccupied with the ill child, so it may be that when the eating disorder sufferer gets well, it may open up other difficulties in the family that were overshadowed by the illness. This is true of other illnesses that create anxiety within the family system but in eating disorders communication itself, within the patient herself and between family members, becomes the focus.

Targeting language and communication – internal language enhancement therapy

Internal language enhancement therapy (ILET) aims to do what its title says: to restore the richness of internal language (how we think) from (under stress conditions) concrete thinking, that is, thoughts that contain only the literal meaning of language (e.g., 'sweet' meaning containing sugar as against being kind (see example of ILET below)) to symbolic function, defined as thoughts that contain metaphoric and ironic meaning, are tested against reality, previous experience and awareness of the consequences of actions. This increases the ability of eating disorder sufferers to understand and think about the meaning of their feelings, with the aim of promoting an independent, well functioning mind, a strong sense of self and the ability to understand their own and others' emotional responses. As a result, parents can begin to see and trust that their child is able to think clearly and make decisions that reflect reality, rather than being preoccupied with body and food issues. All being well, this allows the parental 'compensatory thinking' to become redundant and for family life to return to normal, although perhaps with some changes in order to create a space for the growing mind and needs of their child.

The eating disorder conundrum

There is a conundrum at the heart of eating disorders. Therapists, from both psychodynamic and cognitive–behavioural orientations, may well have experienced sitting in a room trying to talk with their patient about the patient's emotional world, while their patient can only think and talk about her food intake or the shape of her body. One way of thinking about this problem is that the patient and therapist are each talking a different language. The therapist is speaking in what we might describe as 'symbolic language', where possibly we might talk about emotional relationships or what it means to the patient to starve, binge or purge, or try to persuade the patient of the reality of her situation. The patient, on the other hand, is talking in 'concrete' language, where she speaks only of how fat her body feels or her refusal to eat fats and carbohydrates, and is preoccupied with calorie intake. Faced with this conundrum, depending on the therapeutic orientation of the therapist, one option may be to employ a more cognitive–behavioural approach and join the patient in talking about food intake or how to help her see her body in a more positive light. However, this approach does not target the underlying 'concrete speak' problem. If the patient is treated with a psychodynamic approach, then a different problem may arise. If the patient is in the 'concrete mode', then speaking about emotions and underlying conflicts raises anxiety because she is unable to understand the emotional meaning of what is being said and we know that increased anxiety leads to increased symptoms (Bruch, 1982; Schmidt et al., 2012). Sometimes the therapist might employ a combination of an insightful (psychodynamic) and cognitive–behavioural approach as different phases of treatment, or possibly to separate the medical, behavioural and emotional approaches within a team of professionals. However, this presupposes that the patient is able to join the therapists in their symbolic and metaphoric understanding of the inner world, which is mostly not the case. Recently, there has been an emphasis on just allowing patients with severe anorexia to talk about everyday non-threatening topics. It has been noted that symptoms do not get exacerbated but the therapy is no more successful than other treatments that anyway have a poor success rate (Schmidt et al., 2012).

Recent research tells us that these approaches, while to varying degrees helpful, do not offer a consistently satisfactory treatment outcome, not even reaching 50%, including enhanced cognitive–behavioural therapy (CBT-E) (Fairburn & Cooper, 2011; Fairburn et al., 2013, 2015). This is not surprising, given the communication problems.

However, with the increased understanding offered by advances in neurobiological research allied with insights offered by psychoanalytic theory and the development of language function, we are now able to think about eating disorders in a very different way. By translating the patient's concrete understanding of her inner world into symbolic language, it allows the patient access to the meaning behind her concrete thoughts and behaviour. When we know what we think about what we feel, we become more rounded as a personality and in doing so discover a sense of who we are. With apologies to Descartes – 'I think (about what I feel), therefore I am'. When left untreated, eating disorder sufferers, particularly those suffering from anorexia, may come to rely solely on their intellects and expend their energy in keeping out all emotional information that becomes increasingly anxiety provoking. The behavioural counterpart of 'keeping everything out' of extreme starvation is, unfortunately, all too familiar. We know that people who suffer from anorexia are really quite poor at interoception – that is, making sense of messages from the internal organs or state of how the body is feeling (Fotopoulou & Tsakiris, 2017). As a consequence, they rely more on the outside world, or exteroception, as a means to try to make judgements ɛ world. Thus, we see sufferers choosing to eat what others eat rather than on the feeling of being full or, for that matter, being able to accept the fe being full. This is discussed further when we come to talk about maternal ‚‚‚‚uc-cupation and its importance.

The average time before referral to specialist services is around two years; this is generally accepted to be too long (Schmidt et al., 2012) as, left untreated, eating disorders usually worsen (why this happens is discussed in Chapter 5). Adolescence, of course, is an 'at risk' time when we are constantly reacting to, and learning about, our world and our feelings. If an eating disorder begins, we may find ourselves trapped in, or flipping in and out of, concrete thinking that serves to raise our anxiety, and which, in turn, leads to more concrete thinking. When we are unable to decipher meaning, the work of learning about feelings in adolescence is interrupted and we stop learning. This makes the world a much more confusing place. Ideally, the moment parents notice a change in how their child is talking about eating and food is the time to find help, as it is much easier to treat an eating disorder early, before it becomes entrenched.

The theoretically integrative ILET approach allows us to gain a deeper and broader understanding of the workings of the mind in eating disorders or any of the illnesses that exhibit a change of state from being able to think about what makes us anxious to a state where we are compelled to act in place of thought; for example, binge drinking, cutting, or other forms of self-harm.

While this book is necessarily quite heavy on research and is perhaps most useful for fellow professionals, I hope that anyone with an interest in eating disorders will be able to gain insight into this distressing and confusing illness and emerge less distressed and less confused in the process. Once we understand that eating disorder pathology is linked with tipping in and out of, or getting stuck in, the 'concrete' state, then we can see that our patients are neither 'mad' nor 'bad' for exhibiting seemingly incomprehensible thoughts about food and bodies but that they are just firing on the 'wrong' pathway. This shared understanding can reduce the very real anxiety of both sufferers and their families.

The development of an eating disorder

In order to develop an eating disorder, quite a lot of boxes need to be ticked. As the brain develops it creates pathways to process complex emotional reactions from both the internal and external world. This enables us to think about what we feel and make sense of it. Sometimes these pathways are fragile and, especially during adolescence, can become overwhelmed by anxiety so that access to symbolic functions is denied. This can result in our minds being hijacked by an emotional response that is un-thought out (Arnsten, 2005; Aron et al., 2007; LeDoux, 1996, 2003).

As we progress through the book, I will attempt to explain in detail what happens to the brain in eating disorders and its implications for treatment. For now, we can understand it as the mind changing from the ability to think about the meaning of what is making us anxious and what we might need to understand or do as a response to feeling discomfort in our bodies to the need to do something to our bodies to solve what is now felt as a body 'problem'.

This emotional hijacking fundamentally affects how we think. From having access to full language functions, including metaphoric and symbolic understanding of meaning (frontal lobe functions, which also include reality testing, planning, memory in language and creativity), there is a sudden shift to a state where we can only think concretely – where words lose their symbolic, metaphoric and ironic meanings. An example of this is the sentence, 'I am fed up to the back teeth and cannot stomach any more'. If we are able to access our symbolic functions, we understand it to mean that we have had enough of a situation. But if we are in a concrete state, then we understand it to mean that 'I have eaten too much food and I cannot bear it in my stomach' – literally meaning that the food cannot be kept in the stomach, as opposed to the metaphor meaning that an idea or situation cannot be tolerated.

Understanding this change of state from symbolic to concrete language, following an emotionally stressful event or thought, helps us make sense of why someone suffering from an eating disorder thinks the way she does about her body shape or the number of calories in certain foods. With the change of state, the meaning of the stressful event disappears but, and this is the important factor, the sufferers do not know that they have changed state. From their point of view, they are only acting on what their brains tell them is the problem and they do not question something that feels as if it is the only and right thing to do. For example, if a good friend has just rejected you, creating distress and anxiety, then, if you remain symbolic, the meaning might be that you feel loss, upset and despair and that your life may feel empty. But when you change to the concrete state, the symbolic meaning has disappeared and the only thought available is that you feel literally empty inside your body. When you are trapped in the concrete paradigm, if your body experiences a feeling of emptiness, the logical action is to fill it up, that is, to binge. Or, instead of feeling uncomfortable emotions such as anger, envy or sadness in the symbolic state, in the concrete state you might feel that your insides are full of disgusting 'stuff' and you will attempt to get rid of it by starving or purging or possibly excessive activity.

An Example of ILET

As an example of this way of approaching and understanding this change in language I shall describe a vignette of a patient, whom I shall call Katherine, a woman in her late forties who had three children and an emotionally needy, but critical, partner. She had suffered from bulimia from her teenage years and had made several attempts at getting treatment. The results of these treatments were periods of absence of the symptoms but which later returned. She did not have a clear understanding of what an eating disorder was or what caused it or why she binged when she did. In an ILET session, Katherine was asked to report on her most recent binge. She described that while driving her children around, running errands for them, she noticed that she had to fill up her car with petrol. She went to a petrol station and bought her preferred binge foods and subsequently binged and vomited. In line with the ILET protocol, the therapist enquired about the exact last thought before she became preoccupied with needing to buy her binge food. Katherine replied that it was just as she noticed that the car was low on petrol and she reported the last thought as 'I'm running on empty – I must fill up'. She recognised that her thinking had changed, as suddenly all she could think about was getting to the garage that sold her usual binge food, even though it was some way away and there was another garage nearby. She made her way to the more distant garage and filled up on petrol – and her favourite sweet things. She waited until she returned home to binge and vomit. She could give no explanation of why she had binged and vomited.

She was then closely questioned about what exactly was happening at the precise moment just prior to the sudden preoccupation with buying binge food. It turned out that her children were being dismissive of her and ungrateful at the precise moment she noticed the low petrol gauge. It transpired that all weekend she had been busy taking care of her family and she felt taken for granted and criticised, no matter what she did. Employing the ILET protocol, Katherine and the therapist set about resymbolising the concrete thought 'I am running on empty – I must fill up'. Rather than the petrol tank needing filling up, it was understood to mean that she continuously empties herself by caring for others while feeling uncared for herself and that she needed someone to be 'sweet' to her. Her internal language had become concrete, that in 'wanting someone to be "sweet" to her', 'sweet' had lost its symbolic meaning of 'caring for', leaving her craving the literal 'sweet' sugary binge food to 'fill her up on sweetness'. This approach enabled us to touch a deep need to be understood and cared for. Katherine found the children's demands and her partner's criticisms emotionally overwhelming especially as she was trying so hard to be a good mother and wife while holding normal ambivalent feelings towards them. Her less than optimal early care had left her with poor emotional processing skills; difficulty dealing with her anxieties and her ability to understand the minds of others was compromised. These mixed and confusing emotions had provoked the change of state from symbolic function to the concrete state and her language became impoverished. By the adding of symbolic and metaphoric meaning to her concrete understanding and experience, she was able to better understand her own emotional needs.

There was no interpretation or behavioural suggestions, just the translation of her own thoughts from incomprehensible concrete 'filling up the petrol tank and somehow bingeing' to a metaphorical understanding of meaning – 'I feel emptied by constantly trying to please my family and I just want them to be sweet to me'. This promoted insight into her feelings of distress in a manageable way. Once we had identified her deep and upsetting need for care, we were able to look at how her past childhood solution of caring for others in place of, and in the hope of, being cared for, was not working in the present. This allowed us to think about how she now puts herself in the role of helper and carer in the expectation of being shown gratitude and love but gives little opportunity for others to show their care for her. Her strong feelings of anger, sadness and resentment clashed with her need to be the perfect mother and wife to repair a very difficult and neglectful childhood. She was able to acknowledge these ambivalent feelings and how she might serve others less and create opportunities for them to care for her. Thus, from this one episode of bingeing, we were able to reach deep insights by adding metaphor and symbol. The insights were generated by the patient herself in a very non-threatening way and allowed her to think about her childhood and its lasting effect on how she relates to her family and friends. In neurological terms, recognising this way of relating and the distress it generated reduced the anxiety and subsequently (in ILET terms) the brain would be less likely to add danger signals to the complex and overwhelming emotional information. Schore (2012) would describe this process as 'broadening the affective window'. More examples of the ILET technique can be found in Chapters 6 and 8.

Adolescence and eating disorders

Many people point to the role of the external world in causing eating disorders or at least encouraging them (Lake et al., 2000). Some may suggest that young girls and women are influenced by the celebration of thinness (Blowers et al., 2003). Fashion magazines and thin models are said to play a role in creating an eating disorder. It could be that if the potential sufferer is (as suggested above) unable to attend to her inner emotional experiences and is more externally focused, then copying 'thin models' might be a factor. However, this work does not support this simplistic view – the reality is far more complex. Models will not cause an eating disorder in a healthy girl but could influence a girl who is already vulnerable. Thus, it is good practice to showcase healthy weight models but it is not sufficient to blame the development of an eating disorder on the existence of thin fashion models. If society in general considers fat disgusting (itself a concrete shorthand to describe people who are seen by others as showing on their bodies that they lack control over their appetite, are believed to be greedy or literally taking up too much space), and views a woman's body as representative of her many attributes, then it is understandable that women can be affected by these judgements. However, for an eating disorder to develop, the young person needs to be neurologically vulnerable.

It certainly behoves wider society to encourage young women and girls to develop a strong sense of who they are and to be respected for what they can achieve, not objectified or seen as less valuable. They should feel able to express their views – which is, in itself, a protective factor against developing an eating disorder. We also need to reduce the anxiety-provoking double messages that we give to young women – we expect them to be both equal in school and the workplace and to remain stereotypically feminine; to both hold the responsibility for men's sexual behaviour and yet strive to be attractive to men; to be both mothers who put their children first and to hold down jobs and careers and be breadwinners. We need to create a milieu that discourages a 'body' culture so that vulnerable young women and men are not reinforced in their 'concreteness' but are encouraged to develop their symbolic minds so that they can understand the meaning behind society's symbols rather than get trapped in the 'concrete' world. This is especially important during adolescence when, along with the concomitant hormonal changes and the paring down of redundant neural connections in the frontal lobes in preparation for the adult brain, the brain is most vulnerable to emotional hijacking. For our own safety and survival as adults, we need to accurately judge the external world with an independent mind. We cannot afford to be like children who rely on the minds of others.

During this period of synaptic pruning and rewiring, teenagers' ability to understand their emotional world and realistically assess the environment deteriorates (Blakemore & Mills, 2014). This process mimics the paring down of connections in the brain that happen around the age of 2–3 years. Connections that are needed during infancy give way to those required for latency (between 4–5 years and the beginning of puberty) and they, in turn, give way over a period of up to ten years to those needed to develop the adult brain (the adult brain settles down somewhere between 23 and 25 years). In the case of the 2-year-old and the teenager it is the same process, of being confronted with reality in the face of unattainable desires, that matures the frontal lobes and promotes maturity.

I think that we are all familiar with the teenager who refuses to wear a warm, but possibly 'un-cool', coat on a freezing day. Of course, they then learn that ignoring reality leaves them very cold indeed. Frontal function (reality testing and planning) increases with experience and the adult brain is promoted. During adolescence we tend to see concrete body thinking on occasions, but the majority of teenagers will pass through this phase without developing an eating disorder and eventually choose to wear warm clothing when appropriate.

An eating disorder can arise if the naturally turbulent time of adolescence is overlaid on an already poor ability to attenuate anxiety (self-soothe) (Oskis et al., 2012), the teenager has a fragile sense of self (not really knowing her own mind) (Seeley et al., 2007), has possibly experienced an insecure attachment (in her early life) (Micali et al., 2016; Taylor, 2000), has an impaired theory of mind (difficulty understanding how other people think) (Cardi et al., 2015; Russell et al., 2009), has a rather low ability to process emotions (not easily able to understand and make sense of her own or other people's emotions) and a poorer than average ability to comprehend figurative language (less able to understand the meaning of metaphoric and ironic language) (Amanzio et al., 2008). Adolescence is, in any case, a high-risk time due to the demands of separation from relying on parents and individuation (defining their own personality), the requirement to negotiate peer group relationships and pressures as well as the need for teenagers to prove themselves academically and get ready to enter the world of adult pressures of work and relationships (including sexual) (Ambwani et al., 2016). For this 'at-risk' group, much of the complexity of the emotional world would be very difficult for them to fully understand if they are less able to understand language that is both complex and contains metaphoric–ironic–figurative meaning.

Those young people who go on to have an eating disorder and who are very vulnerable to switching into the concrete mode are particularly susceptible to seeing fat as disgusting (this is discussed later in relation to insula function in the brain) and their bodies needing to be perfect, in order to make them feel they have value. But there is a world of difference between wanting to follow fashion and going a 'bit body' during adolescence and the consistent use of the body in place of the mind. In this situation, there is no limit to the amount of weight needing to be lost, no matter how dangerous or ugly the result. The symbolic mind and symbolic internal language has shut down and the inside of the mind has become the inside of the stomach. If there is something 'bad' inside, then it has to be 'got rid of' and 'fat' is the concrete shorthand for what is seen as unacceptable. We might say that eating disorders have nothing to do with either food or bodies.

It might be useful here to mention the difference between men and women in presentation of an eating disorder. For men, body image concerns are different from those of young women. Rather than a drive for thinness, men are more likely to want to gain weight than lose it as they strive for a lean and muscular build (Strother et al., 2012). During a binge, men report feeling less out of control than women do. Another interesting difference is that, for men, anger can trigger a binge episode, while research indicates that women seem to binge in an attempt to restrain their sense of anger (Weltzin, 2005). While there is a different pattern to male eating disorders, the underlying neural processes are the same: young men, too, define their sense of self and develop an adult brain. They, too, come to terms with the notion of their gender identity and, just as young girls, under the sway of adolescence changes in how the brain processes emotions, young men can get trapped in the concrete state and look to their bodies to try to negotiate the demands of their emotional worlds.

An intriguing observation about members of this patient group is that they present, emotionally, as roughly the age they were when they first began to develop their eating disorder. It is as if their emotional development and learning about their inner world, or that of other people, stopped in its tracks when they were no longer able to process their emotions in language and instead dealt with unmanageable emotional stimuli that had got 'stuck' in the body by finding concrete body solutions. On becoming well, patients frequently describe themselves as feeling older and more mature – and indeed their brains no longer resemble that of an adolescent, but of an adult who has an ability to test reality and plan for the future.

Melding the different disciplines

As mentioned above, there seems to have developed a level of separation between disciplines in the approach to thinking about, and in the treatment of, eating disorders, with cognitive–behavioural approaches, insight-orientated therapies and organic psychiatry mostly keeping their own company. In my opinion, this exclusivity weakens each of the approaches, as all of these disciplines are underpinned by, and benefit from, being informed by neurobiological understanding of the developing brain; how certain environmental pressures and experiences can influence the manner in which neurological pathways are created and subsequently function. Creating this work was rather like trying to play three-dimensional chess with all the disparate elements at times having minds of their own and attempting to scuttle back to their original homes. It is necessarily quite dense as I meld them. I hope you will bear with me on the journey that culminates in describing a new way of thinking about eating disorders and the new treatment, internal language enhancement therapy (ILET) which has been designed to link the collapse of symbolic thought (following an overwhelming, complex, negative emotional trigger) to its concrete counterpart and subsequently to resymbolise the material. This is in order to promote the use of the symbolic language neural pathway and to allow patients' overused concrete/body neural pathway to degrade, thus diminishing acted out symptoms and promoting the maturation of the frontal lobes, or what can be described as a move from the adolescent to the adult brain.

ILET

Integral to the ILET approach is the stance taken by the therapist, whose job it is to lead the patient to discover the workings of her own mind. Nothing is 'put into' patients other than their own rediscovered thoughts. The therapist takes an open-minded, curious stance alongside the patient, rather than the role of someone who knows the patient's 'real' thoughts and proffers 'insights', which this patient group generally finds anxiety provoking, owing to their compromised symbolic language capacity.

Psycho-education is at the core of the approach. Merely knowing how the brain has developed in response to internal and external factors has seemed to dramatically reduce anxiety in the consulting room and may be a large factor in anxiety reduction for this patient group. Patients have reported that the theory not only 'feels' right to them and describes their inner world, but also makes intellectual and experiential sense.

Initially, in ILET, content is secondary to mental processing. The therapist shows the patient how to access her own thoughts. This allows for the development of a good therapeutic alliance, rather than the therapeutic situation possibly exacerbating symptoms should the patient be faced with incomprehensible complex emotional interpretation that increases anxiety and triggers the concrete state. Alternatively, if both patient and therapist concentrate on food and the body, then there is a lost opportunity to understand meaning.

It is my experience that many patients can come out of quite lengthy psychoanalytic treatments with their eating disorder relatively intact. Their discourse seems insightful but is often understood at an intellectual level. Conversely, patients who have been treated by CBT have usually significantly reduced their eating disorder behaviour but this is not underpinned by self-knowledge or an increased sense of a well functioning sense of self. The effect is one of brittleness, and the techniques that they have learned may keep the symptoms at bay for a while but under pressure these seem to reassert themselves. A fuller description of, and outcome measures for, other treatments commonly used in treating eating disorders can be found in Appendix B.

Either the symbolic or concrete pathway

An important understanding presented in this book is that the neurobiology of emotional processing is a discontinuous model or, in other words, an either/or model. We process emotions through either the symbolic or the concrete pathway. It is not a continuum where we can be both a bit concrete and a bit symbolic. Traditional treatments assume that patients can be both symbolic and concrete at the same time and be 'moved along' a continuum towards greater insight by the application of treatment (Treasure & Schmidt, 2013). By viewing eating disorder pathology as the result of failure to engage the symbolic processing pathway (which includes reality testing, future planning, memory in language, creativity and, most importantly, symbolic language), it leaves the patient with no option but to process emotions concretely by feeling them to be located in the body. These two pathways represent two discrete states. When in the concrete state, there is no access to symbolic thought and, therefore, the concrete thoughts are accepted as representing reality. Later in the book, the concept of a change between states is explored further and underpinned with research in the fields of the developmental neurobiology of emotional processing, attachment, alexithymia and language processing.

Change of state

As has been mentioned above, at the heart of this new approach is the notion that, for eating disorder patients under certain pressures, there is a change of state from symbolic to concrete functioning and that it is this dramatic loss of symbolic function that creates the behaviours known as an eating disorder, including the patient's rationale for the behaviours. As we go through the book, it is explained how the brains/minds of eating disorder sufferers develop a fragility/brittleness in symbolic emotional processing, predisposing them to becoming overwhelmed by complex and negative emotional stimuli which creates enormous anxiety. One result of this overwhelming is the engagement of the 'fight-or-flight' pathway that is corporeal (body) and concrete in nature. In support of this hypothesised state change is the evidence that the eating disorder population is poor at attenuating anxiety (self-soothing), is alexithymic (has difficulty putting words to feelings), may have experienced an insecure attachment to their primary carer, be poor at understanding complex metaphor and irony, and is, thus, compromised in the ability to comprehend a complex emotional environment.

Early development

The early environment is crucial in the development of the brain and how we relate to others and ourselves. The parent (or carer) and the child need to learn to fit to one another – an undemanding child might not make her needs known or may be very unsettled and does not respond to the care given. A very anxious, unsupported, stressed, depressed or exhausted mother might not be consistently able to follow her child's communications or to soothe her child's anxieties if she herself is very anxious. The child needs to experience a secure attachment, where the care given is consistent, loving and boundaried, but again this might not be possible for myriad reasons. If these needs are met, then the child will be in a good position to be able to attenuate or bring down her own anxiety (self-soothe), develop a strong sense of self (know what she thinks and feels and recognise the boundary between herself and others) and become emotionally literate in order to understand what she and other people are meaning. Sometimes the interplay between these elements may be less than optimal and may result in compromised neurological functioning that, it is argued, can contribute to the development of an eating disorder. A major underlying factor seems to be raised anxiety that is unable to be attenuated (reduced/self-soothed).

As a result of these characteristics, people who go on to express an eating disorder may also be poor at comprehending emotionally complex language, in particular, complex metaphor and irony. It is this deficit, it is suggested, that may trigger a danger signal that overwhelms the symbolic emotional processing pathway and creates the conditions for triggering the neural pathway that only allows for a concrete understanding of the internal and external world. It is suggested that this collapse in symbolic function is instantaneous and that the person with an eating disorder is unaware of the change in state and, thus, continues to accept her thoughts as valid. In this circumstance, it is perfectly understandable that, in order to reduce the cognitive dissonance (the difference between reality and feelings about the body), she would rationalise why her concrete understanding is valid (my body feels too big and uncomfortable, I know that I am under my healthy weight but I should be comfortable in my body and being comfortable is very important to me and so I should eat less). As mentioned above, when there is a lack of making sense of bodily feelings (poor interoception) the task of making sense of emotional responses becomes that much harder.

The two pathways

While this approach relies heavily on developmental and neurobiological research and ideas, it must be stated that when it talks about neurological processes, the descriptions are necessarily schematic. The processes are highly complex and the explanations offered refer to general processes. As mentioned above, the description of how the brain processes emotions follows the work of Banich (1995a,b), LeDoux (1996), Arnsten and Li (2005), Aron et al. (2007), and Fossati (2012).

In general terms there are two pathways available for emotional processing: one where the information from the amygdala has been perused by the symbolic left hemisphere language functions, and one where it has not. A broader and deeper discussion of how brains develop and function can be found in Siegel (1999). His description of the amygdala and the limbic system sets the scene for later discussions.

He describes the amygdala as: 'A cluster of neurons that serves as a receiving and sending station between input from the outer world and emotional response'. Along with the related areas of orbitofrontal cortex and anterior cingulate, which are sensitive to social interactions, the amydala coordinates perceptions with memory and behaviour. These circuits are widely connected to other regions that directly influence the functioning of the brain as a whole system.

The limbic system registers incoming information about the state of the body and activates and regulates the autonomic nervous system. The limbic system appraisal of stimuli and brain/body emotional arousal can be described as the basis of social processing. What is important to note is that this process, and the significance assigned to stimuli, is a non-conscious process and, depending on its actions, influences whether conscious awareness is involved.

The result of these processes is that, in response to fear, the brain is non-consciously wired to create a 'self-fulfilling prophecy'. As Siegel writes: 'If the amygdala is excessively sensitive and fires off a "Danger!" signal, it will automatically alter ongoing perceptions to appear to the individual as threatening'". He posits that this 'self-fulfilling prophecy' may be the basis for phobias and other anxiety disorders. It is certainly useful in understanding the situation that eating disorder sufferers find themselves in – in that when complex emotions are perceived as a danger signal, then access to symbolic frontal functions is denied.

Emotional processing begins with information gathered by the amygdala, which we can think of as the 'receiving station' (see Figure 1.1). The amygdala's role is to pick up any danger signal before we become consciously aware of it. While the 'fight-or-flight' pathway is usually only employed on occasion, all stimuli are routinely examined for potential risk by the 'fast and dirty' amygdala route. The memory systems triggered by this crude pattern matching are not encoded in language (Frampton & Rose, 2013).

The amygdala route plays a vitally important role in keeping us safe, as it is not very useful if we are admiring a lion's pelt rather than running away for our lives. The information gathered by the amygdala is sent up to the insula, which functions like a 'junction box', where there are two possibilities. Either (1), if a danger signal is attached, it alerts the insula to close access to the symbolic functions and the information does not get 'thought about'. The information returns to the amygdala, which then triggers the anxiety 'fight-or-flight' response experienced in the body (see Figure 1.1). Craig (2009, 2011) suggests this can become

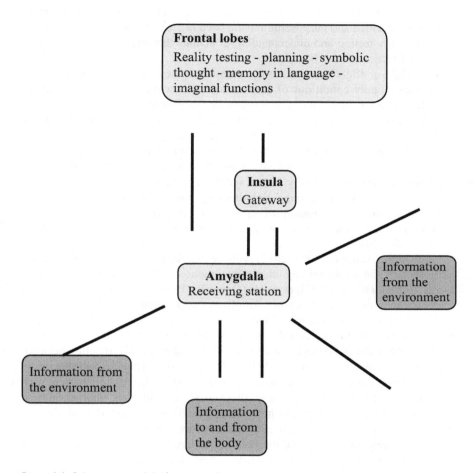

Figure 1.1 Schematic model of emotional processing

self-fulfilling in that the incoming information can be repeatedly pattern-matched for danger and returned to the amygdala, never having access to symbolic language. Or (2), if there is no danger signal, the insula 'sends up', or engages the frontal lobe functions. This route employs symbolic and frontal function (involved in extracting information from the environment (reality testing) and planning functions) and allows for a more abstract representational understanding of the emotional environment in context, having, as it does, access to memory in language. In this case, emotions can be thought about and are attached to past experience. This then creates a store of learned experiences that can be pressed into service when assessing similar future events. The symbolic pathway, after engaging the language, reality, memory and planning functions, finally returns the information to the amygdala, the area of the brain that also involves bodily action. In this case, actions are decided and purposeful, having been related to past experiences in the light of reality testing and understanding of actions that have consequences (the planning functions).

The 'fight-or-flight' concrete/body pathway is designed to be brought into service only under conditions of extreme stress; however, in the case of eating disorders, overwhelming emotional stressors can play the same role as physical danger signals and repeatedly lead to un-thought-out 'fight-or-flight' responses. In this case, there is no understanding of the meaning of the emotional experience, only a body response. In this extremely anxious emotional state there is some access to language, but it is of a concrete nature allied to the body experience, has limited or no ability to use symbol and metaphor and, thus, no way of 'thinking' one's way through a challenging emotional problem. Once these two routes used for emotional processing are reconnected, there is a new sense of integrated consciousness and an experience of a sense of self (Seeley et al., 2007; Uddin, 2015).

Nunn and co-authors (2008, 2012) propose that the clinical picture of anorexia nervosa may be explained by insula dysfunction. Their model derives from Damasio's somatic marker hypothesis (Damasio, 1994) where there is a fast and unconscious processing of sensory data from the periphery and internal organs. The processing of these feeling states requires intact functioning of the insular cortex for what Damasio terms the mapping of the emotional state of the body.

Nunn and colleagues suggest that there may be damage or dysfunction between the structures that are parsimoniously linked by the insula. They describe the insula as having the dominant role in balancing those parts of the brain that deal with adaptation to the environment and as also being responsible for internal homeostasis. Their hypothesis is that in individuals who have predisposing risk factors, there may be sub-optimal functioning of networks that pass through the insular cortex, and they have described the possible underlying neurological milieu that might result in eating disorder pathology. They give weight to the environment that might trigger, in general terms, eating disorder pathology, but do not account for why specific triggers result in eating disorder behaviours or, in other words, what it is that specifically triggers the 'fight-or-flight' concrete pathway – what it is that might cause the insula to malfunction.

This book suggests that particular kinds of stressors, embedded in lack of comprehension of complex emotional language stimuli, may trigger the insula to label the incoming information from the amygdala as a threat, and that lack of access to higher function input results in a change in language function from symbolic to concrete thought and speech.

It is suggested that the more frequently the concrete/body pathway is engaged, the more easily it will be triggered. (Hebb's axiom, 1949 – neurons that fire together wire together.) This is possibly for two reasons. First, there will be reduced opportunity to process the emotional field, no opportunity to learn about how to solve or come to terms with complex emotional material, and, thus, no attenuation of anxiety.

Second, when a pathway is triggered it becomes reinforced, making it more likely to be employed than a less frequently used pathway which, over time, will deteriorate, much in the way that concert pianists will find playing more difficult when they have not practised.

When one's mind can only conceive of the world in concrete form, where the body takes the place of the mind, then understanding the emotional and symbolic world is rather like deciding to eat this book to gain an understanding of it rather than to take in the contents with one's mind. Eating disorder sufferers are occasionally or, perhaps in some cases, constantly trapped in such a world, where the only thing that makes sense is to manipulate the body or to measure it in calories. This is the result of the network that manages 'conflicts' between the emotion-based (basal) processing system and the representation-based (frontal) system not being able to integrate information coming from both these sources (Arnsten & Li, 2005; Aron, et al., 2007, 2016; Banich, 1995a,b).

For this group, intellectual functions can remain intact and, if of considerable power, can be favoured over emotional processing as a style of coping when the healthy/optimal emotional processing is unavailable. However, by definition, an intellectual understanding is unable to guide an emotional response and cannot reflect the feeling state.

The ILET method was developed to address communication as being the problem, not the body symptoms or the consumption of food, important though these are and may need to be dealt with as a priority in some cases. When the patient is enabled to understand her own mind, that is, what her thoughts and feelings are about the multitude of emotional stimuli that are bombarding her, she can begin the process of creating and defining a unified sense of self. The role of the therapist in this approach is designed to mimic that of the early mother–child relationship; translating and ameliorating the wordless primitive feeling state of the baby's world into shared language that allows for symbolic understanding and eventually communication with the other. It directly addresses poor interoception by finding the trigger to the change of state and naming what was, up until then, wordless bodily reactions.

It is important that any treatment addresses the problem with consumption of food. The ILET approach is that the patient learns to identify her uncomfortable bodily reactions as a change in pathway (and thus state) and not as a body reality. For example, a patient we shall call Amy had a very low body mass index (BMI) of 14 (a healthy BMI is between 19 and 25) and experienced very little resistance to eating or gaining weight. The first 19 pounds gained did not impinge on her particularly negatively; conversely, she was proud of her achievement. She understood that 'when I go a bit body' (by which she meant that when she experienced a bodily reaction of feeling too fat or needing to control the calories that she intended to take in), she had to search for the missed emotional trigger and activate the symbolic pathway by trying to understand the fine-grained symbolic and metaphoric meaning of it. In her case, she was able to identify the trigger to state change as being the precise moment when she realised that her boyfriend had lied to her. By thinking about the meaning of the lie (why he might have lied) and her response to it, she was eventually able to make a very difficult decision.

The mentalisation therapy approach to treatment

An allied treatment approach to the ILET method is described in the work of Skarderud (2007). He has based his work on that of Fonagy & Bateman (1997), who have concentrated on mentalisation therapy for borderline patients. While Skarderud acknowledges that eating disorder patients are not to be identified entirely with this group, he suggests that, similarly to borderline patients, the attachment process in eating disorder patients may be impaired.

A major difference between Skarderud's work and the ILET approach is that the mentalisation approach is not designed specifically to target the cause of why a patient might be tipped into the concrete state. This approach does not seek a specific trigger or conceptualise the problem as a change in state (as a response to emotional stimuli that overwhelm the emotional processing capacity of the brain).

While the ILET treatment approach has a lot in common with mentalisation theory, if not technique, its aim might fairly be described as more focused and briefer, and it rests on the premise that it is possible to accurately and rapidly resymbolise eating disorder patients by directly engaging and reinforcing the symbolic emotional processing pathway. When this pathway is engaged, it is hypothesised, it prevents the triggering of the concrete body pathway. This should lead to a rapid reduction in illness behaviour and allow the patient access to the contents of her mind, which might be described as the building blocks of the sense of self.

Affect regulation theory and approach to treatment

Allan Schore's work on affect regulation theory (Schore, 2012) describes what happens when there is a dysregulation of affects under stress. His work focuses on how the right and left hemispheres interact and describes their particular properties when emotional hijacking takes place, or, in Shore's understanding, the patient is either hyper-dysregulated or hypo-dysregulated. Schore concentrates on how these states of dysregulation need to be understood and handled in the psychoanalytic psychotherapy consulting room. Shore's aim, by being highly attuned to his patients, is to broaden their tolerance for emotional stress. Again, while there is much in common in the theoretical and empirical research between ILET and Schore's new paradigm of psychotherapy, ILET homes in on the change in internal access to language from a symbolic to a concrete understanding and vice versa. Schore's highly esteemed work is intended to increase the effectiveness of medium- to long-term psychotherapy but does not necessarily address the dilemma of patients for whom psychotherapy *per se* is too daunting, incomprehensible, and anxiety provoking.

ILET theory suggests that taking an active stance in psycho-education and building a good therapeutic alliance by adopting the position of curious enquiry replicates closely the attuned mother who is mirroring and helping the child to understand how she experiences the world. It is suggested that the key to the process is accuracy. If the patient feels heard and understood, then she is less anxious and can feel attached to the process. ILET specifically and meticulously finds the event that triggers an emotion system response and works with the patient to resymbolise and explore all aspects of the material. It is suggested that one benefit of this approach is that the treatment is relatively brief (around twenty sessions) but its intention is to home in on the active element of the disorder.

Outline of chapters

In order to make the complicated research sections of the book more comprehensible, I shall summarise the main points of each chapter before presenting the research. Each chapter builds on the research presented in the previous one until, in Chapter 4, the evidence from each discipline is integrated into a new understanding of the development of an eating disorder.

Those readers wishing to gain an overview of up-to-date eating disorder research will find it in the bibliography.

Chapter 2 begins with a description of the psychoanalytic understanding of eating disorders and covers the important work of Hilda Bruch, a psychoanalyst who specialised in the theorising and treatment of eating disorders and whose ideas are still very relevant and, interestingly, are increasingly supported by our growing body of neurological research.

This is followed by a description of the development of the 'self' (a psychoanalytic concept) that is quite different to the term 'self-esteem' or how one rates oneself as a person. I am not sure of the value of the concept of 'self-esteem' other than as a measure of how one feels about oneself. The development of the self encompasses the notion of a growing self-agency or a sense of knowing who we are, what we think, and of being a separate, active individual in the world. This section then considers the work of psychoanalysts Klein and Bion and their emphasis on the role of the mother to mediate the child's anxieties, and what may happen if this process becomes distorted.

The next section traces the neurological underpinnings of eating disorders, and describes cognitive deficits that seem to be present in this patient group. It also looks at how they perform on cognitive testing, which fills out the growing picture of fragility in neurological functioning. The research on alexithymia (the inability to put feelings into words) is looked at in relationship to eating disorders. The aim of Chapter 2 is to add to the picture of how some brain functions may become fragile when processing emotion. It describes our present understanding of how emotion is processed and the relationships between alexithymia and brain function and alexithymia and emotional intelligence. We then look at the neurobiological evidence underpinning emotional processing and the role of the right hemisphere in verbal communication. There is a concentration on the role the mother plays in the development of language, or proto-language, particularly how her right hemisphere communicates with her baby's right hemisphere. This leads on to a discussion about metaphorical thinking in relationship to eating disorders. Finally, there is a description of the psychoanalytic approach to the concept of symbolisation.

Chapter 3 describes a conceptual gap in the understanding of eating disorders and a lack of a unified theory. As the field of eating disorders has grown, there has never been a shared understanding of how an eating disorder comes into being. As a result, treatments have been developed in an *ad hoc* way and research has focused on trying to find out what works. The most used and researched treatment, CBT, is a very practical treatment that concentrates on removal of symptoms and does not concern itself with causation of the illness. There follows a discussion of the contributions and limitations of CBT and psychoanalytic ideas and treatment, which, as mentioned above, also presents difficulties in practice. Finally, given that the current categorisation of eating disorders leads to research bias, it is argued that a new model and treatment approach is needed.

Chapter 4 introduces a new conceptual framework to understand the development of symbolisation from a developmental neuropsychoanalytic perspective in the genesis of an eating disorder. It then discusses the importance of maternal preoccupation in relation to right-hemisphere function. The development of the self is then related to how emotions are processed and their relationship to underlying neurological structures.

There is then a discussion of the role of right-hemisphere function, and in particular right-hemisphere language functions, related to the triggering of one or the other of the two pathways available for emotional processing. This leads to a discussion and synthesis of interhemispheric communication, low emotional intelligence, alexithymia, dreaming and the imaginal functions.

Finally, the work of Segal on the psychoanalytic theory of symbol formation is integrated with neuroscientific research evidence on emotional processing. This is followed by a discussion of the development of symbolic thinking and its implications for the treatment of eating disorders.

Chapter 5 introduces a new model of the mind for eating disorders and subsequent diagnosis of an eating disorder. It also introduces a new model of mental functioning in eating disorders based on the notion of change of state from symbolic to concrete mental function. Finally, it introduces the idea of a complex emotional trigger overwhelming the symbolic language functions that can provoke state change.

There follows a discussion of the processing of literal vs figurative language; how metaphor processing and concrete thought in schizophrenia might be related, as well as how metaphor comprehension and Alzheimer's disease might inform the understanding of concrete thought in eating disorders.

This chapter goes on to discuss the nature and content of what constitutes a complex psychological trigger and how the figurative/metaphoric content of this emotional trigger degrades as it collapses towards concrete functioning. There is an examination of this critical moment of state change using examples of trigger material.

Chapter 6 describes a new treatment, ILET, that draws on the model of mental functioning in eating disorders outlined above. Patients treated with ILET have generously given permission for this material to be used and, of course, all identifying information has been changed.

ILET works to reverse the state shift from being trapped in the concrete world of the body and encourages the opening up of the pathway to symbolic thought. The patient is taught how to work back to discover the stressful trigger by employing some techniques from CBT and dream analysis borrowed from psychoanalytic theory and practice. When this trigger has been discovered, the patient is shown how to open up the symbolic pathway with the judicious use of metaphoric and symbolic language. This allows her to think about the meaning of the stressful event or thought and to find real world solutions to real life problems. According to ILET theory an eating disorder only appears when we are in the concrete paradigm, so the more often the symbolic pathway is used the stronger it gets (Hebb, 1949) and, as a consequence, the eating disorder symptoms fade.

The process of how ILET is delivered is closely tied to the realities of how the brain functions. A very important aspect of the treatment is to teach the patients about how their brains work and what happens when they have an eating disorder episode. By doing so, this reduces the patients' anxiety. They come to understand that they are neither 'mad' nor 'bad' but it is just the emotional short-circuiting of their ability to think symbolically while their anxiety levels are high. Also, they are informed that the more frequently they 'go concrete', the more easily that pathway will be triggered in future and, vice versa, the more they can trigger the symbolic pathway, the more it is strengthened and then favoured over the concrete/body pathway. Most importantly, the therapist takes the position of helping the patients to discover, or rediscover, the contents of their own minds in order to become able to think symbolically about their emotions. It is only later in the therapy that the therapist might offer an insightful comment. To do so too early may well feel incomprehensible and intrusive, thus raising anxiety and, as we know, that may well lead to the expression of more symptoms.

Chapter 7 compares and contrasts the most widely used treatment for eating disorders, CBT, with ILET in terms of delivery and theoretical underpinning. This is in order to explore and illuminate the stubborn inability of CBT to pass the 50% 'cure' rate in eating disorders and to put forward possible solutions to the theoretical gaps described in the CBT method which, it is suggested, are resolved by the ILET approach to the treatment of eating disorders.

Chapter 8 follows 'Emily's' treatment with ILET in order to give readers a better understanding of how ILET is delivered and illuminates some potential difficulties that can arise. She has very generously given her permission for our work together to be published. Along with other patients described, all identifying information has been changed.

Chapter 9 provides an overview of the topics covered in the book.

The neurobiological contribution to understanding the development of an eating disorder

Neurobiological underpinnings of eating disorders

Summary

Chapter 2 begins by discussing the neurobiological contribution to understanding the development of an eating disorder. This section traces the neurological underpinnings of eating disorders, and describes cognitive deficits that seem to be present in this patient group. It also looks at how they perform on cognitive testing, which fills out the growing picture of fragility in neurological functioning. The research on alexithymia (the inability to put feelings into words) is looked at in relationship to eating disorders.

The aim of this chapter is to illuminate how some brain functions may become fragile when processing emotion, referencing the literature in the fields of developmental neuropsychology, neuropsychoanalysis and psychoanalytic thought. It describes our present understanding of how emotion is processed and the relationships between alexithymia (an inability to put our feelings into language) and brain function, and alexithymia and emotional intelligence (how we understand our own and others' emotional responses). We then look at the neurobiological evidence underpinning emotional processing and the role of the right hemisphere in verbal communication. There is a concentration on the role the mother plays in the development of language, or proto-language, particularly how her right hemisphere communicates with her baby's right hemisphere. This leads on to a discussion about metaphorical thinking in relationship to eating disorders. Finally, there is a description of the psychoanalytic approach to the concept of symbolisation.

We begin the chapter by setting the scene for how babies develop a sense of an inner world in the context of relationships. The latest neuropsychoanalytic research introduces the concept that to develop a sense of who we are, we not only need a close and appropriately responsive early experience but there is also a need for the actual proximity of two bodies as well as an attuned interaction. This should allow for the healthy development of interoception (the communication from the body to the brain, giving accurate information on the state of the body). When this basic requirement goes well, it aids the development of mentalisation (or how we think about and represent the world to ourselves). This comes under the heading of developing a 'sense of self'.

The literature cited in this chapter supports the hypothesis that eating disorder adolescents who exhibit cognitive deficits, particularly in executive function and attention, have difficulty in developing constructive problem-solving strategies in social interactions. There is also research support for the difficulties they express in executive functioning possibly leading to faulty interpretation of others' body language that, in turn, will have an effect on understanding the minds of others and one's own mind.

The literature suggests emotional intelligence is low in eating disorder patients and, taken in conjunction with the research on early attachment, suggests it, too, is impaired in this population. Perceptual and information-processing capacity is primed by affective information as it enters the perceptual system and it is the perception and appraisal of non-verbal emotional behaviours, including bodily sensations evoked by emotional arousal, facial expressions, tone of voice and gestures displayed by others, that is particularly difficult for eating disorder patients.

The research discussed in the section on emotional processing lies at the heart of this work. It describes the 'discontinuous model of neural emotional processing' that, it is suggested, accounts for the thinking and behaviours that make up a diagnosis of an eating disorder. The case is thus being built up that, as a consequence of unsuccessful maternal preoccupation leading to insecure attachment, alexithymia and low emotional intelligence, eating disorder patients are at risk of 'emotional hijacking', leading to the triggering of the 'fight-or-flight' pathway with no access to higher executive function.

The section on the neurobiological evidence that describes the processing of emotions underpins the concepts of emotional intelligence and alexithymia and extends the evidence for there being neurological deficits in eating disorder sufferers. The picture that emerges in eating disorders is that when care fails to regulate excessive levels of low emotional arousal and/or excessive levels of high negative emotional arousal, there can be permanent alterations in the development of the orbitofrontal cortex, which, in turn, affects activity in the amygdala and other sub-cortical structures. The consequences of this damage, it is suggested, are lack of efficient interhemispheric transmission and impaired interhemispheric transmission required for reflective function, poor understanding of non-verbal cues and metaphorical or figurative meanings of words, and of comprehension of alternative meanings. In eating disorders these functions are sub-optimal and may account for some of the difficulties seen in this group. The literature relating alexithymia to a reduction in rapid eye movement (REM) during dreaming phases of sleep supports the hypothesis that consolidation, integration and processing of affect-laden information is likely to be reduced in eating disorder patients. Divergent thinking and the use of fantasy in order to find novel solutions to emotionally taxing problems, it is suggested, is also lowered in the eating disorder group, along with the capacity for symbolic and imaginal thinking. There is growing evidence that the emotional care given to infants influences not only the development of cognitive and representational abilities but also the maturation of areas of the brain involved in emotional awareness and emotion regulation, creating the conditions for the expression of an eating disorder.

A section then traces the research into right hemisphere function and extends the work on maternal preoccupation and alexithymia. It supplies the neurological evidence for the right hemisphere containing an integrated map of the body state, insula function and memories of past emotional experiences, especially negative ones. When this information is unable to be integrated with higher cortical functions, it is suggested, the conditions are created for bodily feelings to be misrepresented – a situation that obtains in eating disorders where an affect is unable to be differentiated from a bodily feeling.

Complex negative emotional social discourse and metaphor are difficult for eating disorder subjects to process and reflects possible right hemisphere dysfunction. Since it is now accepted that the right hemisphere and left hemisphere together, rather than the left hemisphere alone, are responsible for language comprehension and production, the sub-optimal functioning of the right hemisphere possibly affects how language is understood and processed in the eating disorder population. A complex emotional field may act as a trigger to activate the 'fight-or-flight' 'concrete' emotional processing pathway leading to eating disorder behaviour.

The result of recent work into how language is processed in the brain has been to open up research into right hemisphere and left hemisphere processing of language meaning by focusing on the complexity of the stimulus. The coarse coding model of language processing supplies the fine-grained explanation of why eating disorder patients may have difficulty in comprehending novel, metaphoric and ironic emotional communications and how this may trigger the concrete fight-or-flight emotional processing pathway.

This neurological approach to the understanding of how the internal and external environment influences the development of the brain links the early developmental environment with how the internal and external world is experienced in later life and how language is processed and understood.

Understanding the nuances of complex communications that contain unusual metaphoric or ironic content requires second-order theory of mind. Thus, damage in theory of mind subsequent to faulty maternal preoccupation, it is suggested, detrimentally affects the ability to process emotional information that has multiple possible meanings, in particular complex metaphor and irony.

Eating disorder patients present with certain features: alexithymia; insecure attachments; low emotional intelligence; poor theory of mind; impaired right hemisphere function; possible REM deficits; reduced ability to use fantasy; a tendency to concrete rather than symbolic thought processes; and difficulty in processing complex metaphor and irony. This leaves them vulnerable – when exposed to a complex novel emotional field – to processing emotions via the concrete body pathway in response to complex negative emotional challenges.

The previous areas covered by the literature review – neurological involvement in eating disorders, the process of symbolisation and the origins of, and the ability to use, rich metaphorical language – begin to set the scene for a deeper and more fine-grained understanding of the difficulties faced by this patient group.

This is followed by a section that concentrates on the work of Hilda Bruch, the psychoanalyst who pioneered working with eating disorder patients and who specialised in the theorising and treatment of eating disorders, whose ideas are still very relevant and, interestingly, are increasingly supported by our growing body of neurological research.

She identified the distortion or paucity of a sense of self as lying at the heart of an eating disorder. The development of the self, it has been suggested, depends on successful early maternal preoccupation. However, in order for this to take place, both the mother and child must be able to take part. Either party may have deficits or distractions that prevent a successful outcome. She suggested that in eating disorders the mirroring and containing process breaks down, leading to the baby's inner world being poorly represented and to a disturbance in the development of symbolisation. She posited that eating disordered patients are impaired in their ability to self-reflect and distinguish between inner and outer reality, and there is an absence where the integrated self should be.

The work of Hilda Bruch leads on to considering the psychoanalytic contribution to the understanding of the development of symbolisation, which mirrors the recent neuroscientific research into brain development that ideally culminates in mature symbolic functioning. It considers the work of psychoanalysts Klein and Bion and their emphasis on the role of the mother to mediate the child's anxieties, and what may happen if this process becomes distorted. The neurobiological and the psychoanalytic approaches support and strengthen each other and allow for the introduction of mental content rather than just process. The psychoanalytic explanation of the primitive nature of concrete thinking helps us to put the work with eating disorder patients in its context, while the neuroscience perspective indicates how much weight should be put on the content.

The neurobiological contribution to understanding the development of an eating disorder

Neurobiological underpinnings of eating disorders

There is now an area of research into eating disorders that crosses the divide between so-called 'hard' and 'soft' science. Psychoanalysts have theorised that faulty attunement (Winnicott, 1960, 1967, 1971, 1975) leads to a deficit in the development of the self. Fonagy and Target (1996) have described in fine grain how this deficit will express itself, from the inability to self-soothe through to the inability to mentalise. Fotopoulou and Tsakiris (2017) have illuminated this process even further by proposing that 'embodied mentalisation' is the result of sensory and motor signals that are progressively integrated and become the foundations of the minimal self. They also propose that signals from other bodies that are physically close (think of a mother holding and feeding her child) become incorporated into the child's capacity for mentalisation. Because human babies are so dependent in early infancy, they suggest that there is a 'homeo-statically necessary' requirement for such close interactions, particularly in the development of interoception. They suggest that the very bodily foundations of the self and its beginnings in interoception develops within a close relationship with another person and that such experiences of physical closeness or, in their words, 'proximal intercorporeality' 'sculpt' the mentalisation process and, hence, the creation of the minimal self.

The neurological correlates of these observed phenomena are increasingly the subject of research, and there has been a growing body of literature in the field of neuropsychological functioning in eating disorders in the past two decades. Some of the results have been mixed but there has been a significant number that support the hypothesis that eating disorder adolescents may have underlying cognitive deficits (Mendlewicz et al., 2001; Szmukler et al., 1992; Witt et al., 1985). The areas that have been measured on standardised neuropsychological tests to exhibit deficits in executive functioning are: visual–spatial ability, divided and sustained attention, verbal functioning, learning and memory organisational deficits, tactile–perceptual deficits, psychomotor coordination deficiencies and non-verbal problem-solving difficulties. These deficits are not mutually exclusive and thus they may exacerbate the overall cognitive deficit. Some authors (Lauer et al., 1999; Szmukler et al., 1992) have suggested that the cognitive deficits found could be the consequence of starvation and may be reversed, but this is not a sufficient explanation for the cognitive deficits in bulimia nervosa, or why, even after re-feeding and weight gain, some cognitive functions do not improve.

Cognitive deficits in eating disorders

Lena and co-authors (2004), in a review of the literature on the role of cognitive deficits in the development of eating disorders, suggest that because symptoms are usually present 6–24 months before diagnosis is made, aetiological agents are active before symptoms appear. However, this may be a mistaken use of statistics, as it is very common for there to be a delay before the patient is diagnosed, owing to the secretive nature of the illness and family attempts either to address the problem themselves or, in many cases, deny the severity of the problem or that the problem exists at all. This statement should not be taken to mean that there are no pre-existing cognitive deficits, just that the time lag between appearance and diagnosis may have other explanations. Lena and colleagues (2004) suggest that

> when a specific group of cognitive deficits exist at a particular degree of severity they interfere with the development of self-esteem, assimilation of changes in body image during adolescence, identity formation, interpersonal relationships and autonomy, which in turn, may potentiate the development of an eating disorder.

These authors suggest that when specific cognitive deficits are present to a specific degree and in a specific combination, this may trigger a cascade of reactions, which could be an important variable in the development of the disease, alongside other risk and protective factors

There has been a good deal of research in recent years exploring the neuropsychological functioning of patients with eating disorders (Blanz et al., 1997; Ferraro et al., 1997; Gillberg et al., 1996; Grunwald et al., 2001; Heilbrun & Worobow, 1991; Rieger et al., 1998; Smeets & Kosslyn, 2001; Waller et al., 1996; Witt et al., 1985). These researchers have studied various psychosocial domains that, they suggest, underlie the relationship between neuropsychological deficits in certain cognitive areas and eating disorder development in children and adolescents. They also point to the importance of, and the need for, neuropsychological evaluations on initial assessment. Lask and co-authors (1997) and Lena (1987) demonstrate that individuals who are at high risk of developing anorexia nervosa exhibit a preoccupation with food and dieting, are often obsessively involved in athletic activities, exhibit perfectionist tendencies concerning school work and other activities, have a severely distorted body image, and have poor self-esteem. Nussbaum (1992) and Woodside (1995) suggest that this group tends to exhibit a high need for control over its environment and exhibits conflict regarding issues of identity.

Bulimia nervosa can be described as an attempt to control, avoid, or minimise the impact of disturbing feelings and impulses (Nussbaum, 1992; Steinberg & Shaw, 1997). This group of patients frequently indulges in impulsive behaviour and modes of thinking and they can be disorganised, narcissistic and suggestible in nature (DaCosta & Halmi, 1992; Lehoux et al., 2000; Steinberg & Shaw, 1997; Strasburger & Brown, 1998). In addition they may abuse drugs or alcohol or sex, self-mutilate and indulge in shoplifting (DaCosta & Halmi, 1992; Lledo & Waller, 2000; Shenker & Bunnell, 1992; Strasburger & Brown, 1998; Toner et al., 1987). These researchers suggest that the high rate of relapse may be due to only addressing the eating behaviour and not the underlying cognitive deficits.

Difficulties with executive functioning may lead to faulty interpretation of others' body language which, in turn, will have an effect on understanding the minds of others and one's own mind or, as some researchers call it, self-esteem, which is not a distinct or simple concept. High achieving adolescents may attempt to overcome cognitive drawbacks by becoming vigilant, or perfectionist, in their academic work. Faigel (1975), Hamsher et al. (1981) and Szmukler et al. (1992) have suggested that the greater the number of cognitive deficits, the poorer the prognosis following treatment.

Alexithymia and eating disorders

Alexithymia is the inability to recognise and describe emotions. The term was first coined by Sifneos (1973). It is thought that this problem reflects a deficit in the cognitive processing of emotions (Taylor, 2000). Corcos and co-authors (2000) have demonstrated that eating disorder patients have alexithymic tendencies.

There is support for the hypothesis that eating disorder adolescents who exhibit cognitive deficits, particularly in executive function and attention, have difficulty in developing constructive problem solving strategies in social interactions. Striegel-Moore (1993) has described the tasks of adolescence as developing a sense of self-government, the ability to take responsibility for one's self and others, and the ability to exhibit self-control over behaviour and affect and of changing the relationship with parents from one of dependency to one of mutuality. Nussbaum (1992) has described how problematic it is for eating disorder adolescents to achieve autonomy in the face of parental overprotection and concern and over-ambition for the child (Johnson et al., 1992; Lena, 1987). It is suggested by researchers in the neurological field that eating disorder behaviours are an attempt to wrench control over the confusing cognitive and, subsequently, emotional tasks of adolescence in a bid for self-control and autonomy (Nussbaum, 1992). Certainly vomiting and purging behaviours may be an attempt to decrease anxiety (DaCosta & Halmi, 1992; Heilbrun & Worobow, 1991; Thackwray et al., 1993).

When there is an inability to process and understand language-free, visual and non-verbal cues, there is difficulty in reading other people's body language. Thus, social interactions can be very challenging to the adolescent, resulting in misattributing or oversimplifying causes for others' behaviours (Little, 1993; Rourke et al., 1989). There may be a fall back on to earlier over-learned strategies that are narrow and may not be adaptable to novel social challenges. The Eating Disorder Inventory (EDI) measures interoceptive awareness – the ability to accurately recognise and identify self and others' emotions, an ability that is very poor in patients with anorexia. Without this ability, it is very difficult to create and maintain healthy relationships. The usual physical and emotional changes present adaptive challenges to all adolescents, but they are particularly challenging for young people with neuropsychological deficits.

Specific cognitive deficits may impair the ability to engage in realistic self-appraisal, to accurately assess stressful situations, and to formulate appropriate solutions to specific problems (Fox & Mahoney, 1998; Huntington & Bender, 1993). Killen and co-authors (1994) found symptomatic girls to be more physically mature than asymptomatic girls. He suggested that deficits in visual–spatial, attentional, and executive functioning domains result in the inability to assimilate physical changes. In Killen's study, the more mature girls were faced with the task of assimilating greater physical changes, and he suggested that because they were unable to do so, they exhibited more severe symptoms.

Steiger and colleagues (1999) found that, compared to normal controls, bulimia nervosa patients were hypersensitive to interpersonal experiences. They found that, after negative interactions, the patients were prone to greater self-criticisms that were followed by bingeing episodes. The case is thus put forward that bingeing is to be understood as a coping mechanism used to decrease negative affect produced by failed interpersonal encounters. Waller and co-authors (1996) found that bulimia nervosa is associated with 'an attentional bias toward ego threats that are self-directed, thus any negative social interaction may cause perceived threat of social isolation and rejection'. Heatherton and Baumeister (1991) suggest that this is then followed by cognitive-narrowing strategies that allow normally inhibited behaviours such as eating.

It has been suggested that there might be a causal overlap between bulimia nervosa and attention deficit hyperactivity disorder (ADHD) (Rapport, 1993) as both conditions exhibit impulsive behaviour that is sporadic and out of control. As with eating disorder subjects, ADHD subjects make more errors and take less time to consider alternative options before making their test selection (Rapport, 1993).

With the advent of neuroimaging techniques, evidence of brain alterations has been provided. Positron emission tomography (PET) scans show sulcal widening, ventricular dilatation and cortical atrophy in anorexic patients (Herholz, 1996; Katzman et al., 1997, 2001; Kingston et al., 1996; Krieg et al., 1989; Lankenau et al., 1985; Lask et al., 1997). Most of these changes ameliorate with weight gain (Herholz, 1996; Kingston et al., 1996; Krieg et al., 1989) but some abnormalities persist (Dolan et al., 1988; Katzman et al., 1997, 2001). However, the extent to which brain abnormalities found in eating disorder patients are associated with functional cognitive consequences remains unclear (Katzman et al., 2001; Kingston et al., 1996; Palazidou et al., 1990).

There are many factors in the environment, including heredity, birth injury, and exposure to toxic substances that can cause brain abnormalities; therefore, neuro-cognitive abnormalities in eating disorder patients may precede onset of the eating disorder (Palazidou et al., 1990). These researchers suggest that children between the ages of 9 and 14 who present with body image disturbances, fear of fat and restrictive eating patterns should be monitored and screened for both mild and severe cognitive impairments early in their assessment.

Testing cognitive abilities

When testing subjects with anorexia, Gillberg et al. (1996) found that they performed significantly poorer on block design and object assembly performance. In particular, they noted that there was a sub-sample of their subjects which was also diagnosed with autistic-type conditions and these scored lower on digit span arithmetic comprehension and coding, which is characteristic of autistic disorders. They also tended to become obsessed with details when attempting to solve tasks, and showed themselves unable to look at the bigger picture and think in a more abstract way. Bourke et al. (1985, 1992), Schmidt et al. (1993) and Mansour et al. (2016) have also reported this inability of symbolic functioning in patients with anorexia. They suggest that this difficulty may contribute to the development of an eating disorder in adolescents owing to faulty perception when they attempt to comprehend their environment. Nunn and co-authors (2008) suggest that neurobiological processes mediate between underlying neurobiological abnormalities and 'surface level' cognitive and behavioural symptoms of anorexia and bulimia nervosa.

Bulimic subjects exhibit more errors on neuropsychological tests of problem-solving strategies (Ferraro et al., 1997), impaired attention term memory, problems in forming abstract concepts, deficits in visu processing and difficulties in initiating an appropriate strategy in a fre task. Bulimic subjects also display a trade-off between speed and accuracy performing the Digit Modalities Test, indicating cognitive impulsivity (Fe .aro et al., 1997). Lena and colleagues (2004) suggest that chaotic or disordered eating patterns serve as a coping mechanism for adolescents who use them as a means to experience a sense of autonomy and internal control. Perfectionism, a well-documented trait in eating disorder sufferers, is an indication of a rigid strategy employed to maintain control (Lena, 1987; Nussbaum, 1992). They do not elaborate on what is being controlled but it might be suggested it is to ward off catastrophic feelings of lack of self-worth, as diminished self-esteem is correlated with the development of an eating disorder (Johnson et al., 1992; Striegel-Moore, 1993). Johnson and co-authors (1992) noted that a significant subgroup of their eating disorder patients had developed anorexia following a rejection by their peers. Lena and colleagues (2004) conclude that 'the presence of neuro-psychological difficulties may create unfavorable adolescent experiences that may result in diminished self-esteem, and in turn may result in faulty coping behaviors, such as dietrestricting or binging, to combat feelings of worthlessness'. However, this does not explain the choice of the body as the stage on which all these concerns are acted out.

Emotional processing, alexithymia and brain function

LeDoux (1996) described the brain mechanisms that underlie emotions and which explain the neuroanatomy and neurophysiology of emotional processing. Taylor and co-authors (1997) reviewed the workings of the emotional brain and neurobiological studies. They demonstrated that 'certain facets of the emotional intelligence construct correlate with functional activity in parts of the brain involved in the cognitive processing of emotions'. They also suggest that the development of cognitive functions and neural mechanisms that underlie and underpin emotional intelligence is related to, and influenced by, early attachment relationships. They also report on the relationship between emotional intelligence and alexithymia.

Salovey and Mayer (1990) defined the core capacities of personal intelligence as 'the ability to monitor one's own and others' feelings and emotions, to discriminate among them and to use this information to guide one's thinking and actions'. They describe the affect system as functioning in both a perceptual and information processing capacity with the emotional intelligence system being primed by the affect-laden information as it enters the perceptual system.

Gardner (1983) described intrapersonal intelligence as the ability to access one's own feeling state, and interpersonal intelligence as the ability to read the moods, intentions and desires of others. Salovey and colleagues (1993) found that high emotional intelligence is equated with ease of identifying and describing feelings in oneself and in others. This group is at ease with the emotional world and is able to regulate states of emotional arousal in themselves as well as in others. An aspect of emotional intelligence that is a particular difficulty for eating disorder patients is the perception and appraisal of non-verbal emotional behaviours; these include bodily sensations evoked by emotional arousal as well as facial expressions, tone of voice, and gestures displayed by others.

Bar-On (1997) has developed a self-report inventory for assessing emotional intelligence that covers adaptability and stress management skills as well as intra- and interpersonal intelligence and is based on Mayer and Salovey's (1997) modified definition that emphasises 'the ability to think about feelings'. Mayer and Salovey point out that there is a conceptual overlap between emotional intelligence and psychoanalytic concepts, particularly with Freud's ideas in his 1926 paper *Inhibitions, Symptoms and Anxiety*. In this paper, Freud proposed that anxiety is generated by the ego regarding its safety, in order to mobilise defences against forbidden impulses and fantasies. Included in this were depressive affects which signal to the ego that there is a lost attachment to a loved and need-gratifying person. However, Freud never let go of his earlier view that affects come from the instinctual drives. Contemporary psychoanalysis views affects as a primary motivator and the basis for assessing and communicating the state of the self (Spezzano, 1993). However, in relation to eating disorders, Freud's (1926) work, on both instincts and signal anxiety, illuminates the core problem of fear of disinhibition, losing control, difficulties in attachment and the development of the self. Gardner (1983) suggests that if we feel, we know who we are, which is the core of human subjectivity and a central feature of emotional intelligence.

Alexithymia and emotional intelligence

Alexithymia has been linked with deficits in cognitive representation of emotions and with poor ability to use affects, signalling that there is an inverse relationship between emotional intelligence and alexithymia (Krystal, 1988; Taylor et al., 1997). Alexithymics have difficulty identifying or describing feelings, a limited capacity for imagination, and an externally orientated style of thinking. Subjects with high degrees of alexithymia experience problems in accurately identifying emotions in the facial expressions of others (Lane et al., 1996; Parker et al., 1993) and have little capacity for empathising with others' emotional states (Beckendam, 1997; Davies et al., 1998; Krystal, 1979; McDougall, 1989; Taylor, 1987). Bagby and co-authors (1993) found that alexithymics had difficulty discriminating between different emotional states while Parker et al. (1998) and Schaffer (1993) found that this group had a limited ability to think about and use emotions to negotiate stressful situations. It is this limited ability to regulate emotions via cognitive processing that may make alexithymic individuals more susceptible to medical and psychiatric illnesses (Taylor et al., 1997).

Schutte and co-authors (1998) developed a self-report scale for measuring emotional intelligence and found a strong negative correlation with the self-report Toronto Alexithymia Scale (TAS-20). These findings confirm that alexithymia and emotional intelligence are inverse, but strongly overlapping, constructs.

Emotional processing

According to LeDoux (1989), the key structure in the basic emotional processing system is the amygdala, which evaluates a stimulus's affective significance, including internal stimuli from within the brain of thoughts, images and memories. This is particularly the case in regard to fear and anger. This process operates outside conscious experience (LeDoux, 1989) and underlies conscious awareness and linguistic processing of emotion (LeDoux, 1996).

Two circuits have been identified by which sensory stimuli reach the amygdala (LeDoux, 1986, 1996). One is a direct pathway from the thalamus to the amygdala that allows for a rapid appraisal and may result in the fight-or-flight concrete response, and another is the symbolic pathway from the thalamus to the neo-cortex and then to the amygdala. This enables the executive cognitive functions in the brain to appraise the stimulus in more detail, which includes the stimulus's relationship to other stimuli and also to past experiences, leading to a more nuanced, informed and appropriate emotional response.

The work of Nunn et al. (2008) has concentrated on the insula as the junction box that either opens up the pathway to the executive cognitive, symbolic functions or returns the impulses to the amygdala and into the concrete body realm, where the danger signal is translated into experienced anxiety in the body.

Their work is in line with that of Connan et al. (2003) and Steinglass and Walsh (2006) in that they have postulated a disturbance in neural circuits between the cortex (frontal, somatosensory and parietal) and sub-cortical structures (amygdala, hippocampus, thalamus, hypothalamus and striatum). Their model extends previous work in the field by predicting that it is not cortico–striatal–thalamico–striatal system dysfunction *per se*, but more extensively distributed neural networks, mediated by the insular cortex, that modulate and stabilise the direct circuits.

They propose that

> these modulatory circuits include the insula as a central point of integration and regulation of information and that insular dysfunction contributes to a failure of integration and regulation of autonomic, sensory and affective stimuli. This would then account for the core features of anorexia, its co-morbid features and the common findings on neuroimaging and neuropsychological testing.
>
> (Nunn et al., 2008)

Once in the realm of conscious feelings, other higher-level cognitive systems can then regulate the emotional reactions. These higher-level cognitive systems evolved alongside acquisition of language and other modes of symbolisation. This very significant development has given human beings the mental equipment to differentiate between emotional states and, most importantly, to reflect on the meaning of subjective experience (Rolls, 1995; Taylor & Bagby, 2000).

However, the pathway that leads directly from the thalamus to the amygdala allows the emotional system to act independently of the neo-cortex and can lead to 'emotional hijacking' (Arnsten & Li, 2005; Aron et al., 2007; Banich, 1995a,b). This can occur if the neural pathways from the prefrontal cortex to the amygdala are compromised. Thus, how well cognition can regulate emotion seems to be determined by both the quality of the representations in the cognitive systems and the strength of the neuronal pathways from the prefrontal cortex to the amygdala. However, even though the neurobiology of consciousness is still not completely understood, it is suggested by LeDoux (1996) that 'emotional feelings are experienced when representations of the amygdaloid and neocortical appraisals of stimuli, along with representations of the triggering stimuli, enter working memory and become integrated with representations of past experiences and representations of the self'.

Working memory is considered the basis of all conscious experience and is the major part of the information processing system. It allows behaviour to be guided by ideas, thoughts and other symbolic representations rather than be 'hijacked' by immediate emotional reactions to stimuli (Baddeley, 1992; Goldman-Rakic, 1996; Kihlstrom, 1987; Kosslyn & Koenig, 1992). LeDoux (1996) cites the accumulating evidence that the selection of information that will be attended to and held 'on line' at any given time requires the involvement of the lateral prefrontal cortex, the anterior cingulate cortex and the orbitofrontal cortex.

Neurobiological evidence underpinning emotional processing

In their seminal review of the neurobiological underpinnings of emotional processing, 'Emotional intelligence and the emotional brain: Points of convergence and implications for psychoanalysis', Taylor et al. (1999) discuss the formation of somatic responses over processing emotions via language in the presence of alexithymia and low emotional intelligence.

Lane and colleagues (1998) developed the Levels of Emotional Awareness Scale (LEAS) that assesses individual differences in the cognitive skill of recognising and describing emotions in oneself and others. They found that high scores on the scale indicated greater awareness of emotional complexity in self and others. They tested twelve healthy women and found that their performance on the LEAS correlated significantly with changes in blood flow in the right anterior cingulate cortex when emotions were induced. They speculated that alexithymia and low emotional intelligence might be associated with a deficit in anterior cingulate cortical activity during emotional arousal.

LeDoux (1996) and Heilman (1997) pointed out that the anterior cingulate cortex and other areas of the limbic system are functionally intertwined with higher areas of the brain, in particular in interhemispheric communication via the corpus callosum. This interhemispheric communication plays a role in certain aspects of conscious awareness of emotional processing. The right hemisphere is, to a greater extent than the left hemisphere, involved in the perception and expression of non-verbal emotional behaviour (facial expressions, prosody, gestures) and the left hemisphere is preferentially involved in verbal functioning in right-handed individuals. The interpretation of information is also carried out in the left hemisphere (Gazzaniga, 1992, 1995) as well as assigning meanings to conscious emotional experiences. This ability is central to emotional intelligence and deficient in alexithymic individuals. Taylor and co-authors (1997) found that highly alexithymic individuals often misinterpret the somatic sensations of emotional arousal as symptoms of disease.

While the left hemisphere's interpreting function relies heavily on language to process information in the service of reflective function (Gazzaniga, 1992), there is also right hemisphere involvement in language, particularly in understanding the metaphorical or figurative meanings of words. As well as understanding the meanings of non-verbal cues, it also allows for comprehension of alternative meanings that result in a deeper and broader understanding of the environment (Ornstein, 1997).

Hoppe (Hoppe & Bogen, 1977) proposed that alexithymia might be associated with a functional impairment in interhemispheric communication when he observed that 'split-brain' patients exhibited alexithymic features. Hoppe's work has been supported by the work of Zeitlin et al. (1989) and Parker et al. (1999), who also found that the deficits are bidirectional. Performing emotional processing and imaginal functions effectively requires interhemispheric cooperation (Banich, 1995a,b; Christman, 1994; Pally, 1998). As Teicher et al. (1996) succinctly put it, 'our capacity to appropriately identify and evaluate the affect of others, and in turn to communicate affect, depends on a healthy interaction between right-hemisphere emotional perception, and left-hemisphere linguistic processing and reason'.

There has been interest in the relationship between alexithymia and dreams. Patients with high levels of alexithymia often have difficulty in recalling dreams, and the content of their dreams closely resemble waking thoughts or life events (Apfel & Sifneos, 1979; McDougall, 1989; Taylor, 1987). Levitan (1989) suggests that structural features of dreams can supply information about an individual's capacity for representation, symbolisation, and abstraction. It has been demonstrated that alexithymic students experience 50% less REM sleep, and dreams reported by alexithymic students were significantly less bizarre and imaginative in content than the dreams of non-alexithymic students. Researchers Bauermann et al. (1999a,b) suggest that alexithymia is associated with a variation in both the neurophysiology of REM sleep and the content of its psychological counterpart, the dream.

REM sleep is thought to play a role in processing of 'procedural-implicit' memory and in consolidation, and integration and processing of affect-laden information (Levin, 1990; Macquet et al., 1996: Panksepp, 1998). Levin (1990) found that increased REM sleep and dreaming are associated with increases in the ability to use fantasy, divergent thinking and holistic problem solving. Thus, the reduced REM sleep of alexithymics suggests that they have a limited capacity to process intense emotional experiences, and the qualitative difference in their dreams is consistent with a less developed capacity for symbolic and imaginal thinking.

Taylor and co-authors (1999) conclude that

> low emotional intelligence is associated with an interhemispheric transfer deficit, which reduces coordination and integration of the specialised activities of the two hemispheres, as well as with underactivity of that part of the anterior cingulate cortex involved with selective attention and working memory. There may also be a reduced amount of REM sleep and associated deficits in the processing of 'procedural-implicit' memory and affect-laden information. According to this proposal, states of emotional arousal evoked by activation of the amygdala may remain unregulated for two reasons. First, the unconscious inhibitory feedback from the prefrontal cortex to the amygdala is reduced because of an impoverished representational world that limits the ability of this part of the prefrontal cortex to perform a more detailed cognitive appraisal of complex emotional stimuli. Second, the limited ability to represent and contain emotions with words and fantasies, and to reflect on their meanings, restricts the use of conscious cognitive processes to modulate arousal by way of cortico–amygdala pathways. The reduced ability to modulate arousal of peripheral autonomic and endocrine systems, especially in response to highly stressful situations, may over time create bodily conditions favorable to the onset of physical illness.

They also suggest that, as well as differences in temperament, the quality of early attachment relationships is the critical variable in the development of emotional intelligence. This process is nurtured in the relationship between mother (or primary carer) and child that fosters the representation of self and others through the mechanism of mirroring the infant's emotional expressions (Emde, 1988; Gergely & Watson, 1996; Stern, 1985). This process is continued by the creation of pleasurable playful interactions where the child is taught words to name and to talk about feelings (Dunne et al., 1991; Taylor et al., 1997).

Fonagy and Target's (1997) work looking into attachment relationships emphasises the importance of attunement. Parents who are themselves alexithymic will most likely have impaired attunement to their infants' emotional states and non-verbal emotional communications. Beckendam (1997), Schaffer (1993), and Scheidt et al. (1999) found that alexithymia is associated with insecure attachment styles. Schore (1994, 1996) posits that when carers fail to regulate excessive levels of low emotional arousal and/or excessive levels of high negative emotional arousal, there can be permanent alterations in the development of the orbitofrontal cortex, which, in turn, affects activity in the amygdala and other subcortical structures. Thus, there is growing evidence that the emotional care given to infants not only influences the development of cognitive and representational abilities but also the maturation of areas of the brain involved in emotional awareness and emotion regulation.

LeDoux (1996) has argued that it is possible, in later life, to learn the skills required for emotional intelligence but it may be a laborious job and sometimes may not be possible if there is very low emotional intelligence. He describes this process as 'rewiring'.

The role of the right hemisphere in verbal communication

In his 2005 paper 'A neuro-psychoanalytic viewpoint', commenting on the work of Knoblauch, Schore focused on the functions of the right hemisphere as a precursor to the development of verbal communication. The early evolving right lateralised system (Chiron et al., 1997) is centrally involved in implicit learning (Hugdahl, 2002) and also enables the organism to cope with stress and new challenges (Wittling & Schweiger, 1993). Schore suggests that the right brain that evolves in the preverbal stages of development is both the 'I-system' and the biological substrate of the dynamic unconscious (Schore, 2002, 2017).

The right hemisphere has been linked to implicit information processing, unlike the more conscious processing which is the domain of the left hemisphere (Happaney et al., 2004). The early-maturing right hemisphere is also centrally involved in the maintenance of a coherent, continuous and unified sense of self (Devinsky, 2000). Miller and co-authors (2001) describe the non-dominant frontal lobe process as 'one that connects the individual to emotionally salient experiences and memories underlying self-schemas and is the glue holding together a sense of self.'

Schore (1994) suggests that deficits in implicit subjective and intersubjective functions reflect impairments in the right hemisphere's central role in verbal communication and self-regulation. It is suggested that these impairments underlie attachment disorders. Decety and Chaminade (2003) suggest that self-awareness, empathy and identification with others mainly depend on right hemisphere functions that are the first to develop.

Schore's paper concentrates mainly on the right hemisphere functions that are in play when carrying out the psychoanalytic process. He suggests that the almost exclusive focus of research has been on the verbal and cognitive outputs rather than on the hidden prosodic cues and visuo-affective transactions that take place in the consulting room. Schore suggests that studying only left hemispheric activities does not allow for understanding of socio-emotional disorders that arise from limitations of right hemispheric affect regulation.

Schore describes implicit processing as being particularly relevant to the quick and automatic handling of non-verbal affective cues that develop before symbolic verbal communication. He describes most relational transactions as relying heavily on a substrate of affective cues that evaluate each emotional communication and which are carried out at an implicit level of cuing and response, which is too rapid for simultaneous verbal translation and conscious reflection.

Stuss and Alexander (1999) suggest that attachment experiences are "affectively burnt in" to the right hemisphere, thus imprinting an internal working model that encodes strategies of affect regulation that act at implicit non-conscious levels. These non-verbal attachment communications of facial expression, posture and tone of voice are the product of the operations of the infant's right hemisphere interacting with the mother's right hemisphere. This interaction influences the maturation of the processing of emotion in the limbic circuits of the right brain (Devinsky, 2000). Trevarthen (1990) described what she called proto-dialogues, which were defined as coordinated visual eye-to-eye messages, tactile and body gestures, and auditory prosodic vocalisations that induce instant emotional effects. These she called the essential vehicles of attachment communications.

Bourne and Todd (2004) refer to the adaptive importance of 'optimal transmission of affective information to the right hemisphere'. These early experiences may be regulated or dysregulated, imprinting either secure or insecure attachments, creating a resistance against, or vulnerability to, future psychopathologies. Thus, intersubjective deficits of these disorders represent right and not left brain dysfunctions.

Schore suggests that there is a common misconception among scientists and clinicians that the left hemisphere is uniquely specialised for all language functions. It is now well-established that the right and not left hemisphere is dominant not only for prosody but also for the processing of emotional words (Kensinger & Schacter, 2006) the detection of one's first name (Perrin et al., 2005), humour (Borod et al., 2000), laughter (Meyer et al., 2005), social discourse (Bryan & Hale, 2001) and metaphor (Sotillo et al., 2005). The right hemisphere is, thus, dominant for the broader aspects of communication (van Lancker & Cummings, 1999) and for subjective emotional experiences (Wittling & Roschmann, 1993). Dysfunction in the right hemisphere can result in a two-way disturbance of how one relates to the environment that can lead to disorders of under- and over-relatedness between the self and the world.

Damasio (1994) suggests that the right brain is centrally involved in the analysis of information received by the subject from her own body, and it is this hemisphere that contains an integrated map of the body state. Of particular interest is the insula, a structure embedded in the right temporal lobe that, along with the orbital cortex (located in the right prefrontal lobe), plays a significant role in the processing of bodily-based information. Visceral responses become accessible to awareness and are mediated through the right anterior insular cortex, while the right orbitofrontal cortex is involved in the implicit subjective evaluation of the condition of the body and differentiates an affect associated with a bodily feeling. Craig (2011) has found that emotional depth and complexity are related to the degree of expansion of the right anterior insula and adjacent orbitofrontal cortices.

Nunn and co-authors (2008), in their paper 'The fault is not in her parents but in her insula—a neurobiological hypothesis of anorexia nervosa', suggest that it is at the level of the insula that the neurological deficits which lead to the expression of an eating disorder lie.

The right hemisphere holds representations of emotional states associated with past events and when a similar scenario is encountered, it is the right hemisphere that retrieves past emotional experiences that are then incorporated into the reasoning process. Shuren and Grafman (2002) found that it is the right hemisphere that responds to negative emotional stimuli and suggest that negative transference is specifically mediated by the right brain (there is some neuro-imaging support for these assertions by Christakou et al. (2009)). Andrade (2005) suggests that in classical psychoanalysis, only pathologies that have their roots in the verbal phase and which relate to specific memories are available to be treated. Pathologies that arise from the preverbal stage, where implicit memories are to be found, are not amenable to psychoanalytic treatment based on interpretation.

Andrade suggests that the formula to treat patients whose difficulties lie in the preverbal stage is 'empathetic–introjective reciprocal identification' or perhaps, put another way, the same functions as maternal preoccupation. Knoblauch's responses to a patient's non-verbal moment-to-moment shifts in body, posture, rhythm, tone and facial expression triggers his own right brain autobiographical memory system and influences his feedback to the patient. This, in turn, then impacts the patient's self-regulatory functions. It is this approach that Knoblauch suggests is the mutative factor in his new version of psychoanalysis that allows for somatic as well as psychic change.

Schore (2011) quotes Freud: 'The unconscious is the proper mediator between the somatic and the mental, perhaps the long-sought "missing link"' (Freud, 1915). Schore adds, 'In light of the above recent data from developmental and neuropsychoanalysis, I suggest that psychoanalysis is not the "talking" but the "communicating" cure'. I might add that communication first requires two minds; it then progresses to one person communicating effectively with himself or herself that only then can expand to become effective communication between two minds.

The importance of metaphoric understanding in eating disorders

Metaphorical thinking and eating disorders

Eating disorder patients can be described as thinking in the concrete mode or as having become 'concretised' (Buhl, 2002; Pearlman, 1999). The symptoms with which they present are concrete in nature, having a cognitive and emotional over-concern with body shape and weight. It has been suggested by Skarderud (2007) that for eating disordered individuals there is an immediate equivalence between bodily and emotional experience that takes the place of symbolic and metaphoric thought. Enckell (2002) describes 'concretised metaphors', where metaphors are not experienced as indirect expressions but as immediate and bodily experiences of a concrete reality. The 'as if' of the metaphor as a figure of speech is turned into an 'is'. An example of this is a patient I treated who, when first assessed, complained about her consumption of biscuits. It turned out that there was no pattern as to when she might binge on them and she found it strange that she did so, as she did not like the taste. On exploration of the circumstances around the most recent binge, it was no surprise to find that just prior to the binge an event had occurred that had distressed her, although she was consciously unaware of it at the time. She recognised in hindsight that a change of state had occurred when she began foraging for biscuits to the exclusion of everything else that was happening at work. The trigger event was explored, and the theme that emerged (which was the same for other binges) was anger and frustration that a colleague could make such outrageous demands on her. The patient laughed when I suggested 'that it took the biscuit' for her colleague to behave in such a manner. The patient's metaphorical understanding of the inappropriateness of her colleague's demands came under pressure, as it would have required a sophisticated response to an emotionally demanding field. The emerging metaphorical understanding that his request 'took the biscuit' degraded until all she was aware of was a compelling need to 'take the biscuit' unconnected to the surrounding complex emotional stimulus.

Metaphor and language processing

Aristotle described metaphor as giving something a name that belongs to something else. It is commonly defined as 'being a word or phrase that is applied to an object or action that it does not literally denote, in order to imply a resemblance' (*Concise Oxford Dictionary*, 2011).

Wright (1991) describes metaphor thus:

> Metaphor is the linguistic tool of the explorer. It is through metaphor that the explorer describes the unknown. There is no word for the unknown, so something has to be found that will bring this new something into a relation with what is already known. The unknown is 'the thing without a name' so it has to be named by linking it to something else that is already named. Metaphor means literally carrying across of something from one location to another.

Skarderud (2007) suggests that the essence of metaphor is to understand and experience one phenomenon through another phenomenon. He describes metaphors as a sub-group of symbols based on the perception of physical realities, such as feeling up or down or burdened by heavy thoughts. He goes on to suggest that metaphor is at the core of mental representations and human understanding as it utilises imaginal thinking. In eating disorders, he suggests that the body functions as the source for metaphors and that 'sensorimotor experiences and bodily qualities and sensations, like hunger, size, weight and shape, are physical entities that may also represent non-physical phenomena'.

Lakoff and Johnson (1999) strongly argue against the tradition in Western philosophy that considers cognition and rationality as separate from the body. These two philosophers have posited that metaphors should not be viewed solely as a phenomenon of a conscious multi-stage process of language interpretation but, rather, as a model for the general function of mind, including memories, feelings and dreams. They see the production of metaphor as immediate conceptual mapping via neural connections based on perception, and have suggested that the mind is always embodied. They suggest that sensorimotor experiences constitute the basis for conceptualising. In their model of the function of the mind there are three premises: '(1) the mind is inherently embodied, (2) thought is mostly unconscious, and (3) abstract concepts are largely metaphorical'.

The French philosopher Maurice Merleau-Ponty (1907–1961) posited that all linguistic meaning is ultimately metaphorical. In order to use metaphors as a figure of speech, language has to be 'stretched' from its concrete meaning to create a new symbol. Wright (1991) discussed this further, in his book *Vision and Separation: Between Mother and Baby*. When this process fails, I suggest that the attempt at symbolisation falls back, as it were, to its original concrete state but with some residual meaning from the original attempt. For example, 'there is a lot on my plate' (i.e., I have too many things to do or take in), or 'I cannot stomach the situation' (i.e., I cannot tolerate what I see); an anorexic patient feels that there is too much food on the plate that is impossible to eat or that she might have to vomit the contents of her stomach. The stimulus thought would then be lost in the concrete behaviour. Enckell (2002) describes the reduction in the capacity to use functioning metaphors as the collapse of the symbolic room between the body and emotion/cognition.

Krause (2008) reviewed the then recent work on the neuroscience of figurative language. It is worth quoting his opening paragraph as an excellent example of metaphoric versus literal language.

> Sometimes a cigar is just a cigar. Then again, mischief is the hot smoke that curls off the end of a lit intellect. And sometimes a diamond in the rough is indeed just an ancient deposit of highly compressed carbon. But no facet of humanity's evolved 'genius,' as Aristotle put it more than 2,300 years ago, sparkles so brilliantly as our unique capacities for extra-literal description and comprehension.

In the light of the latest research using functional magnetic resonance imaging (MRI), Broca's and Wernicke's areas are not confined to responsibility for grammar (Broca's) or word meanings (Wernicke's). These functions are now accepted as being carried out in other parts of the brain as well. Conversely, Broca's and Wernicke's areas also contribute to the processing of other important tasks. Thus,

Krause suggests that the 'modularity' hypothesis is no longer sufficient but should be re-thought in the light of evolution (Krause, 2008).

Steen (2007) supports the views of Krause and defines language (as opposed to communication) in adaptive terms. He suggests that language is a system of communication that is central to understanding, influencing and predicting the behaviour of others. Steen accepts that the left hemisphere is involved in both language and problem solving, but he looks at the whole issue of language in a framework of practical and adaptive use.

Steen posits that for language to be seen in the light of a system of communication requires the concept of theory of mind. For communication to be purposeful it must assume the presence of other independent minds capable of being influenced. The communication has to serve the needs of both the speaker and the receiver. Steen suggests that it is not sufficient to understand merely the literal content but should also include what the speaker is 'really saying'.

Krause describes how the standard model of figurative language, or the 'indirect' or 'sequential' view, has given way to a new understanding of the processing of figurative language comprehension. Rather than the right hemisphere being responsible for figurative understanding, he suggests that while the right hemisphere appears to play an important role, factors other than figurativity *per se* might be involved.

The 'sequential' or 'indirect' view maintains that, initially, the brain analyses passages for the literal meaning, and if this makes no sense it then reprocesses the words in an attempt to extract an appropriate figurative meaning. This prevailing view, based on work by Winner and Gardner (1997), was of a dichotomous model of laterality with the left hemisphere being responsible for processing literal language and the right hemisphere only engaged to decode figurative expressions. Rapp and colleagues (2004) challenged this relatively simplistic view. In well-designed studies, Rapp predicted that, consistent with the laterality model, metaphorical sentences should stimulate greater brain activity in the right lateral temporal cortices. However, they found that the strongest signal came from the left hemisphere. Thus, they put forward the view that there was some right hemisphere involvement but the true picture is far more complex. Giora (2007) argued that, in fact, Winner and Gardner's results had been misinterpreted and that laterality in terms of figurative language was not proved. Nunn and colleagues (2008) argue against strict modularity that language processing requires the coordination of the whole structure of the brain, both left and right, and if one part of the system is not functioning correctly, this could cause a problem somewhere else in a distributed network.

Eviatar and Just (1999) took the research in this area further in their study 'Brain correlates of discourse processing: a functional magnetic resonance imaging (fMRI) investigation of irony and conventional metaphor comprehension'. Sixteen subjects were presented with ironic sentences as well as literal and simple metaphorical expressions. The results showed that all three conditions stimulated the classical language area of the left hemisphere (left inferior frontal gyrus, the left inferior temporal gyrus and the left inferior extra striate region). Metaphorical sentences activated the same areas but to a significantly higher degree than literal or ironic statements. Different areas of the left hemisphere (the right superior and middle temporal gyri) were significantly more sensitive to ironic statements than to any others and the right inferior temporal gyrus was differentially sensitive to metaphorical meanings.

As all the different kinds of stimuli had activated the same classical language regions of the left hemisphere, Eviatar and Just concluded that the exclusive right hemisphere theory of figurative language was untenable. In addition, both irony and metaphor triggered further activation in the brain; metaphor particularly in the left hemisphere and less strongly in the right hemisphere, while irony vigorously stimulated a disparate region of the right hemisphere.

They concluded that, for whatever reasons, metaphors were processed in a slightly dissimilar manner than the literals. Most interestingly, the metaphorical and ironical expressions were processed differently in relation to one another.

The possible explanation given by the authors attributed the distinction between metaphor and irony to the character of the sentences rather than their category. However, Eviatar and Just chose conventional or salient metaphors that had been 'lexicalised' and thus did not provoke the need for novel thought in order to understand their meaning. These simple idiomatic metaphors, such as a fast worker being compared to a 'hurricane', might be processed most efficiently in the left hemisphere as a unit similar to the processing of long words and literal phrases.

Eviatar and Just suggested that irony requires more interpretation and is more complex, as it implies an association between the speaker's thoughts and those of someone else. They discussed developmental studies in the light of theory of mind. They remarked that first-order beliefs (modelling what another person knows) can be correctly attributed by healthy children and adults who can also express an understanding of metaphor, but not necessarily irony. However, subjects who can make second-order attributions (modelling what another person knows about what a third person knows) proved usually capable of also understanding irony. Happé (1994) devised a more naturalistic and subtle probe for everyday mind-reading skills work. Her 'strange stories' extended the theory of mind research by introducing ironic tableaux that discriminated between autistic spectrum subjects who scored relatively well on the simpler Sally Ann task.

Happé suggests that the group of individuals who are both intellectually able and have substantial theory of mind skills remain disabled none the less, due to the fact that their social and mind-reading skills developed late and missed the developmental context in which these skills are normally embedded. The result is that their skills are atypical and inutile.

This research has opened up an area of study regarding right hemisphere and left hemisphere processing of language meaning that focuses on the complexity of the stimulus. This opens the possibility of linking the early developmental environment with the development of theory of mind and processing of complex emotional stimuli. Happé's work suggests that the more complex the stimuli, that is, in terms of unusual metaphoric/ironic content, the greater is the requirement for a high functioning theory of mind to be able to understand the nuances of the communication.

Schmidt and co-authors (2007) looked at 81 subjects in their creative and well-designed study, 'Right hemisphere metaphor processing: characterising the lateralization of semantic processes'. Three different phases were designed to investigate the processing by the brain of different types of literal and figurative sentences. They used a divided visual field technique to measure left hemisphere and right hemisphere reaction times following the reading of experimentally relevant portions of sentences.

Phases one and two of the study compared reaction times between unfamiliar (non-salient) metaphors (e.g., 'This city is a chimney') and familiar and non-familiar literal (e.g., 'The children's shoes were covered in dirt' and 'Janice used fans axes'). Phase three was a comparison between familiar and very unfamiliar metaphors (e.g., 'Alcohol is a crutch' and 'A bagpipe is a newborn baby').

They found a right hemisphere time advantage for processing sentences with moderately unfamiliar metaphor endings and a left hemisphere advantage for literal–familiar sentence endings. However, there was a time advantage for the right hemisphere in processing literal–unfamiliar and novel metaphors. They also found that there was a left hemisphere advantage for familiar metaphors and a right hemisphere advantage for the highly unfamiliar metaphors.

These results supported the 'coarse coding model' of semantic processing and did not support the old indirect/sequential processing and dichotomous laterality paradigms.

> The coarse coding model predicts that any sentence depending on a close semantic relationship (e.g., The camel is a desert animal) will activate the left hemisphere, and that any sentence relying on a distant semantic relationship (e.g., either The camel is a desert taxi, or The camel is a good friend) will activate the right hemisphere, regardless of whether the expression is intended metaphorically or literally. More hackneyed stimuli can be efficiently processed in a fine semantic field in the left hemisphere. Novel ones with multiple possible meanings, however, must be dealt with more methodically in a much coarser field in the right hemisphere.
>
> (Schmidt et al., 2007)

Recent research by Kircher et al. (2007), 'Neural correlates of metaphor processing in schizophrenia', looked at concretism in schizophrenia. Their findings were that the dysfunction of key regions, the inferior frontal and superior temporal gyri, in the neuropathology of schizophrenia, seems to underlie the clinical symptom of concretism. This dysfunction is reflected in the impaired understanding of non-literal, semantically complex language structure. Thus, while there is evidence demonstrating the right hemisphere's important role in complex syntactic and semantic processing, Kircher et al. suggested that it was the also the failure to recruit the identified areas of the left hemisphere that may underlie the concretism of schizophrenia.

The work of Amanzio et al. (2008) compared conventional and novel metaphor comprehension between 20 Alzheimer's sufferers and 20 matched controls. They successfully predicted that the Alzheimer's patients would perform relatively well on salient metaphors but significantly less well on non-salient metaphors.

The results were discussed from a sceptical point of view, but they lead to a hypothesis that the distinction between performance for the patient group might be a result of the involvement of the prefrontal cortex, as dysfunction in this area is affected by the disease and because executive ability is required to compare and combine material in order to appreciate figurative meanings.

This recent research leads the way in viewing the neurological processing of language as a complex integrated process. This suggests that rather than a specific area of the brain being responsible for the processing of information, it is the complexity of the demand for processing the meaning of stimuli that requires input from many different structures. If one connects these requirements with the research on early deprivation, then a possible result begins to suggest itself: that the damage in theory of mind subsequent to faulty maternal preoccupation detrimentally affects the ability to process emotional information that has multiple possible meanings.

Impaired reflective function in anorexic patients has been described as 'concretism' by Buhl (2002), 'concrete attitude' by Miller (1991), 'psychic equivalence' by Bateman and Fonagy (2004, 2010) and Fonagy et al. (2002), and 'concretised metaphor' by Enckell (2002).

Skarderud (2007) describes patients with anorexia as preoccupied with food and calories, weight and size to the point of a pervasive obsession. They exhibit a lack of 'conscious awareness of the metaphoric connections between their concrete symptoms and underlying emotions and sense of self'. He goes on to argue that the problem for the anorexic patient is not that thinking is metaphorical, but that the sufferer is 'used by' the concrete metaphor which is acted out in the body, rather than using metaphoric language to understand her thinking and direct her behaviour.

Enckell (2002) suggests that concretised metaphors are an attempt at a regression or a lack of development of symbolic capacity. Campbell and Enckell (2002) suggest that the concrete presentation is a reaction to a threat of inner fragmentation. Skarderud (2007) suggests that in order to understand anorexia (but this may apply to all eating disorders to some degree), it is important to look not only for the possible metaphoric meaning of the behavioural and cognitive symptoms, but also for the compromised reflective function, the capacity for making mental representations of metaphorisation. He suggests that this brings us closer to understanding the eating disorder pathology and why it is so difficult to engage this group of patients, due to their being 'trapped in the concreteness of body symbolism'.

Lakoff and Johnson (1980, 1999) described the concept of primary metaphors. They suggested that primary metaphors are acquired automatically and unconsciously through neural learning and are experienced as 'real'. These bodily experiences are considered universal and account for the similarity of these metaphors across cultures and languages. They then suggest that these primary metaphors may be developed, in language, into linguistic conventions and used consciously. They describe complex metaphors as important parts of our conceptual apparatus and of how we think and feel (Lakoff & Turner, 1989; Turner, 1995). Rizzuto (2001) states, 'To understand internal reality means to understand a human being who not only knows, but who also feels that knowledge'.

Kitayama (1987) describes how, in borderline and psychotic states, there can be a collapse in the capacity to use functioning metaphors. He described how a psychotic patient could not sleep, as he was kept awake due to a constant light. The man had called his former girlfriend 'my sunshine', and it turned out that thoughts about this girl had kept him awake. Skarderud (2007) states that concretised metaphors are widely accepted as a corollary of psychotic or borderline functioning and particularly in eating disorders.

Barth (1988), Chessick (1984/85), Geist (1985), and Goodsitt (1997) argue that anorexia nervosa sufferers are really suffering from a disorder of the self, and that the 'concretistic' symptoms maintain the cohesion and stability of a tenuous sense of self. Buhl (2002) refers to concretism as a developmental fault and describes serious eating disorders as manifestations of disorders in the development of personality and a reduced capacity for abstract thinking. Killingmo (1989) refers to a 'deficit pathology' characterised by an inadequately developed ability to distinguish and understand emotional states and needs.

Rizzuto (2001) refers to how there is a 'clinical restriction of language' in many bulimics and anorexics. She describes how there is typically a minimal use of metaphor by these patients when trying to identify common somatic reactions that accompany a variety of affects. Skarderud (2007) suggests, 'One way of conceptualising the psychotherapeutic enterprise may be as an activity that is specifically focused on the rehabilitation of this function.'

Psychoanalytic contributions to the understanding of eating disorders

The main tenets underlying the psychoanalytic understanding of eating disorders. The work of Hilda Bruch

The psychoanalytic view is that disordered eating, weight and allied symptoms appear to be related to core problems of development (Bruch, 1973). The literature in this area is mainly theoretical, with clinical examples rather than well-designed outcome studies. The best outcome studies relate to trials of interpersonal therapy (IPT) or cognitive analytic therapy (CAT), both of which are focused shortened forms of psychodynamic treatment. In general, they perform as well as CBT treatment, but that means that the 'gold standard' treatments only produce less than a 50% cure rate. As Fairburn et al. (1991) have demonstrated that if one removes the behavioural element to the treatment and only utilises the cognitive element, whether that is addressing irrational thoughts or relationship difficulties, the reduction in symptoms is the same even if the treatment process takes longer, as in the case of IPT and CAT. Therefore, it poses the question as to what is or are the active ingredient(s). De Groot and Rodin (1998) suggest,

> A therapeutic posture of sustained empathic enquiry contributes to the patient's curiosity about her own subjective world. Feeling understood in a therapeutic relationship and feeling assisted in organizing and understanding one's subjective experience contributes to the gradual unfolding of the psychological sense of self.

The work of Hilda Bruch has been seminal in the development of the thinking about eating disorders. With the advent of CBT treatment approaches to eating disorders, much of what Bruch theorised and described has been neglected. Her observations have, however, stood the test of time, and later empirical work has vindicated the accuracy of her observations.

Bruch was quite radical and scientific in her critique of the failings of traditional psychoanalysis, where the patient expresses her secret thoughts and feelings and the analyst interprets the meaning. This, she felt, was a devastating re-experience of the maternal controlling relationship (which she posited as fundamental to the development of an eating disorder) where 'mother knew how the patient was feeling' and thus interfered with the development of a true self-awareness and trust in the patient's own psychological faculties. The therapeutic goal, in her view, was to make it possible for the patient to uncover her own abilities and resources and inner capacities for thinking, judging and feeling. It is the capacity for self-recognition that needs to be experienced, which, in her view, creates a change in the involvement of the patient in the therapeutic process.

Bruch described a patient attending a session in an unusually excited mood, as if something great had happened. Bruch explained that the patient had taken a shower 'because I wanted to', which indicated that the impulse had come from her own feeling state which she had recognised. It is the growing awareness of one's own impulses and resources that are not yet matured that might lead to delinquent behaviour. The patient may not be aware of the immaturity of her desires and might assert her independence by following all kinds of impulses. Bruch describes this as a transitional period that needs to be handled sensitively, with the errors and misconceptions in a patient's thinking accurately labelled by the therapist. She does not advocate an uncritical supportive attitude on the part of the therapist, which she suggests can lead to an impasse in the therapy and might even require a change of therapist.

Bruch suggested that a non-interpretive approach increased patients' cooperation. She described how the therapist needed to pay minute attention to the discrepancies in patients' recall of events and to the misperceptions and misinterpretations of past and current events. The when, where, who and how should be elucidated in order to uncover emotional stresses of which patients had been completely unaware. She also described the inability to identify bodily sensations and to recognise the implication of interactions of others. She came to the conclusion 'that correct or incorrect interpretation of enteroceptive stimuli and the sense of control over and ownership of the body needed to be included in the concept of body awareness or body identity'. She suggested that when the body does not conform to the socially acceptable image (although we might now understand this to mean that the patient is trying to make sense of her inner world by conforming to some external image), the deviant body size itself is related to, or even the result of, disturbances in hunger awareness or of other bodily sensations. She was very prescient in suggesting that the evaluation of the enteroceptive awareness needs to be included when considering the notion of body image. This would include body concept, body identity, and body percept, but the important factor is the correctness or error in cognitive awareness of the bodily self, the accuracy in recognising stimuli coming from without or within, the sense of control over one's own bodily functions, the affective reaction to what is being experienced in the body. She also added the rating by others of the desirability of one's body. Thus, Bruch suggested that body image is made up of many factors that might be grouped under the umbrella of trying to define who one is and what one thinks, but with only the body to work on in a concrete mode of thought.

Thus, Bruch puts at the heart of the therapeutic process the need to help the patient to come to a more realistic awareness of her functioning self, both related to the body and symbolically. The aim is to integrate all the experiences into a functioning whole, monitoring the changing impulses and experiencing them as being under the patient's own control. Bruch describes the therapeutic encounter as a place for the therapist to witness the development of the patient from discussing feelings about her body and how these are related to other aspects of her self-awareness. She describes how the patient gradually understands how the distortion of what she calls the 'structural as well as [her] functional body concept' (i.e., the symbolic understanding as well as the concrete body experiences) are closely interconnected with experiences and interactions with significant people in the patient's life.

Another area of understanding introduced by Bruch long before we had the current understanding that neuroscience affords us is that of disturbances in size awareness. She described the denial of a starved appearance as pathognomic for anorexia. The patient cannot 'see' how thin she is; as an example, Bruch quotes a patient who only knew of her thin condition when she felt her bones. She understood that a realistic body image is a precondition for recovery and that regaining weight was not a sufficient condition. Thus, she understood that there were underlying mechanisms operating which prevented the patient from attending to objective reality or – viewed from a neurobiological perspective – that access to symbolic executive functions is impaired.

Bruch emphasised the importance of being listened to as a bridge to building a sense of self where the patient's own desires and impulses count (Winnicott, 1967). Cognitive distortions are thus repaired as she learns to rely on her own thinking. In Bruch's view, if the patient's own thoughts are not clarified and seriously attended to, then what she called 'counterfeit' communication would result and much meaningless verbal exchange would occur.

Most importantly, Bruch paid attention to the use of language between patient and therapist, suggesting that what the patient hears may be very different to what the therapist intends (Bruch, 1982). She likened the difficulties eating disordered patients have with language to the similar difficulties of schizophrenic patients (Lidz & Lidz, 1952). She posited that what is usually described as 'resistance' may well be the result of discrepancies in meaning and use of language, even though the exchange may be composed of ordinary words.

Bruch's underlying thesis as to the cause of this state, where the patient literally does not know how she feels, emotionally or physically, is that it is the expression of a faulty self-awareness. The problem is conceptualised as related to deficiencies in the mother–child interaction when there is an absence of a regular and consistent appropriate response to child-initiated behaviour which results in a gross deficiency of active self-experience (Murray & Cooper, 1997). Bruch also talks of the therapeutic importance of 'constructive ignorance', which sees both patient and therapist pose the question, 'What is there that I do not know?' This allows the therapeutic couple to become true collaborators and removes the feeling that the therapist has some secret knowledge (i.e., 'mother knows for you'). It is suggested that if the deprivation of early learning has been severe or total, then the resulting remedial action can only be partially successful. If it is not too severe, then the move to conscious control of the eating functions can, with practice, resemble true autonomy.

The origins of the problems expressed as an eating disorder, Bruch posits, originates with difficulties within the early mother–child relationship. When the mother misses or misinterprets the cues for hunger, or, for that matter, other communications, from her baby the process of connection between the physiological state of nutritional depletion and a psychological experience of hunger is a complex, unpleasant and compelling sensation which results in searching for food. It is, therefore, very important that the therapist and the patient understand the brain chemistry involved in hunger and satiation in order to begin the work of separating the physiological from the psychological. This view is supported by the recent work of Ward et al. (2000), who reviewed the organic factors and their interplay with the psychosocial and familial. They suggest that aetiological theories of eating disorders need to encompass both organic and psychosocial factors and that they are allowed to interact in complex ways, because if the focus is exclusively on either aspect, it is a disservice to patients.

Bruch reports the work of Harlow et al. (1966) on monkeys separated from their mothers at birth who were unable to 'read' facial expressions, understand, or send messages to, other monkeys when reintroduced to monkey society after being reared as isolates. Harlow's work is often misquoted by suggesting that cloth-covered 'mummy' substitutes provided more 'warmth', allowing the monkeys to cling, but when researched in more detail it becomes clear that the active ingredient seemed to be the lack of response from the 'mother' rather than the cling factor. Another interesting factor was that the isolates ingested larger amounts of fluids than the controls (Miller, 1969) and became visibly fat: the more that was offered, the more they drank. The conclusion was that the seemingly innate function of hunger requires early learning experiences in order to become organised into functional mature behaviour.

This leads us to the work of the child psychoanalysts/psychologists to describe the development of the self within the mother–child relationship.

Development of the self

The development of the self is a major area of theorising and research in the analytic world. Bion (1962) extrapolated from Klein's (1930) work to describe how repeated internalisation of the mother's mediated or processed image of the infant's thoughts and feelings provides a containment of the child's primitive fears and anxieties. Fonagy and Target (1996) suggest that a parent who cannot think about the child's mental experience deprives the child of the building blocks required for a viable sense of self. McDougall (1989) describes how mothers function as the baby's 'thinking system'. She posits that it is only the mother who can interpret her baby's cries, bodily gestures and reactions to stress. This mediating process not only requires taking in the baby's communications, but also giving back to the baby a manageable or digested version of these primitive communications. This healthy outcome, which contributes to the psychological birth of the infant (Mahler et al., 1975), requires quite a sophisticated set of responses and it is this process, it is hypothesised, that either breaks down or is deficient in some way.

The ideal early environment requires a secure containing relationship where the baby's affective signals are accurately interpreted by the parent who is able to reflect on the baby's mental states that underlie its distress (Brazelton, 1982). It needs to involve a subtle combination of mirroring and the ability to communicate a contrasting feeling (Fonagy et al., 2002). It is, thus, suggested that the parent's reaction, which needs to be the same – yet not the same – as the baby's experience, creates the possibility of generating a second-order (symbolic) representation of the anxiety. The mother will transmit this complex communication of understanding and soothing through the media of her voice and touch. This, Fonagy suggests, is the beginning of symbolisation. If all goes well, representations of feelings within the child grow in tandem with parental reflection and moderation of the child's inner experience, gradually creating coherence between physiological and emotional reactions.

Disturbance in the development of the self

If this mirroring process breaks down, for whatever reasons, the resulting experience for the baby is a psychological world where inner experiences are poorly represented. This internal psychic situation then creates a pressure to find alternative ways of containing these primitive and unprocessed physiological and psychological experiences. It is suggested by Fonagy et al. (2002) and Fonagy and Target (1996) that the expression of such an experience may be various forms of self-harm or aggression towards others. The attempt to reduce psychic and physical disturbance would normally be carried out by accurately identifying the source of distress and processing it in language, from which might flow a resolution of the problem, or at least an acceptance.

The reasons behind failure of attunement may be a reflection of parental pathology or may be constitutional factors in the child. We do not have to look too far into the past to remember how the 'refrigerator mother' was supposed to have caused autism in her child rather than it being the child's cognitive deficits, leading to avoidance and an inability to make sense of complex emotional stimuli which extinguished the mother's attempts at attunement (Rutter et al., 1997). Trauma or depression may affect the mother's ability to respond to her child, leading to a 'pretend' mode of communication not related to the infant's communication (Murray & Cooper, 1997). The material fact is, if the mother is unable to respond in a sufficiently attuned way, the infant is at risk of internalising the mother's own experience or defences, resulting in the baby's distress being either avoided or mirrored back without first being 'metabolised'. For example, the mother might panic at the child's distress and become panicked herself, or she may avoid thinking about the child's distress by disassociating (Buhl, 2002). Either way, the mother is not in close emotional contact with her child. This does not allow for any meaningful communication from child to mother and then back from mother to child. This gives no opportunity for the child to use the communications to build a repertoire of feeling states as the foundational components of the self. The baby loses the opportunity to experience a recognisable version of its mental state in the mother's mind, as well as to acquire a symbolic representation of those mental states. Stein and colleagues' (2001) work, looking at how mothers with eating disorders interact with their babies when feeding them, found that these mothers are particularly controlling of their infants, using more verbal control, especially strong control. Stein found that it was maternal dietary restraint that was the one feature of eating disorder psychopathology associated with the use of verbal control.

Fonagy and Target (1996) suggest that children who do not have the experience of receiving from the mother images that are, at the same time, recognisable but also modified, may have difficulties separating reality from fantasy. They suggest that this leads to a restriction to 'an instrumental (manipulative), rather than signal (communicative) use of affect'. They posit that instrumental use of affect is a key aspect of the tendency of borderline patients to express and cope with thoughts and feelings through physical action. They put forward the suggestion that delayed or absent secondary representation of affect constrains the development of the child's psychic reality.

Segal (1957), in her seminal paper on symbol formation, describes how, in psychotic patients,

> The symbolic equation between the original object and the symbol in the internal and the external world is, I think, the basis of the schizophrenic's concrete thinking where substitutes for the original objects, or parts of the self, can be used quite freely, but they are hardly different from the original object: they are felt and treated as though they were identical with it.

Fonagy and Target (1996) describe the integration of the two primitive modes of experiencing mind (equivalence and pretence) as normally beginning in the second year of life and being partially completed by the fifth or sixth years. It is this integration that provides the basis for mentalisation – defined as the ability to 'read' other people's minds, making their behaviour meaningful and predictable. Thus, there is a build-up of multiple sets of self–other representations available to be called upon to negotiate the interpersonal world. The concept of mentalisation involves a self-reflective and an interpersonal component that allows for the capacity to distinguish inner from outer reality. It is this ability that supports and underlies the capacity for affect regulation, impulse control, self-monitoring and the experience of self-agency, which they consider to be the building blocks of the self.

Fonagy and Target (1997) describe the lack of reflective function in borderline patients as a result of an unstable sense of self. They posit that the patient 'lacks an authentic, organic self-image built around internalised representations of self-states'. Bion (1962) described this state as patients being unable to label their affects, leaving them confused and feeling uncontained. McCann and co-authors (1994) found that eating disordered mothers who had high levels of dietary restraint restricted their child's intake of forbidden food, that is, sweet food, even though their children were failing to thrive. This could be interpreted as supporting the hypothesis that this group of mothers first had difficulty viewing their child's needs as separate from their own, and then behaved in as concrete a way to their child's misperceived emotional needs as they did to their own.

The absence or vacuum at the core of where the integrated self should be creates, as Britton (1998) would describe it, 'a nameless dread'. He suggests that this creates desperation for a sense of meaning which leads to taking in reflections from others that do not resonate with anything in the child's own experience. This allows for internalisation of the parent's state, in place of the child's own version of his experiences. This state of affairs is described by Fonagy as being close to Britton's 'alien self', in which 'once internalised, the alien presence interferes with the relationship between thought and identity: ideas or feelings are experienced that do not seem to belong to the self. The alien self destroys the sense of coherence of self'. Fonagy goes on to suggest that the weakened sense of self can only be restored by constant and intense projection. In contrast to the neurotic case, Fonagy suggests that the projection is not motivated by superego pressures, but by the need to 'establish a basic continuity of self-experience'.

Adult attachment and maternal brain oxytocin response to infant cues

In their research by Strathearn et al. (2009), mothers with secure attachment, on viewing their own infants' smiling and crying facial expressions, have been shown to have greater activation of brain reward regions (including the ventral striatum) and the oxytocin-associated hypothalamus/pituitary region. Peripheral oxytocin response to infant contact has been demonstrated to be positively correlated with brain activation in these regions and significantly higher in secure mothers than in insecure/dismissing mothers. In the case of securely attached mothers, their infant cues (positive or negative) may act as an essential reinforcer and motivator of maternal care, while for mothers with a dismissing attachment style, when they viewed their infants' sad faces, there was an increase in anterior insula activation which, it was suggested may mediate negative emotional experience by signaling 'norm violations' (Montague & Lohrenz, 2007). Anterior insula activation has been found by Vrticka et al. (2008) to be positively correlated with dismissing attachment scores.

Mothers with secure attachment patterns may produce more oxytocin when interacting with their infants, which, in turn, increases the experience of reward which may, in its turn, reinforce and contribute to the mother's ability to provide consistent nurturing care. In the case of insecure/dismissing mothers, sad affect may inhibit normal caring and may lead to insecure attachments in the child. It is this group of children who tend to have some difficulties in affect regulation (Strathearn et al., 2009).

The psychoanalytic approach to the concept of symbolisation

The ability and the necessity to symbolise psychic material lie at the heart of the analytic enterprise where the 'symbolisation of disjunctive experiences is the mechanism by which psychoanalysis effects its cure' (Laplanche & Pontalis, 1973).

Much has been written on symbolisation in psychoanalysis – particularly in the field of psychosomatics by both the French and American schools. McDougall (1978) described the concrete functioning of patients as just the recording of events; the French school called this *pensée operatoire*. Kanzer (1966) places emphasis on the motor aspect of the transference where actions may have an integrative function. Laplanche (1981) describes as pathological symbolisation the repetition of finding symbols for early wounds, and Bates (1979) describes a symbol as expressing an intention to communicate and as an image that is communicated affectively as well as verbally.

Freedman (1985) suggests that the model for change in psychoanalysis is the progression from a present image that is symbolised through a stage of revisualisation of archaic core fantasies, through finally to the establishment of new sublimated forms of representation. He describes as symbolic equations what Werner and Kaplan (1963) describe as protosymbols; 'the construction of imagery privately held'.

Rose (2000) suggests that change inevitably creates anxiety because of loss and coming into confrontation with the unknown, and one function of symbols is to manage the anxiety of change. In the service of change, he suggests that it is more technically useful to examine the communication aspects of symbols.

Segal (1957) describes the process of symbol formation thus:

> The word 'symbol' comes from the Greek term for throwing together, bringing together, integrating. The process of symbol formation is a continuous process of bringing together and integrating the internal with the external, the subject with the object, and the earlier experiences with the later ones.

In her elegant seminal paper, Segal (1957) discussed the process of symbol formation in patients who exhibit a 'disturbance or inhibition in the formation or free use of symbols' particularly by psychotic or schizoid patients. Segal's starting point was Jones' (1916) paper, where he made the following statements about unconscious symbolism:

> A symbol represents what has been repressed from consciousness, and the whole process of symbolisation is carried on unconsciously.
>
> All symbols represent ideas of 'the self and of immediate blood relations and of the phenomena of birth, life and death'.
>
> A symbol has a constant meaning. Many symbols can be used to represent the same repressed idea, but a given symbol has a constant meaning which is universal.
>
> Symbolism arises as the result of intrapsychic conflict between the 'repressing tendencies and the repressed'. Further, 'Only what is repressed is symbolised; only what is repressed needs to be symbolised'.

Segal further quotes Jones' distinction between sublimation and symbolisation. In order for a symbol to be formed, the affect invested in the symbolised idea is unable to be transformed or modified into sublimation that, he implies, is a more sophisticated function. Segal summarises Jones thus: 'when a desire has to be given up because of conflict and repressed, the object of the desire which had to be given up can be replaced by a symbol'.

It might be added that this only happens when the process of sublimation, which requires higher-order functioning, fails. Segal demonstrated these ideas in her work with psychotic or schizoid patients who showed a disturbance or inhibition in the formation or free use of symbols.

Segal gave what have now become two classic examples of symbol formation versus sublimation. In one case, a man suffering from schizophrenia was asked by his doctor why, since his illness, he no longer played the violin, to which the patient replied, 'Why? Do you expect me to masturbate in public?' Segal suggests that for this patient the violin was completely equated with his genitals and, thus, to touch it in public became embarrassingly impossible. The second patient dreamt that he and a girl were playing a violin duet. His associations to the dream were of fiddling and masturbating, and, thus, the violin represented his genitals and playing it represented a masturbation phantasy of a sexual relation with the girl. Segal suggests that for this patient playing the violin was an important sublimation of his sexual desires. In addition, she states that when the meaning of the dream became conscious, it did not prevent him from playing his violin, while for the first patient there was an equivalency between the unconscious and the way the violin was used on the conscious level.

Segal agrees with Jones' view that only those substitutes that replace the object without any change of affect should be called symbols. Klein (1930) did not agree with this view but, rather, tried to show that children's play, which she described as a sublimated activity, is a symbolic expression of anxieties and wishes.

Klein described the inhibition in symbol formation in a 4-year-old autistic child who was preverbal. He did not play meaningfully with toys, exhibited no affection or anxiety, and did not pay any attention to his surroundings (Klein, 1930). Her conclusions regarding the child's analysis were that if symbolisation does not occur, then the whole development of the ego is arrested. Klein chose to interpret the child's unprocessed primitive aggression as the spur to creating powerful defences against his phantasies of harming his mother's body that had turned bad because of his attacks on it.

Jones' definition of a symbol was narrow and did not correspond to common linguistic usage and, thus, excluded most of what was understood to be a symbol in science and everyday language. Segal chose to widen the definition of a symbol to cover symbols used in sublimation. Thus, she connected two processes that, one might argue, were distinct. She added that, 'it is difficult to establish a connection between the early primitive desires and processes in the mind and the later development of the individual, unless the wider concept of symbolism is admitted'. She proposed that there seemed to be a 'continuous development from the primitive symbol' as defined by Jones to 'the symbols used in self-expression, communication, discovery, creation, etc.'

Thus, the analytical view is that the child's interest in the outside world is effected by a series of displacements from early objects to ever-new objects. This view of a continuous process of emotional experience being symbolised in language and then laid down to memory is supported by the new discipline of neuropsychoanalysis.

Watt (1990) has suggested 'large areas of corticolimbic circuitry are tailor made to perform precisely those correlations between increasingly complex perceptual templates and states of pleasure and "unpleasure" that are the hallmark of the ego'.

Segal goes on to describe the process of symbolising as a relation between the ego, the object and the symbol. She describes symbol formation as an activity of the ego attempting to deal with the anxieties stirred by its relation to the object. According to Segal, there is a fear of bad objects and a fear of the loss of good objects, and when there is a disturbance in the ego's relation to objects this is reflected in disturbance of symbol formation.

The seminal point she makes is that disturbances in differentiation between ego and object lead to disturbances in the differentiation between the symbol and the object symbolised. This lack of differentiation then creates the concrete thinking characteristic of psychoses.

Segal suggests that symbol formation should always be viewed in the context of the ego's relation to its objects. This is described using Klein's concepts of the paranoid–schizoid position and the depressive position. Klein viewed the oral stage of development as falling into two phases, the earlier being the point of fixation of the schizophrenic group of illnesses and the later the point of fixation of the manic depressive illnesses.

In this earliest period of object relations, the object is split into either ideal and good or entirely bad. The aim of the ego is either total union with the good object or annihilation of the bad object along with the bad parts of the self. During this early phase, the thinking is omnipotent and the sense of reality is intermittent and precarious. The ego is in union either with the good object or with the bad. There is no sense of just an absence of the object. This period is dominated by hallucinatory wish fulfilment as described by Freud, when the thought creates the object that is then felt to be available. Klein adds that this is also the time of the bad 'hallucinosis' when, if the ideal conditions are not fulfilled, the bad object is equally hallucinated and felt as real.

Segal then describes the Kleinian construct of projective identification, a primitive defence mechanism by which

> the subject in phantasy projects large parts of himself into the object, and the object becomes identified with the parts of the self that it is felt to contain. Similarly, internal objects are projected outside and identified with parts of the external world which come to represent them.

Klein suggests that it is these first projections and identifications that are the beginning of the process of symbol formation.

Segal's contribution was to describe the early symbols as felt by the ego not to be symbols or substitutes, but the original object itself. To differentiate these primitive symbols, she coined the term 'symbolic equation'. Segal suggests that it is the symbolic equation between the original object and the symbol in the internal and external world that is the basis of the schizophrenic's concrete thinking.

The object is felt and treated as though it is identical to part of the self. The non-differentiation between the thing symbolised and the symbol is reflective of the disturbance between the object and the ego. Segal then states,

> Parts of the ego and internal objects are projected into an object and identified with it. The differentiation between the self and the object is obscured. Then, since a part of the ego is confused with the object, the symbol—which is a creation and a function of the ego—becomes, in turn, confused with the object which is symbolized.

Most importantly, Segal describes the development of the ego and the changes in the ego's relation to its objects, which are gradual, as is the change from early symbols (symbolic equations) to fully formed symbols in Klein's depressive position. When the depressive position has been attained, the object is experienced as a whole object, along with ambivalence, guilt, fear of loss or actual loss and mourning, plus a striving to recreate the object. Processes of introjection become more pronounced than those of projection. This is of a piece with the work of repairing and restoring and re-creating the object inside. It is through the repeated experience of loss, recovery and re-creation that a good object is securely established in the ego.

Segal suggests that it is the increased awareness of ambivalence, the lessening of the intensity of projection, and the growing differentiation between the self and the object that create a growing sense of reality, both internal and external, plus the internal world becomes differentiated from the external world. The omnipotent thinking of the primitive phase gives way to more realistic thinking. When there is recognition that whole objects are both good and bad, the ego will become increasingly concerned with saving the object from its aggression and possessiveness, which suggests that there is some inhibition of the instinctual aims. These objects are now felt to have been created by the ego and, therefore, are never completely equated with the original object. This situation is described as a powerful stimulus for the creation of symbols. When these internally created symbols are re-projected into the external world, they endow the external world with symbolic meaning and increase the sense of reality.

Unlike in symbolic equations, Segal suggests that the symbols created by the experience of loss and re-creation of the object within the individual allow for unconscious freedom in the use of symbols. The symbol is recognised for having its own properties and can be respected and used as a symbol because there is no confusion with the original object.

Importantly, Segal suggests that even when this stage of development has been achieved, it can be reversed if anxieties are too strong. There can be a regression to a paranoid–schizoid position at any stage of the individual's development, and projective identification may be resorted to as a defence against anxiety. Thus, symbols that may have been functioning as symbols in sublimation revert to concrete symbolic equations. Segal's explanation for this is that in massive projective identification the ego becomes again confused with the object, the symbol becomes confused with the thing symbolised and, thus, turns into an equation.

Segal describes symbols as governing the capacity to communicate. She suggests that all communication is made by means of symbols. When schizoid disturbances in object relations occur, it is posited that communication is similarly disturbed. This is because the differentiation between the subject and the object is blurred, and also because the means of communication are lacking because symbols are experienced in a concrete way and are, therefore, unavailable for use in communication. Segal suggests that words are felt to be objects or actions, and it is for this reason that they cannot easily be used for purposes of communication.

Segal goes on to say that symbols are also needed in internal communication. She suggests that when people are described as being 'in touch' with themselves, it is because they have an awareness of their impulses and feelings that is the product of an actual communication with, in her conceptual framework, their unconscious phantasies. This is effected via a constant free symbol formation where there is conscious awareness and control of symbolic expressions of the underlying primitive phantasies. Thus, the main difficulty, Segal suggests, is that schizoid patients not only cannot communicate with professionals but, more importantly, they cannot communicate with themselves. She describes this state as part of the ego being split off from any other part with no communication available between them.

Thus, Segal says that the capacity to communicate with oneself using symbols is 'the basis of verbal thinking, which is the capacity to communicate with oneself by means of words. Not all internal communication is verbal thinking, but all verbal thinking is an internal communication by means of symbols – words'.

In her final point, Segal suggests that when the depressive position is attained, there is a capacity to symbolise, the result of which is to lessen anxiety and resolve conflict. This capacity is then used to deal with earlier unresolved conflicts by symbolising them. Anxiety was generated by these early, unresolved conflicts due to the extreme concreteness of the experiences.

Segal also suggests that there is instability in the system when there is insufficient working through of early object relations. This instability can precipitate the move back to early paranoid–schizoid functioning where symbolic equations invade the ego. However, Segal's work could also be understood as a metaphor to describe a neurobiological process.

She ends her paper by stating that

If the ego in the depressive position is strong enough and capable of dealing with anxieties, much more of the earlier situations can be integrated into the ego and dealt with by way of symbolisation, enriching the ego with the whole wealth of the earlier experiences.

Chapter 3

A conceptual gap

Current ideas in eating disorders and the
need for a new treatment approach

Summary

This chapter lays the foundation for the need for a new treatment approach to
eating disorders.

The current main theoretical approaches are critiqued for their theoretical
strengths and weaknesses. The best practice model that uses elements from the
different theoretical streams, while crossing theoretical divides, rather ignores the
question of the need for a unified theory to explain the illness process and, thus,
to provide a rationale for treatment. Rather, it seems to have chosen treatments on
the basis that each problem is addressed as a separate element.

While there has definitely been a move to try to make current treatments for eating
disorders more efficient and the neurological perspective, that there are deficits
that underlie this illness, is beginning to gain ground, there remains a conceptual
gap in the approach to treating eating disorders – we need a new approach. In the
previous chapters, we have explored how the brain is built within a relationship
and how it can become fragile when trying to process complex emotional material, leading to overuse of the 'body concrete' pathway that is then favoured over
the symbolic pathway when under emotional stress. It is, perhaps, now time to
introduce a treatment approach that follows neurobiological realities. It can be
argued that current approaches do not sufficiently consider neurobiological function, its subsequent effect on the ability to process emotion, or the degradation
of the use of language in eating disorder sufferers, as central to treating eating
disorder pathology.

Traditionally, from the time when eating disorders were first described, the
empirical approach was employed. No particular theory was pressed into service
and the treatment became very *ad hoc*. Whatever worked was used. This has led
to a very patchy service within and between countries with no rationale as to why
one treatment should be used over any other.

As a consequence, a 'best practice' model has been accepted which borrows
from several theoretical approaches. It mainly falls into the 'maintenance model'
approach, which is concerned with what breaks the behavioural cycle rather than
why the thoughts and behaviours are there; that is, it is less concerned about what

causes the disorder. The present best practice treatments might utilise behavioural components such as CBT-E, family therapy, individual counselling and psychoanalytic psychotherapy, as well as psycho-education. However, the psychodynamic approaches will be theoretically at odds with the more behavioural approaches. This 'joint' approach certainly covers most bases, but stubbornly still does not break the 50% 'cure' rate. This would suggest that this general approach has a scattergun effect, some of the bullets hitting their target and some not.

The scattergun approach suffers from a lack of a coherent theoretical base, which, it is suggested, weakens the ability to generate ideas for new treatments. There is a need for a unified theory that offers an explanation of the genesis of an eating disorder (how it comes into being) and a treatment based on a theory – in this case, one which targets and repairs specific neurobiological (and subsequently social) deficits.

The current approaches can broadly be put under two headings; cognitive–behavioural and psychoanalytic or psychodynamic. This chapter assesses the strengths and weaknesses of these two approaches and the treatments derived from them.

Lack of a unified theory of eating disorders

There is, at present, no unified theory as to how eating disorders come into being. The various schools of thought approach the collection of behaviours categorised as anorexia nervosa, bulimia nervosa, binge eating disorder or eating disorder not otherwise specified (EDNOS) from their different perspectives.

Although Cooper and Steere (1995) found no single aetiological factor to account for the development of an eating disorder or for variation among individuals, the research in this area allows no clear conclusions.

The research into discovering possible aetiological factors suffers from methodological weakness. The studies suffer from selection bias due to the clinical sample coming from specialist treatment centres, a dearth of appropriate control groups, results that might be ascribed to general psychiatric disorders and uncertainty as to whether the findings are causes or consequences of the eating disorder (Stice, 2002).

There are considered to be genetic factors involved in the transmission of an eating disorder, with Wade et al. (2000) suggesting the heritability to be 58%. However, this research, too, has been criticised. Severe stressful life events have been implicated in roughly 70% of eating disorders. In one study (North et al., 1997), the 25% of eating disorder patients who had suffered a severe negative independent life event had a better prognosis. This suggests the eating disorder is a reaction to an emotional event that overwhelmed the emotional coping capacities of the patient.

To date, family factors show no clear pattern in the creation of an eating disorder. It is unclear whether it is actually having a psychiatrically ill member that creates the disturbance that is seen in the family, rather than the family behaviour causing the illness, or the interaction between the two. It has been found that there are three times more affective disorders in first- and second-degree relatives of eating disorder patients (Cooper & Steere, 1995) but this is also true of psychiatric disorders in general. However, broad measures and loose definitions of what constitutes disturbance might not be able to pick up fine-grained difficulties in families that have a member who goes on to suffer an eating disorder.

An area of research that has been fruitful in pointing to a mechanism of transmission is early mother–child interactions. The general outcome from this research seems to point to a lack of attunement in interactions between an eating disorder mother and her young baby. This lack of attunement is evident particularly where hunger, food, body shape and size are concerned (Stein et al., 1995).

As mentioned above, there are two main theoretical approaches to the treatment of eating disorders: cognitive–behavioural and psychoanalytic. Other neurological approaches, such as Tchanturia and colleagues' (2003, 2017) innovative work that addresses the underlying cognitive/neurological deficits in eating disorder patients, as well as a motivational enhancement approach, are increasingly making a contribution. While difficulties in interpersonal processes, emotion regulation and anxiety are more recently considered a core part of conceptual models of eating disorders, the experimental findings to support this are limited; however, the research data support the role of emotional functioning in the development and maintenance of eating disorders (Harrison et al., 2010).

Contributions and limitations of cognitive–behavioural treatments

The most widely employed and researched approach, CBT (plus all the treatments that derive from it, e.g., CBT-E), is quite comfortable with being theory-free. It is, on the whole, mainly concerned with eliminating behaviours that are considered pathological and identifies negative thoughts that are deemed to underlie the target behaviours. Its aim is to challenge the rationality of these thoughts in a sophistic way.

Underlying CBT is the assumption that the mind functions as a continuous model. This may be appropriate for some illnesses, but does not accord with observed mental phenomena in eating disorders. By assuming that eating disorder patients are thinking in a normal, if irrational, manner and that these expressed thoughts can be modified by exposure to Socratic argument, CBT loses the opportunity to relate to the patient in terms that the patient can comprehend. Long-drawn-out 'proofs' that the patient will not balloon if she eats three meals a day is useful in regulating food intake, but does not address the underlying difficulties in understanding her feeling states and can offer no solution to being trapped in a concrete world.

Treatments that are based on CBT principles regard the expressed ideas around food and weight as irrational, rather than a sign of a mental state that is concrete in nature and possibly closer to psychosis (in terms of fixed ideas) than neurosis.

The CBT view has a fundamental weakness in that it prescribes how the illness is viewed and, therefore, treated. However, due to the general paucity of outcome research into psychodynamic treatment of eating disorders, the main thrust of evidence-based medicine has been in the cognitive–behavioural field.

In many ways, CBT is quite a simplistic approach. While, on the one hand, it usefully identifies triggers to abnormal eating, it then offers unsophisticated solutions: for example, the patient is advised to avoid being alone in the kitchen, if that is the trigger to the abnormal eating behaviour. It does not enquire as to what, if anything, the behaviour signifies, as the behaviour is labelled irrational and, therefore, unworthy of contemplation in itself. With no concept of unconscious processes, which are not under the scrutiny of reality testing, the utterances of the patient are easily dismissed rather than understood as attempts at communication, both internally and externally, that may carry vital information.

The basis of behavioural theory is learning theory. Somehow or other, these maladaptive behaviours have been adopted and used as a technique to reduce anxiety. There is a notion that the behaviours are an attempt by the patient to control her life, which otherwise is not, or is felt not to be, under her control. This rationale is often put forward by the patient (and accepted by CBT professionals) in an attempt to *post hoc* rationalise behaviour that is not understood by either party. CBT has very recently acknowledged the existence of processes outside of consciousness, but these ideas have not yet infiltrated the treatment approach to eating disorders.

Contributions and limitations of psychoanalytic ideas and treatment

On the other hand, the psychoanalytic approach to eating disorders offers a theoretical rationale that describes a possible aetiology of an eating disorder. However, this approach, too, suffers from difficulties in both delivery of the treatment and lack of specificity in targeting the processing of emotions, and it, too, uses a scattergun approach to rectify specific deficits.

Psychoanalysis places importance on early stages of development as being key to good mental health. Under some conditions, when developmental stages are not achieved or go awry, later development cannot take place or pathological symptoms are produced.

Maternal preoccupation in the days, weeks and months after birth is seen as a very important phase. It is hypothesised that this is when the infant is libidinised, or brought to life, by the mother's close attention to her child's needs, particularly in the area of reducing her baby's anxiety when he cries for food or attention. When there is a successful outcome to maternal preoccupation, a coherent sense of self-agency, or 'self', develops. The function of maternal preoccupation is the use of the mother's own feeling state to take in her child's primitive communications and to detoxify the primitive dread and anxiety felt by the helpless infant. In her touch and voice, she is able to ameliorate and contain the baby's anxiety, allowing the baby to develop a sense of agency, an ability to self-soothe and, later on, to manage her own anxiety. As well as promoting accurate interoception (messages of the body-state to the brain), these communications are also the proto-language basis of later verbal communication. When this process is distorted and the baby has not experienced the containment of her anxiety (Williams, 1997), she can feel overwhelmed not only by her own anxiety, which has been undigested by the mother and remains toxic, but also receives the mother's anxiety, which she transmits to her child. The child can be overwhelmed by the 'double dose' of anxiety and is deprived of help to ameliorate it. Thus, the work of connecting the child to his or her own feeling state via appropriate handling (i.e., tone of voice, touch, comprehension of the child's primitively stated needs followed by appropriate action) might be compromised. This situation leaves the baby vulnerable to developing pathology. The infant may not experience feeling connected up between its primitive needs and an appropriate response. This weakens the sense of 'self' and self-agency. In this state of being, the child cannot internally process feeling states and join them up with language function or understand and process external events. This creates a scenario where the child learns to rely on the judgement of others rather than emotionally process for herself.

Segal's contribution to understanding the process of symbolisation, which she posits is at the root of verbal language, was to detail the steps (in Kleinian terms) that, if all goes well, result in full symbolic and metaphoric functioning or, in other words, the depressive position has been achieved. Segal describes symbols as governing the capacity to communicate, and all communication is made by means of symbols. Thus, a person's ability to be 'in touch' with herself is dependent on her awareness of her impulses and unconscious phantasies. The alternative state is to languish in the paranoid–schizoid position, where thinking is concrete and internal communication, as well as meaningful communication with others, is unavailable.

Most importantly, in psychoanalytic terms of reference, the capacity to communicate with oneself using symbols is 'the basis of verbal thinking, which is the capacity to communicate with oneself by means of words. Not all internal communication is verbal thinking, but all verbal thinking is an internal communication by means of symbols – words' (Segal, 1957). Jones (1916) suggested that 'when a desire has to be given up because of conflict and repressed, the object of the desire which had to be given up can be replaced by a symbol'.

While psychoanalysis does provide the understanding of how an eating disorder can come into being (and is increasingly supported by neurobiological research), there are practical obstacles to its widespread use. These are: the need for an analyst who has received between five and ten years training, of whom there is a scarcity, the cost of such treatment, and the time needed to treat the patient, which could stretch into several years several times a week.

Bruch (1982) touched on the difficulties that patients may have in the analytic situation. She suggested that the 'all-knowing' analyst replicates the controlling 'all-knowing' mother (whom she thought to be at the base of the eating disorder) and raises the anxiety and resistance of the patient. Elsewhere, she talks of the concrete nature of the patient's thinking, leading to miscommunication between therapist and patient. When a patient is operating in the concrete mode, a discrepancy in meaning is opened up between her and the therapist. Should a Kleinian analyst/therapist interpret only the transference (as is the practice) and place the interpreted aggression firmly in the patient, the concrete mode of operation of the patient is likely to increase her anxiety. If she is unable to symbolise and cannot understand metaphor, the patient is left with no ability to understand the 'as if' of the analytic situation. Words will not have shared meanings between the psychoanalyst or therapist and the patient, as the symbolic and metaphoric meanings will have been lost for the patient. Thus, interpretations, such as saying to the patient that she wants to attack and destroy the good things in the analyst, are not understood in a symbolic or metaphorical way. When a patient is concretely occupied with putting things into her stomach or getting rid of them via vomiting, transference interpretations are not understood as a reference to primitive envy, but as an attack on the patient by telling her that she is a really nasty evil person who is a destructive killer. The patient can only fail in this scenario and become very anxious and more symptomatic.

In the psychoanalytic paradigm, there is no specific moment of transformation between concrete and symbolic thinking when treating eating disorder patients, whereas, when treating neurotic patients, the interpretation is the vehicle for helping the patient understand the workings of the unconscious. Thus, both the patient and the analyst, or therapist, are caught up in the belief that they are speaking a shared language, but their understanding veers in different directions. If both parties understand that the patient is functioning from a concrete area of brain function, then communication can be translated rather than interpreted.

What, in the Kleinian approach to psychoanalysis, is considered a seminal paper (Sohn, 1985) on how to treat anorexia, is, on closer inspection, more a guide to what not to do. The patient, who suffered from anorexia, came to Sohn and, as requested, lay on his couch. To break the silence, the patient said that she did not know how this process was supposed to work and she could not freely associate (say whatever comes into her mind by associating to her stream of thought) as is expected. Instead, she suggested to Sohn that he ask her questions and that she would reply to them. Sohn's interpretation was along the lines that she was attacking his position and trying to prevent him functioning as an analyst. He reported that the patient still attended, but was silent for around a year before again attempting communication. If one is operating without the ability to symbolise, then such 'interpretations' will, at the very least, create confusion, if not outright anxiety, at the incomprehensibility of the analyst's communication. As will be discussed later, it is suggested that a complex emotional communication, for this patient group, is a trigger that provokes a move to a concrete state of mind and increases anxiety. Thus, treatments that actually raise anxiety are exacerbating the very problem they are aiming to cure.

In the case of Sohn's patient, I suggest that the patient was telling the truth when she said that she was unable to free associate and seemed not to understand the 'as if' nature of the analyst–analysand relationship. Therefore, she tried to create a framework that was more familiar and comprehensible to her. Sohn might not have wasted valuable time (and risks to the patient's health) if he had agreed with her that, indeed, she found the analytic situation, with its expectations and occluded cues, beyond her ability to comprehend. It might also have been helpful to the patient to acknowledge that she was unable to communicate either with the analyst, by freely using words as symbols, or to use them to communicate within herself. The therapeutic endeavour might have begun in a collaborative manner to try to understand the extent of that patient's difficulties and deficits, rather than be marooned in the *post hoc* rationalisations and confabulations that mask these very real deficits.

Such patients feel bad about themselves in any case and, in my opinion, these feelings are exacerbated when the patient is put into situations where she is bound to fail. If we understand the patient's mind, and how she may understand our communications, then we are better prepared to help lead her away from her concrete solutions to complex, higher-order symbolic, interactional emotional demands.

Skarderud (2007) acknowledges the use of concrete utterances about the body, which he calls concrete metaphors, and urges their use as communication in the analytic situation. However, the very verbal nature of analysis, with its emphasis on free association, dream life and phantasies, might be claimed to be beyond the capacities of most eating disorder patients. Those patients who find their way into psychoanalysis may represent a subgroup for whom the required process is not too daunting. It is also very difficult to assess the efficacy of this mode of treating eating disorders due to the paucity of good outcome research.

Attachment theory-led interventions

Interventions based on the premise that attachment to the main attachment figure is insecure follow the work of Bowlby (1999). His groundbreaking work looking at the importance of secure attachments has informed interventions in eating disorder work, particularly in the case of young children. While attachment difficulties are evident in this patient group, working mainly with this dimension, it is suggested, may be insufficient in older patients. Children are still operating in the concrete mode and, thus, early intervention may offer more chances for reparative work (Lask et al., 1997).

The work on emotional processing

The basic research on emotional processing in regard to developing a treatment for eating disorders is increasing. Tchanturia and colleagues' (2003) work on rigidity and set-shifting shows the way forward and promises to be very important for future treatments, particularly studies in cognitive remediation therapy (Davies & Tchanturia, 2005). Tackling the underlying deficits exhibited by these conditions helps to loosen the grip of the unhelpful mode of behaviour and also lessens the guilt and shame; the patients have a deficit, not a character flaw. Tchanturia's work on cognitive remediation has broadened into the field of emotion skills training and has produced a manual – 'Cognitive Remediation and Emotion Skills Training (CREST)' (Tchanturia et al., 2015). This approach encourages frontal function via story telling, after which the patient is encouraged to switch between the details and the bigger picture. This is good training for the frontal functions, but again does not target the emotions that trigger the concrete state.

Problems with the categorisation of eating disorders leading to research bias

The first problem one is confronted with, when dealing with research into eating disorders, is in the definition and categorisation of the various illness clusters. How this problem is solved must also have an effect on how research is designed.

Until the publication of the fifth edition of *Diagnostic and Statistical Manual of Mental Disorders* (DSM-5) (American Psychiatric Association) in 2013, only 20% of patients suffering from some form of eating disorder were categorised as anorexia nervosa or bulimia nervosa, which left 80% languishing in the EDNOS, or atypical, category. This has now been updated and bulimia nervosa and binge eating disorder were changed from 'at least twice weekly for 6 months to at least once weekly over the *last* 3 months'. This follows Fairburn et al.'s (2007) suggestion that sub-threshold patients respond equally well to standard treatments, and in a similar fashion, as 'proper' eating disorder patients. However, if patients do not differ in response to treatment but only in severity of symptoms, this suggests that eating disorders might be better thought about as lying on a continuum rather than as clusters of symptoms. This is suggestive of a unified underlying 'illness' process at work.

Fairburn suggested that there is a need to create more categories but to treat them in the same way. His 'dismantling' research does look for the effective ingredients of treatment, but just widening the delivery of treatment does not seem to have increased the rather disappointing at best 50% 'cure' rate and does not add to the creation of a unified theory of eating disorders.

It might be more fruitful to study what it is that maybe protects patients formally categorised as EDNOS from expressing the 'full' eating disorder syndrome, rather than including in research only 'pure' full-blown examples of each individual eating disorder. Researching only 'pure' examples also ignores the overlapping of, and movement between, illness categories. It is accepted that becoming bulimic is a move on from anorexia (Fairburn et al. 2007) and is usually taken to imply a loosening of the tight control over appetite, but might equally be evidence of a development of cognitive/emotional abilities.

It may be that eating disorder symptoms, at any level of intensity, can be viewed as either a manifestation of eating disorder patients' achievement of varying levels of cognitive/emotional development or an expression of possible deficits. In particular, it is suggested that eating disorder patients under complex emotional stress may be vulnerable to triggering brain pathways that lead directly to bodily expression that only allow for concrete thinking, as against pathways that are 'sent up' to the language area and, thus, allow for verbal symbolisation. When there is symbolic access, it promotes both full intrapsychic and interpsychic functioning or, in other words, the internal body 'emotion' information can be made sense of as well as being able to accurately understand the external world.

Need for a new treatment approach

It is suggested that the lack of a unified theory to explain the aetiology of eating disorder pathology has hampered the development of new treatments and research.

It has also been unhelpful that CBT has been labelled 'the gold standard' treatment that should be applied in all cases. This is because CBT has been the most researched treatment, but it does not necessarily follow that CBT should be the main or only treatment offered, which it increasingly is. The more CBT is researched, the more 'evidence based' it becomes, leading to it being more widely used. This situation fosters a false paradigm because, as mentioned above, CBT is effective in less than 50% of cases.

It is noteworthy that when the cognitive aspect of the treatment has been removed, the outcome remains the same, as it does when the behavioural aspect is removed. Thus, if one judges CBT purely by empirical standards, the treatment approach leaves a lot to be desired. A particular problem is the emphasis that CBT places on the removal of symptoms, which are seen as the problem. This pragmatic view offers no understanding, other than at a superficial level, of the meaning of the behaviour; it is only interested in the rationality or otherwise of statements.

Fairburn and colleagues (1991, 1993), Wilson et al. (2002) and Bulik et al. (1998) have investigated the active components of CBT treatment, as well as what works for whom under what conditions. However, this looks only at what might be working in the accepted treatment approach; it is not the same as searching for a new paradigm, which might not only explain the underlying causes of this group of illnesses, but also offer a theoretically cogent treatment. With a deeper theoretical understanding of how eating disorders come into being, it might be possible to create a treatment that addresses the specific deficits leading directly to the production of symptoms.

ILET treatment, which is described in Chapter 6, is based on a neurobiological, psychoanalytic and linguistic understanding of the creation of the specific deficits that lead to eating disorder symptoms, and targets these underlying deficits.

A theory that offers an explanation of how an illness comes into being should also be able to contain within it the possibility to predict a 'cure' by reversing the process; in the case of eating disorders, the malfunctioning of the neural emotional processing pathways. Whether ILET will, in fact, produce a 'cure' or whether it is valid and effective compared to other treatments awaits the outcome of clinical trials.

Chapter 4

Filling the conceptual gap

The development of symbolisation from a developmental neuropsychoanalytic perspective

Summary

In Chapter 3, we have looked at the need for a new conceptual framework for understanding how eating disorders come about. By understanding the development of symbolisation from a developmental neuropsychoanalytic perspective, it opens up the possibility of addressing the very difficulties that underlie eating disorder pathology and creating a new theoretical framework from which to address this serious and debilitating illness.

The previous chapters presented research from neurobiology, psychoanalysis, developmental psychology and CBT. This fourth chapter is necessarily quite dense, as it tries to fit together, into one model, ideas and research from different and disparate theoretical traditions. I hope you will bear with me as I layer and integrate the research.

The chapter's overall aim is to trace the development of symbolisation from a developmental neuropsychoanalytic perspective.

The argument put forward is that neurological, psychological and environmental factors are operational in the creation of an eating disorder. The results of deficiencies or distortions in these factors, it is suggested, may lead to: instability in processing emotions (owing to the concrete pathway being easily triggered in preference to processing via the symbolic functions): an impairment of symbolic thought; poor comprehension of symbolic and metaphoric language; and an impoverished capacity to use fantasy. Finally, a rationale is offered as to why neuroscience and psychoanalysis are both deepened by integration with one another that is illustrated by a detailed reading of Segal's work on symbolisation.

As discussed in the previous chapters, it is proposed that the expressed symptoms that are required to make a diagnosis of an eating disorder the result of deficits in the very early environment, in the child' makeup militating against attunement with the mother, or dif mother's capacity to be attuned to her child or both. It is su there is a distortion in the work of maternal preoccupation, fo the baby may be left in a vulnerable neurological state that c attachment. The robustness or otherwise of right hemisphere function, as well as right hemisphere language function, forms part of the picture that underpins emotional processing.

This vulnerability can eventually express itself in instability in processing complex emotional internal states through language, with a consequent inability to use and understand symbolic and metaphoric language. It will be argued that brain pathways to the language area are disrupted under the pressure of an overwhelming, complex emotional trigger, and the concrete body pathway is triggered, creating overwhelming anxiety. When this triggering happens, the result is reduced language function and what language is available is concrete in nature.

When there has been a change of state in the mind of the patient, from symbolic to concrete thought, it is suggested that the patient is unaware of this change and will treat her thoughts as valid. It is proposed that it is this that leads to concrete solutions, acted out on the body, in response to complex emotional challenges.

It will also be proposed that poor interhemispheric transmission, which is related to alexithymia and reduced REM sleep, contributes to the overall picture of an impoverished capacity to use fantasy. The areas of the brain implicated in these deficits are the anterior commissure and corpus callosum, which are interhemispheric conductors and introduce different brain regions to the emotion processing networks (which connect via the limbic system). The involvement of all these structures may account for why eating disorders are so rare and for why metaphor processing is impaired.

Finally, the psychoanalytic work on the development of symbol formation (symbols as the basis for verbal thinking) will be underpinned by the recent work on emotional processing from the neurological viewpoint and supported by the work on alexithymia in eating disorders.

Maternal preoccupation, right hemisphere function and the development of 'the self', emotional processing and underlying neurological structures

As discussed in Chapter 2, Harlow's work with primates demonstrates the necessity of maternal contact and responsiveness in order to develop and understand communication within the primate's social group. Primates reared as isolates eat significantly more and appear fatter than their maternally reared siblings, suggesting that regulation of biological states is affected by maternal deprivation, along with the understanding of social behaviour.

Biologically-driven maternal preoccupation in the days and months following birth creates the conditions for hyper-attention by the mother to her child's needs. The mother meets the most primitive nutritional and comfort needs of the child, embedded in a developing relationship. This relationship, when it functions well, provides for a containment of the primitive anxieties of the baby. The only communication available to the infant is a primitive, relatively undifferentiated cry.

If this cry is to be understood and appropriately acted upon, it requires the mother to decipher it, using her own internal emotional processing (or interoception) as a template. By continually monitoring her baby's state and offering accurate responses within an appropriate timescale, the mother can provide the infant with a containing experience and the beginnings of proto-language. The mother mirrors the child's feeling state back to the baby and allows a sense of self-agency to develop. When this relationship is not sufficiently calibrated or attuned, it is suggested that the vital connections between emotional arousal and proto-language can be disrupted (Fonagy & Target, 1997). This loss, the failure of a baby to experience a version of himself in his mother's mind, can interrupt the acquisition of symbolic representation of mental states. The growing connections between feeling states and language (both internal, by understanding self states, and external, communication between self and other) are considered the fundamental building blocks of the self, and it is suggested by Craig (1996) that it is insecure attachment and faulty development of the self that underlies eating disorder pathology.

Early maternal preoccupation has been shown to have a decisive influence on the rapidly maturing infant's brain (Emde, 1988; Gergely & Watson, 1996; Stern, 1985). These researchers argue that even though there are differences in temperament, it is the early attachment relationship that is the critical variable in the development of emotional intelligence.

In order to mature cognitive and representational abilities, as well as areas of the brain involved in emotional awareness, it is important that the emotional care given to infants is well attuned and modulated. Too little emotional arousal or excessively high levels of negative emotional arousal may result in permanent alterations in the development of the orbitofrontal cortex that affects activity in the amygdala (Schore, 1994, 1996). When the development of emotional intelligence is damaged, it is possible, later, to learn the required skills but not to the same level as if the early environment had allowed optimal development and, in severe cases of very low emotional intelligence, it is suggested that there may be no possibility of 'rewiring' the brain (LeDoux, 1996).

At this stage, it is important to state that it is not only the external environment (i.e., mothering and all that entails), but also the internal environment (i.e., the genetic makeup of the child along with personality factors) that affect the attunement or, in other words, the fit between mother and child. Mothers who may have postnatal depression, who are in mourning, who are unsupported or who function in a narcissistic manner may be unavailable to fulfil the requirements of maternal preoccupation. Alternatively, a child who is unable to demand mother's attention may allow emotionally unresponsive mothering to continue, whereas a more forceful child might draw out of her mother appropriate attention. It might also be that the child may have neurobiological deficits that militate against joining in the 'dance' between mother and child. In addition, some children may be less affected by their mother's anxiety than others. When a parent is alexithymic herself, there is a high likelihood that she will have impaired attunement to her infant's emotional states and non-verbal emotional communications. As has been noted above, there is some evidence that alexithymia is associated with insecure attachment styles (Beckendam, 1997; Schaffer, 1993; Scheidt et al., 1999)

In their research, 'Adult attachment predicts maternal brain oxytocin response to infant cues', Strathearn et al. (2009) looked at how the infant cues of crying and smiling activated dopamine-associated brain reward circuits in new first-time mothers in relation to secure versus insecure/dismissing styles on the Adult Attachment Interview.

They found that mothers with secure attachment, on viewing their own infants' smiling and crying facial expressions, showed greater activation of both the brain rewards regions (including the ventral striatum) and the oxytocin-associated hypothalamus/pituitary region. Peripheral oxytocin response to infant contact was positively correlated with brain activation in these regions and was significantly higher in secure mothers than in insecure/dismissing mothers. This was found to be independent of whether they were breastfeeding. The researchers concluded that the results suggested that individual differences in maternal attachment might be linked with the development of the dopaminergic and oxytocinergic neuroendocrine systems.

Interestingly, they found that there were notable differences between the groups in response to the subjects' own infants' sad facial affect, in that securely-attached mothers continued to exhibit greater activation in the regions of the brain that process reward, as against insecurely attached/dismissing mothers, who exhibited increased activation of the anterior insula, which is a region associated with feelings of unfairness, pain and disgust.

Their findings suggest that, for securely attached mothers, their infants' cues (positive or negative) may act as an essential reinforcer and motivator of maternal care.

The researchers cited studies that suggest reduced peripheral oxytocin responses in cocaine-addicted mothers and pregnant women with lower maternal–foetal attachment scores, and among autistic children and orphanage-adopted children with histories of early neglect.

They concluded that mothers with secure attachment patterns may produce more oxytocin when interacting with their infants, which, in turn, increases the experience of reward which may then reinforce and contribute to a mother's ability to provide consistent nurturing care.

They discussed an unexpected finding, which was the increase in anterior insula activation when mothers with a dismissing attachment style viewed the sad faces of their own infants. Anterior insula activation has been found by Vrticka et al. (2008) to be positively correlated with dismissing attachment scores, which was in line with the understanding of the researchers that the anterior insula may mediate negative emotional experience by signalling 'norm violations' (Montague & Lohrenz, 2007) activation in insecure/dismissing mothers. This, they suggest, may indicate that these mothers see their infants' sad affects as a violation of the affective state that they 'expected' to see. This results in the mother experiencing a more intense negative affect. In addition, Fink et al. (1996) linked insula activation with the retrieval of autobiographical memories, which suggests that dismissing mothers may respond to their own infants' sad affects by recalling negative emotional experiences from their own past.

Thus, Strathearn et al. (2009) assert that sad infant affect may inhibit normal caring responses in insecure/dismissing mothers and may predispose the infant to develop insecure attachments. The children of these mothers tend to have more difficulties in regulating affect. This is in contrast with reward/motivation seen in mothers with secure attachment and their babies.

This rigorously scientific work underpins the observations that underlie psychoanalytic theory of maternal preoccupation and adds weight to both psychoanalytic and neuroscientific approaches.

Right hemisphere function

The commentary of Schore (2005) on Knoblauch concentrates on the functions of the early-developing right hemisphere. Schore and Knoblauch assert that these functions are the precursor to the development of verbal communication and suggest that maternal preoccupation is the communication between the mother's and baby's right hemispheres. The non-verbal attachment communications of facial expression, posture and tone of voice are 'affectively burnt in' to the right hemisphere (Stuss & Alexander, 1999) and imprint an internal working model of affect regulation strategies. It is these proto-dialogues that Trevarthen (1990) called the essential vehicles of attachment communications, and it is this interaction that aids the maturation of emotional processing in the limbic circuits of the right brain (Devinsky, 2000). There are aspects of language processing that are handled by the right hemisphere (especially 'non-linguistic' elements such as prosody and visualisation) that may also be disrupted if the 'emotional brain' is dominating (Schore, 1996).

The function of this biologically driven preoccupation could be understood to, as it were, 'prime' the infant's right hemisphere in readiness for later developing left hemisphere language functions. Disruption in the stimulation and shaping of these right hemisphere functions could be expected to have an impact on the infant's ability to connect feeling states to language. Of particular interest is the right hemisphere's role in coping with stress and new challenges. As discussed above, eating disorder patients have difficultly in attenuating anxiety, and they express rigidity in their thinking (Tchanturia et al., 2003). Schore (1996) has described the functions of the right hemisphere that evolve in the preverbal stage as being involved in the development of 'the implicit self system'. This denotes knowledge of self-states that are below conscious awareness. He also posits that this below-awareness knowledge is the biological substrate of the dynamic unconscious.

I would suggest that the disruption in the development of this unconscious knowledge can be connected to the clinical picture observed in eating disorder patients. When placed in therapeutic situations that demand fluent responses and knowledge of self-states, eating disorder patients typically cannot function. Functioning, as they frequently do, in a concrete paradigm in response to emotional challenges, they become aware of their body state and not their feeling state. A frequent response of patients to their therapists' attempts to communicate in the therapeutic situation is silence, or to speak of how fat and disgusting they feel. Eating disorder patients typically do not understand what is being asked of them in a traditional analytic or psychoanalytic psychotherapy situation and, in fact, generally find the whole process bewildering and threatening (Bruch, 1973; Sohn, 1985). When there is little ability or connection to the well of non-verbal, ongoing, out-of-consciousness experience, being expected to freely associate to ideas as they come to mind is beyond their capacity. An attempt to do so may result in a false analysis or therapy, as there will only be connection to intellectual language and not an expression of the self-state or 'implicit self system' or 'dynamic unconscious'.

It has been controversially asserted by Andrade (2005) that classical psychoanalysis is only effective when treating pathologies that are rooted in the verbal phase. He states that pathologies with their roots in the preverbal implicit memory stage are not amenable to treatment based on interpretations that are designed to relate to specific memories. This could account for why talking therapies have not proved effective in the treatment of eating disorders.

It is interesting to note that the work of Bateman and Fonagy (2004) suggests that different techniques are required with borderline patients who present as concrete in their thinking. Skarderud (2007), in his work with the eating disordered population, has also followed a mentalising technique.

Distortions or deficits in the early maturation of the right hemisphere will impact on the maintenance of a coherent, continuous and unified sense of self (Schore, 1996). Implicit processing requires rapid and automatic handling of non-verbal emotional cues. This ability develops before symbolic verbal language. Schore describes relational transactions as relying heavily on a substrate of affective cues that evaluate emotional communications. This process requires a level of cuing and response that is far too rapid to allow simultaneous verbal translation and, therefore, conscious awareness and reflection. Taylor (2000) and Corcos et al. (2000) have demonstrated that eating disorder patients have alexithymic tendencies and are significantly less able to verbalise their emotional or, for that matter, bodily states.

If one is not connected to emotionally salient experiences and memories which underlie self-schemas, it would be expected that the sense of self would be fragile and/or fractured. With the right hemisphere having a central role in verbal communication and self-regulation, it has been suggested by Schore (1994) that impairments in these functions underlie attachment disorders. The ideal outcome of maternal preoccupation would be optimal transmission of affective information to the right hemisphere; thus, early experiences would have the opportunity to be regulated and create resistance against future pathologies. The obverse would create insecure attachments and vulnerability to pathology (Bourne & Todd, 2004).

Self-awareness, empathy and identification with others also mainly depend on right hemisphere functions (Decety & Chaminade, 2003), and emotional depth and complexity have been related to the degree of expansion of the right anterior insular and adjacent orbitofrontal cortices (Craig, 2004). It is noteworthy that it is these abilities that are reduced or lacking in eating disorder patients (Fox & Mahoney, 1998).

Traditionally, it has been accepted that language functions are lateralised to the left hemisphere but Schore suggests that, as a consequence of such a view, socio-emotional disorders that arise from limitations of right hemispheric affect regulation cannot be understood and are overlooked. The left hemisphere language function is the expression of a more conscious processing but, as Schore (2005) has argued, this conscious language might not be a reflection of the implicit knowledge that makes up the sense of an ongoing self.

I would suggest that possibly one of the main causes of therapeutic failure in the treatment of eating disorders is the failure to distinguish and conceptualise the patients' dislocation between feeling states and conscious language function. The patient may sound as though her language functions are intact and that she is responding 'normally' to the therapy, but the material may be unrelated to her feeling state, both expressively and receptively. Schore is interested in the hidden prosodic cues and visuo-affective transactions in the consulting room and argues for more fine-grained attunement between analyst and analysand, but I suggest that language itself may hold the clues to the occluded right hemisphere functions and, thus, give direct access to the fragmented self-state.

Right hemisphere language function

The right hemisphere is dominant for the broader aspects of communication, including subjective emotional experiences, and is responsible for the processing of emotional words, including detecting one's first name, humour, laughter, social discourse and, importantly, metaphor (Damasio, 1994). Damasio has developed the somatic marker hypothesis that 'made it possible to view emotion as an embodiment of the logic of survival'. In this hypothesis, he suggests that the delicate mechanism of reasoning is affected non-consciously by signals coming from the neural machinery that underlies emotion.

In addition, the right brain is centrally involved in the analysis of information received from the body and contains an integrated map of the body state. In particular the insula, embedded in the right temporal lobe, along with the orbital cortex, is significantly involved in processing information coming from the body. Thus, visceral responses become accessible to conscious awareness that allows an affect to be differentiated from a bodily feeling. In addition, when an emotional event occurs, particularly a negative experience, the right hemisphere retrieves past emotional experiences that are then available to be incorporated into the reasoning process (Shuren & Grafman, 2002). It is precisely these right hemisphere functions of differentiating a body state from a feeling state and dealing with negative emotional stimuli that seem to be operating sub-optimally in the eating disordered population. When pathological responses are employed to deal with emotional stresses, this again interferes with emotional learning. Past experiences are then of no help in solving present difficulties.

The two pathways of the emotional processing system

This section looks in detail at the specific neural pathways employed in emotional processing and suggests the hypothesis that, owing to right hemisphere immaturity, damage or distortion and under the stress of negative and complex emotional stimuli, eating disorder patients' brains will utilise the 'fast and dirty' pathway (see Figure 1.1) which does not include verbal and, thus, symbolic processing of the emotional threat, and will return the information down to the amygdala. This situation, it will be argued, depletes conscious language, leaving it concrete in nature and devoid of its deeper metaphoric meaning. This, in turn, will influence the behaviour of these patients, as they will have no capacity to recognise that their thinking has changed in nature, leading them to behave in a concrete fashion with concrete solutions to emotional problems.

As mentioned above, the amygdala has a central role in the processing of emotions. It is responsible for evaluating the affective significance of an external stimulus as well as information coming from within, which takes the form of thoughts, images and memories. This system, which operates outside conscious awareness, is particularly primed to react to fear and anger (LeDoux, 1986).

As described in Figure 1.1, there are two circuits by which sensory stimuli arrive at the amygdala. The 'body concrete' pathway allows a potential mortal threat to be assessed and the 'fight-or-flight' mechanism is employed if required. The symbolic pathway (employed when there is low threat) engages the symbolic functions and allows for the stimulus to be appraised in more depth and related to past experiences. This, in turn, creates the opportunity for the emotional response and subsequent action to be informed and considered in the light of past experience and present reality.

It is this ability to bring feeling states into the realm of consciousness and then engage the symbolic functions and access memories coded in language that allows for regulation of emotional reactions and, most importantly, attenuation of anxiety. Rolls (1995) and Taylor and Bagby (2000) suggest that this creates the conditions for reflection on the meaning of subjective experience.

When anxiety is high, the pathway that goes immediately to the amygdala is brought into play. This pathway acts independently of the neo-cortex and can lead to 'emotional hijacking' (LeDoux, 1996). In this condition there is a visceral reaction to the perceived threat, without any appraisal of the significance of the threat in terms of objective reality. LeDoux (1996) suggests that this is more likely to occur if the neural pathways from the prefrontal cortex to the amygdala are compromised, as the ability to regulate emotion is dependent on the quality of the cognitive representations and the strength of the neuronal pathways from the prefrontal cortex to the amygdala. The present state of neurobiological understanding of consciousness is incomplete, but it can be said that it is only when representations of neo-cortical and amygdaloid appraisal of stimuli, plus representations of the triggering stimuli, enter working memory and integrate with representations of past experiences and representations of the self that emotional feelings are experienced (LeDoux, 1996).

It is the involvement of working memory, an important aspect of conscious experience, which allows behaviour to be influenced by ideas and thoughts. When one is able to peruse all aspects of a stimulus, including consequences of actions, the response can be measured and appropriate. If 'emotional hijacking' occurs, there is an immediate unthought-out, acted-out response. There will have been no processing of the reality of the threat or the ability to learn from the experience or to judge the consequences of this visceral, literally thoughtless, response. This accurately describes an eating disorder episode where there is a trigger of complex negative emotions followed by a spike of anxiety leading to a concrete, wordless bodily response. When the episode is over and the anxiety reduced, then, it is suggested, there is access to language and memory and subsequent self-reproach, as the consequences of the behaviour can then be understood.

The relationship between interhemispheric communication, low emotional intelligence, alexithymia and the imaginal functions

To be able to identify, evaluate and communicate affects within oneself and others, a well functioning interaction between right hemisphere emotional perception and left hemisphere linguistic processing and reasoning is required (Teicher et al., 1996).

Interhemispheric communication is involved in conscious awareness of emotional processing. The non-verbal emotional information garnered by the right hemisphere is transmitted, via the corpus callosum, to the left hemisphere for interpretation of the emotional experience (Gazzinga, 1992, 1995). This ability to fluently transmit between the right and left hemispheres is central to emotional intelligence. This function is compromised in alexithymic individuals who, as a result, often misinterpret, as disease, the somatic sensations of emotional arousal (Taylor et al., 1997). Also, alexithymic individuals score low on the Levels of Emotional Awareness Scale (LEAS), a measure of emotional intelligence, which is to say that they have difficulty assigning meaning to conscious emotional experiences.

The neurological evidence underpinning poor performance on the LEAS has led to speculation that low emotional intelligence might be associated with a deficit in anterior cingulate cortical activity during emotional arousal (Lane et al., 1998). This and other areas of the limbic system are involved in interhemispheric communication via the corpus callosum (Heilman, 1997; LeDoux, 1996).

As mentioned above, the left hemisphere has the important role of interpreting the emotional stimuli that are experienced via the right hemisphere. The right hemisphere is responsible for the metaphorical or figurative meanings of words, as well as the meaning of non-verbal cues and comprehension of alternative meanings to words. Optimal calibration in the functioning of the two hemispheres allows for a deeper understanding of the internal and external environment (Ornstein, 1997).

When interhemispheric communication is functionally impaired, as in 'split brain' patients, Hoppe (1977), Zeitlin et al. (1989) and Parker et al. (1999) found that subjects exhibited alexithymia. They also demonstrated that these deficits were bi-directional.

For efficient emotional processing and full imaginal functioning, interhemispheric cooperation is essential (Banich, 1995a,b; Christman, 1994; Pally, 1998).

Alexithymia, dreaming and imaginal functions

Alexithymic subjects not only have difficulty remembering dreams but they also exhibit 50% less REM sleep. The dreams they report are significantly less bizarre and imaginative and closely resemble waking thoughts or life events (Apfel & Sifneos, 1979; Levitan, 1989; McDougall, 1989; Taylor, 1987).

The role of REM sleep is thought to be involved with the processing and consolidation of affective information (Levin, 1990; Macquet et al., 1996; Panksepp, 1998). In contrast to alexithymics, subjects with increased REM sleep and reported dreams had increased ability to use fantasy, divergent thinking and holistic problem solving (Levin, 1990).

The picture that emerges suggests that alexithymics have a limited capacity to process intense emotional experiences. The qualitative difference in their dreams is consistent with a less developed capacity for symbolic and imaginal thinking.

The conclusions that can be drawn from this research, which was reviewed by Taylor et al. (1999), are that low emotional intelligence is associated with an interhemispheric transfer deficit. This deficit reduces the coordination and integration of the specialised activities between the two hemispheres. In addition, there is an underactivity of the anterior cingulate cortex, which is involved with selective attention and working memory. Taylor and colleagues suggest that with low emotional intelligence, there are reduced amounts of REM sleep and associated deficits in the processing of 'procedural-implicit' memory.

They give two reasons why states of emotional arousal evoked by activation of the amygdala may remain unregulated. First, there is a reduction in the unconscious inhibitory feedback from the prefrontal cortex to the amygdala, due to an impoverished representational world that limits the ability of the prefrontal cortex to make a detailed cognitive appraisal of the complex emotional stimuli. Second, there is a limited ability to represent and, therefore, contain emotions in language. When this condition obtains, it reduces the ability to use fantasy to imagine different solutions to emotional problems and reflect on the meaning of the emotional stimuli. This inability restricts the use of conscious cognitive processes to modulate arousal via cortico–amygdala pathways.

The psychoanalytic theory of the development of symbol formation, integrated with neuroscientific research on emotional processing, the development of symbolic thinking and its implications for the treatment of eating disorders

This section melds the neuroscientific research findings with the psychoanalytic work on symbol formation.

Introducing psychoanalytic concepts at this stage in the discussion aims to broaden and deepen both the psychoanalytic and neuroscientific approaches to the treatment of eating disorders. Basic neuroscientific research on its own does not necessarily lead to the development of treatments that are able to take into consideration the whole personality or the content of mental functions. The present thrust of research into the neuroscience of eating disorders is to look mainly at specific deficits in mental functioning. A problem with the psychoanalytic approach to eating disorders is that it does not necessarily take into consideration aspects of brain function. This, it is suggested, might allow for either the analysand being drawn into a false analysis, where the material expressed is not connected to the self-state, or possibly the analyst losing the opportunity to be more accurate, and, thus, more effective, in what can then result in a very long and possibly unnecessarily drawn-out treatment.

Blass and Carmeli (2007) write very critically of neuropsychoanalysis. They suggest that neuroscience does not offer an explanation for non-recollection of non-symbolised memories, mental phenomena cannot be accounted for at the neuronal level and 'the application of neuroscience to psychoanalysis rests on unwarranted inferences that may have a significant negative impact on the way psychoanalysis will evolve in future years'. They quote Freud when he described that an advance in human nature took place when Moses prohibited making an image of God. This, Freud explained, if accepted, would have a profound effect. 'For it meant that a sensory perception was given second place to what may be called an abstract idea – a triumph of intellectuality [Geistigkeit] over sensuality (*Moses and Monotheism.* 1939)'.

I suggest that there is not the profound incompatibility between the two allied disciplines that Blass and Carmeli assert. Brain function can perhaps be better understood as working in systems, where difficulties in any one part can impair function. In order to think symbolically in an abstract manner, there must be access to executive frontal functions. When access to this 'symbolic' system fails due to an inability to comprehend certain material, which then triggers the amygdala to send out fear signals via the body, there is a closing down of this 'symbolic' system. While memory in language requires access to these executive frontal functions, it is possible, using certain psychoanalytic techniques, that experiences encoded in implicit memory (mediated more by the amygdala than the hippocampus) can be discerned in dreams and transference (Mancia, 2006).

Yovell (2000) described how his timing of interpretations changed in response to neurobiological insight into the effects of stress on memory formation due to such patients being in a compromised state where their

> hippocampi are already compromised, and with hypersensitive amygdala. In this setting, an exaggerated cortisol response to emotional stress, triggered by their amygdala, may overwhelm their hippocampi, and render them incapable of retaining even the best interpretation. Furthermore, excessive negative affect during a session may lead to nothing more than a traumatic repetition of the original insult in a patient suffering from PTSD.

Thus, he concluded, 'it may actually be better to "strike while the iron is cold," and deliver interpretations during moments of emotional calm, when they can be processed and remembered'. He continued,

> In other words, the discovery of the neurological states underlying different disorders and of the neurological impact of forming memories through interpretation allows us to better predict and understand not only whether a painful or traumatic event will be remembered, but also the methods that facilitate its recollection and the consequences of it being recalled.

I suggest that understanding how brains function under specific duress allows the professional delivering the treatment to attune to the capacities of the patient, especially if a particular technique is discovered to increase patient anxiety and the patient belongs to a group known to have difficulty in attenuating anxiety.

When patients undergo treatment (even in the case of eating disorders where the patient is resistant to treatment), it is their lives and relationships that are the content of the trigger material which, it is hypothesised, provokes an eating disorder episode. Therapists naturally gravitate to trying to communicate about these relationships or, in the case of psychoanalysis, drive derivatives (depending on the school of psychoanalysis). It is suggested that by understanding the neuropsychological deficits and the mode of thinking of the patient, the emotional material can be approached in a way that reduces anxiety and, it is hypothesised, promotes the re-establishment of the pathway to the prefrontal cortex. If the patient's mode of thinking is not taken into consideration, then it is hypothesised that anxiety is increased by presenting material that can overwhelm the ability to process emotions via the symbolic pathway to the prefrontal cortex. Under this pressure, it is hypothesised that the 'body concrete' 'fight-or-flight' 'fast and dirty' pathway (see Figure 1.1) to the amygdala is promoted and reinforced, leading to concrete thinking and acted-out solutions.

I am suggesting that how a patient is communicated with can affect how the brain of the patient responds. Another way of putting it is that neuro-anatomical change can arise from therapeutic treatment, be that psychoanalysis or a specific treatment designed for the purpose. This might be seen by psychoanalysts as a radical proposal but is given support by Cozolino in his book *The Neuroscience of Psychotherapy* (2002).

Following a synthesis of these two theoretical approaches, a model of the mind in eating disorders is presented in Chapter 5, based on both neuropsychological and psychoanalytic concepts.

Symbolisation in psychoanalysis and the work of Segal and Klein

While the American and French schools have extrapolated and refined the concept of symbolisation in psychoanalysis (see Chapter 3), this work will concentrate on the seminal work of Hannah Segal, whose 1957 paper became the basis for later theorising. Segal's work was based on that of Melanie Klein. The aim of this section is to specifically examine how the Kleinian concepts of projective identification and the depressive position meld with neuroscientific understanding of emotional processing pathways.

How the infant's primitive mental equipment perceives her 'objects' and how this relationship matures and changes, is accurately described by Segal (in that her work mirrors the neuroscientific findings), and her work on symbol formation is seen as seminal in the psychoanalytic field (Segal, 1957). It is noteworthy that her theorising was based on her work with severely thought-disordered schizophrenic patients, a group accepted to have neurological deficits.

Segal's endpoint of a fully functioning psyche is, following Klein's work, the depressive position. In this paradigm an individual has achieved full symbolic function, can experience both positive and negative feelings towards the same object (person or experience) at the same time, can employ memory to guide present and future actions, can reflect on the deeper meanings of a situation and is able to create an internal representation of the objects in her world, having let go of needing the actual external object. Thus, there is the ability to symbolise and use these symbols in thinking and to represent the internal world. Paranoid–schizoid thinking is no longer routinely employed. The paranoid–schizoid mode of thinking is primitive, that is, grandiose, narcissistic, lacking in boundary between internal and external phenomena, concrete in nature and lacking in separation of the qualities of the concrete object and the self.

When the depressive position is attained, the resultant capacity to symbolise lessens anxiety and allows the resolution of conflict. This symbolic capacity is then available to process earlier unresolved conflicts.

Most importantly, Segal's theorising includes the possibility of movement between these two states even once the depressive position has been achieved. She describes how, under conditions of high anxiety, there can be a regression to the paranoid–schizoid position, with a subsequent return to the depressive position when that anxiety has decreased.

The endpoint of physiological maturation is described by Fonagy and Target (1996) as the desired result of well-attuned maternal preoccupation where the mother correctly reads the infant's communications and mirrors back to her baby her understanding and containment of his primitive anxieties, via her voice and actions. This activity primes the right hemisphere for the prosodic and emotional content of language and modulation of anxiety. This priming creates the conditions for efficient transfer of non-verbal language information between the hemispheres, via the corpus callosum. This reinforces the potential symbolic emotional processing pathway to the prefrontal cortex to engage the left hemisphere symbolic language function. Prior to this, the baby experiences the world viscerally and much as Segal describes the paranoid–schizoid position.

Neurologically, the infant exists in a world of undeveloped neural pathways, having yet to gain control over her limbs or any body function except rooting and sucking. In her earliest days, the infant can focus at around 10 inches, just the distance to her mother's face (Stern, 1985). There are, as yet, no symbolic functions and the baby exists in an unseparated world where the mother takes the role of the baby's thinking system. As the pathways to the symbolic functions are created, the child slowly develops mastery over language and the ability to symbolise. If, however, language develops without the ability to reflect on self-states (Bateman & Fonagy, 2010) – that is, there is little or no connection between right hemisphere experience and anxiety moderation and left hemisphere ability to employ language-encoded memory, allowing symbolic perusal of the material – expressed language is denuded of its experienced emotional meaning.

Freud, who began his medical life as a neurologist, stated that when he began to formulate psychoanalysis, due to the lack of sophistication of the science of neurology, he hypothesised the existence of various brain mechanisms. He hoped that one day the equipment might exist that would make it possible to investigate whether these brain mechanisms do exist. Freud's exceptional talent was that he was a very fine observer, and it was this accuracy of observation that underpinned his theorising. At times he would put aside ideas that he was working on, stating that due to lack of information he was unable to continue until it was possible to support his thinking with new deductions flowing from his future theoretical work or hard science (Freud, 1915).

> The deficiencies in our description would probably vanish if we were already in a position to replace the psychological terms with physiological or chemical ones . . . We may expect [physiology and chemistry] to give the most surprising information and we cannot guess what answers it will return in a few dozen years of questions we have put to it. They may be of a kind that will blow away the whole of our artificial structure of hypothesis.
>
> (Freud, 1920)

Segal's work on symbolisation freely uses the terms repression and sublimation. She employs Ernest Jones' distinction between sublimation and symbolisation. Jones suggested that for a symbol to be formed, the affect invested in the symbolised idea is unable to be transformed or modified into sublimation. His view was that sublimation is a more sophisticated function. Thus, one might suggest that the formation of a symbol in Jones' theorising might better be described as a concrete symbol applied only to unconscious symbols, as in dreams that were intended to disguise meaning. I might say that due to neurological disruption – when the pathway to the symbolic language functions is inaccessible – all that is available to the mind is the dreamlike concrete symbol. Under these circumstances, the only language available is concrete in nature and lacks metaphorical meaning.

For sublimation to occur, the symbolic language functions must be connected to the broadly right hemisphere emotional functions. In addition, there needs to be access to memory encoded in language which supports fully functioning frontal functions that include forward planning, allowing consequences of actions to be foreseen.

Segal described the process of symbolisation as one in which, owing to emotional conflict, a desire has to be given up and is then repressed to become a dream symbol. Segal theorised that symbols are not repressed objects because they are no longer objects, as there is a confusion between the self and the object and then between the symbol and the object symbolised. This is in line with the current work that suggests that an eating disorder is the concrete manifestation of an emotional state.

We know that in eating disorders it is the complex and negative emotional material that is the trigger for an eating/bingeing/purging episode (Waller et al., 1996). This overwhelming and incomprehensible information, it is suggested, is labelled with a danger signal and is returned by the insula to the amygdala, never reaching the representational functions of the prefrontal cortex.

At this point there is no access to language-encoded memory, no activation of frontal lobe function which extracts information from the environment and can plan for the future, and, in fact, no possibility to sublimate (in psychoanalytic terms) or integrate (from the neurological perspective) emotional experience. The experience of these emotions remains primitive and concrete and is well described as paranoid–schizoid material and primitive defence mechanisms.

Sublimation is the result of perusal of complex emotional information from the point of view of the subject's past and present experiences. It is then possible for this material to enter conscious thought in an occluded manner. Under these conditions, the content of the complex emotional thoughts can be metaphorised and are available to be made conscious through interpretation. When there is no such perusal, there can be no sublimation.

Thus, it could be argued that there is a close relationship between the psychoanalytic observations of Klein and Segal and the neuroscientific research into emotional processing, which strengthens both psychoanalytic theory and practice and the clinical validity of the neuroscientific findings.

In particular, this exercise has illuminated the discontinuous model of neural emotional processing and adds weight to the need to include this understanding in clinical practice. It is suggested that the 'switch' between concrete and symbolic states can be predicted and reversed due to the understanding of what, in the internal and external environment, constitutes trigger material. In particular, the neuroscientific understanding indicates that the reversal of the concrete state to symbolic function need not be the laborious process that it is understood to be in psychoanalysis but, with the opening of the pathway to the higher functions, can be effected relatively rapidly.

Quite rightly, psychoanalysts have understood that the achievement of full symbolic function allows for mature interaction with the internal and external world. It is suggested that the neuroscience of emotional processing should be a necessary, or even essential, element of psychological treatment, offering, as it does, a rationale for the what, when and how of delivering treatment. In eating disorders, the switch from the concrete to the symbolic mode of functioning is quite clear, while in other illnesses, for example, the addictions, it is less obvious but, it is suggested, still relevant.

Symbolisation as a process of integration

The root of the word 'symbol' is the Greek for throwing, or bringing together. It is just this process of integration that is described by both the analytic and neuroscientific schools of thought as the basis of the process of symbolisation. For the neuroscientists, this process is the smooth integration between hemispheres, where the various streams of stimuli coalesce and all the aspects of language are available to facilitate higher-order executive functioning. For the analytic school, it is the culmination of the process of sublimation, when material has been worked on and internal objects are able to be viewed in a nuanced way. When this process of integration fails, there is no distinction between internal and external phenomena, between the subject and the object, and between early and later experiences.

Both schools of thought recognise that these processes have failed in patients presenting with psychotic or schizoid symptoms. Segal (1957) describes this presentation as a disturbance or inhibition in the formation or free use of symbols. Neuroscientists will be looking at excessive levels of anxiety, resulting in the inhibition of the use of executive functions. They might view the resulting concrete state as possible damage in brain function and a sequelae or cause of an illness process or psychological phenomena. In the case of a neuroscientific explanation, LeDoux (1996) has described two possible neurological pathways available for emotional processing. The 'body concrete' is designed for the 'fight-or-flight' response to threatening stimuli. It is when this pathway to the amygdala is overused (i.e., when there is no imminent threat to the organism but the brain believes there is) that the more complex pathway that enables symbolic representation, language and memory is short-circuited.

Segal described her work with two patients that have become classic examples of the difference between concrete symbolism and sublimation (see Chapter 2).

The first patient had a diagnosis of schizophrenia. The second patient, who reported a dream, was considered neurotic.

The important factor in distinguishing between the two cases, Segal suggested, was that when the meaning of the dream became conscious it did not prevent the man from playing the violin but, rather, gave him more access to his unconscious life. As the first man felt that his violin was his penis, he found it as shocking to play the violin in public as it would be to masturbate in public. In other words, there was no distinction between aspects of his body, the object, and his sexuality. In this state of mind there might not even have been any thoughts about an 'other' (i.e., a woman) to whom sexual thoughts might have been directed. All he experienced was shame and an overwhelming feeling that the violin could not be played or, as Segal described it, there was an equivalency between the unconscious and the way the violin was used on the conscious level. Thus, both Jones and Segal define a symbol as those substitutes that replace the object without any change of affect.

It is a moot point whether the genesis of a psychotic illness is to be found in a poor environment, poor genetics, a combination of the two, or a weakness in coping with anxiety. However, when one addresses illnesses that are not considered psychoses but have elements of psychotic thinking (schizoid, in psychoanalytic terminology), one sees the movement between concrete (or paranoid–schizoid) thinking and symbolic (depressive position or sublimated) thinking. I would suggest that this movement between states is the result of fragility in the sense of self, in terms of poor access to ongoing self-states (as defined by Schore, 1996) and subsequent inability to ameliorate anxiety. This state of affairs can also be described as low emotional intelligence and alexithymic.

Klein (1930) suggested that if symbolisation does not occur, the whole development of the ego is arrested. This is very much in line with neuroscientific findings that reduced and unstable ability to access the ongoing self-state leads to an impoverished understanding of the internal and external environment. That is, when, under the stimulus of a danger signal, the 'fight-or-flight' mechanism is operational, and there is reduced capacity for learning and the laying down of memory. Owing to memory being encoded in language, little learning can take place that, in turn, depletes even further the memory store of workable solutions to emotional problems. As this cycle continues, the 'body concrete' pathway to the amygdala is reinforced and the symbolic pathway is neglected, as the more a pathway is used, the stronger it becomes, with the obverse being true that when a pathway is neglected, the connections deteriorate. This state of affairs may result in a preference for concrete thinking and body solutions to complex emotional problems.

Thus, if one generally equates ego functions with frontal lobe functions, which extract information from the environment and are involved in planning and conceptual functions as well as having access to language and memory (Solms & Turnbull, 2003), the preferential use of the 'fast and dirty' pathway back down from the insula to the amygdala (see Figure 1.1) might lead one to expect to see little development, or a stasis, in ego function. With this compromised state of frontal/ego function, it can be hypothesised that there is a reduced ability to mediate between the content of the ongoing self-state and the demands of reality, difficulty in planning ahead, poor extraction of information from the environment and inability to peruse memory and, thus, to bring relevant information to bear in a novel situation. Use of the prefrontal cortical pathway, which involves symbolic language function, allows decisions to be made in the light of ethical constraints, generating a deeper and more nuanced response.

As has been previously discussed, Jones' definition of a symbol simply states that what is not sublimated becomes a symbol. The essence of this symbol is concrete and is the kind of symbol equated with, and undifferentiated from, parts of the self. However, Segal considered this definition of a symbol too narrow and felt it important to widen the meaning. She was concerned that the common usage of the word symbol in everyday language and in scientific parlance would be excluded by this narrow definition. Thus, she chose to broaden the definition to include symbols used in sublimation. She hypothesised a continuous process from the primitive symbol to symbols able to be used in 'self expression, communication, discovery, creation etc.'

Her view was that a child's internal world is created via a series of displacements from early objects to ever-new objects. For this to happen, a child's mental equipment has to develop. Thus, if the child's genetic makeup allows her to be attuned to her mother, and if the environment is such that the mother is free to operate optimally within workable parameters, leading to successful maternal preoccupation, the child's anxiety will be kept within manageable parameters and allow for the development of both right and left hemisphere language. When this optimal situation obtains, the individual is able to contain right hemisphere emotional experience, allow it to cross the corpus callosum to the prefrontal cortex, engage symbolic/metaphoric language, access memory functions, and allows the emotional experience to become symbolised in language.

In psychoanalytic terms, the hallmark of the ego is to mediate between states of pleasure and unpleasure. Large areas of cortico-limbic circuitry are dedicated to performing precisely those correlations between increasingly complex perceptual information and states of pleasure and unpleasure (Watt, 1990).

The analytic description of the symbolic process involves the relationship between the ego, the object, and the symbol. When there is (in analytic terms) a disturbance in the ego's relationship with the object, this will be reflected in disturbance of symbol formation.

The ego attempts to deal with the anxieties created by its relation to the object. When there is emotional difficulty or ambivalence, there is a fear of losing the good object and a fear of the bad object. Thus, if anxiety is high when the 'fast and dirty' pathway to the amygdala is activated, then concrete, simplistic splitting into good and bad predominates. In this state these polar opposites of good and bad are experienced corporeally. The good is allowed to remain inside but the bad has to be ejected. The consequence of this experience is a paucity of symbolic, nuanced thinking. When the pathway to the prefrontal cortex is activated, the whole object can be held in mind with all its good and bad features.

As described above, the more frequently the 'body concrete' pathway is utilised, leading to increased concrete thought, the more it weakens and lessens the probability that the symbolic emotional processing pathway will be utilised, and the ability to relate to the external world will be compromised. The experience of emotional unpleasure, usually created by ambivalent feelings towards an object, will result in a short-term move away from the perceived emotional unpleasure. However, the short-term solution will lead to increased unpleasure when the original emotional problem remains unsolved due to the inability to think about the material in a realistic, rounded way. It is this lack of differentiation between the ego and its object that, in Segal's theorising, leads to disturbances in the differentiation between the symbol and the object symbolised. This lack of differentiation, she proposes, then creates the concrete thinking characteristic of the psychoses.

It is suggested that, due to the creation of unstable neural pathways, a patient may respond to a negative and complex emotional stimulus by experiencing very high anxiety as a result of the insula triggering the concrete pathway. This then forces the patient into a concrete state of mind (the borderline, in analytic terms) and when functioning in this state, there is dissolution of the boundary between the self and the object, which are then experienced as identical. In eating disorders, when there has been a change of state owing to the firing of the 'fast -and dirty' pathway to the amygdala, intolerable and indecipherable negative or mixed feelings become a concrete object; a bad thing inside the stomach and the only solution to hand is to get rid of this bad stuff in the stomach or fat on the body. Vomiting, starving or purging is the logical solution to this concretised anxiety, and the act in itself, it is hypothesised, reduces the anxiety of the intolerable physical/mental state.

Segal uses Klein's concepts where she divided the oral phase into two stages, the earlier being the 'point of fixation of the schizophrenic group of illnesses' and the latter the 'point of fixation of the manic depressive illnesses'. Klein described a splitting of the object into either entirely good or entirely bad (which reflects the primitive workings of the limbic system when no higher-order information has been received). She describes the aim of the ego as being either total union with the good object or annihilation of the bad object along with the bad parts of the self. Thus, if there is no ability to recognise the difference between emotional feelings about an object and the body self, along with vastly reduced ability to access reality, the consequence will be concrete thought processes akin to psychosis and actions that reflect this mode of thinking.

As Klein describes, in this early phase, the thinking is omnipotent and the sense of reality intermittent and precarious. She states that there is no sense of absence of the object. To experience the absence of an object requires left hemisphere symbolic language function to represent the object (Solms & Turnbull, 2003). Without this symbolic language input, the object would always have to be present. Again, eating disorder patients (as is the case with many other conditions) have great difficulty in keeping the therapist 'in mind' and need their 'fix' of being with their therapist, whose efficacy diminishes between sessions. I have noted that patients who become able to symbolise often report how they keep the therapist with them as a voice in their minds.

Freud described the early developmentally primitive state of mind as being dominated by hallucinatory wish fulfilment. He suggested that the object is desired and a hallucination is created which is then experienced as real. Klein extrapolated that the obverse is also felt; when the wish is not fulfilled, the bad object is hallucinated and experienced as real.

With no connections to frontal lobe function, desires would be experienced as if they were real, as there would be no access to reality-testing functions. This is in much the same way that psychotic patients have vastly reduced frontal function and accept internal phenomena as if they were real (Solms & Turnbull, 2003).

Klein (1930) described the process of symbol formation using the concept of projective identification. It is required that large parts of the self are projected into, and identified with, the object and subsequently the object is felt to contain those parts of the self. In the same way, the external world is the recipient of, and comes to represent, projections of the internal world (or internal objects).

This explanation follows the logic of the development of the brain as connections are formed between the hemispheres. In this early stage, distinctions cannot be made between undifferentiated right hemisphere experiences, the concept of self or other, and temporal sequencing. In other words, this early developmental stage exhibits the attributes of the unconscious as described by Freud. It might be posited that it is the successful connecting up of the two hemispheres, in particular regarding language function, that is required for good mental health. When there are difficulties in accessing the ongoing right hemisphere self-state via left hemisphere symbolic language, various symptoms of mental illness might be produced.

Segal's work accurately observed the confusion between the early symbols and the object. She described it as the ego not recognising any difference between the symbol and the object or, in other words, executive frontal functions not being available to make the required distinction.

As described above, Segal's contribution was to explain Freud's (1927) conflation of the original object and the symbol in terms of projective identification. These early symbols were felt by the ego to be the original object, and it was these undifferentiated primitive symbols that she named 'symbolic equation'. Schizophrenic thought, she suggested, was the result of the equation in the internal and external world between the original object and the symbol, where the object is felt and treated as part of the self. This, she proposed, is the result of projection of parts of the ego and internal objects into the object, which then becomes identified with these projects. The symbol, which she describes as created by the ego, is, thus, confused with the object.

Segal has described symbol formation as a gradual process in line with the development of the ego. This is of a piece with the development of neural pathways from primitive function to higher frontal functions. Segal charts the change from early symbols (symbolic equations) to fully formed symbols that can be used for sublimation and are essential for the attainment of the depressive position. As noted above, once Klein's depressive position has been achieved, thinking about an object deepens and is more nuanced. In particular, thinking embraces ambivalence, guilt, fear of loss and actual loss and mourning. There is a striving to recreate the object and there is a lessened need for projection with a concomitant desire for introjection. Segal has written that it is through the repeated experience of loss, recovery and re-creation that the ego establishes a good object.

Segal discusses the growing sense of reality that follows on from an increased awareness of this ambivalence and a lessening need to project negative feelings. As this occurs, there is an increased differentiation between the self and the object that, in turn, creates a differentiation between the internal and external world. The tone of the emotions changes from extreme feelings of anger, hate, murderousness, omnipotence and narcissism to a more caring attitude towards the object, saving it from aggressive attacks and over-possessiveness. This, says Segal, is evidence of inhibition of instinctual aims. At this point, it is suggested that these new objects have been created by the ego and are not identified with the original object. It is this process that creates symbols which are then free to be re-projected into the external world, which is then endowed with symbolic meaning and an increasing sense of reality.

The loss and recreation of the object, which then has its own properties and is no longer able to be confused with the original object, is the basis of the internal object that can now be used symbolically by the unconscious. With access to left hemisphere language and reality-testing frontal functions, the external world can be differentiated from the internal. With full interhemispheric communication, there is access to the internal ongoing self-state which is able to utilise these free symbols, allowing for full symbolic and metaphoric internal language. This full mental capacity is then at the service of complex emotionally demanding stimuli and will produce workable reality solutions.

As mentioned above, this healthy state of affairs is not necessarily stable but can, according to Segal's and Klein's theorising, be reversed, under pressure of anxiety, to the paranoid–schizoid position with all the loss of nuanced emotional thinking and reality-testing functions. Objects again get confused with the self, and splitting and projective identification are employed as defence mechanisms. This state of affairs obtains until there is a reduction in anxiety. Therefore, symbols employed in sublimation return to symbolic equations, which is the result of massive projective identification leading to the ego becoming confused with the object being symbolised. This reversal, it is suggested, is linked to the 'short-circuiting' in the insula back to the amygdala.

This process is very evident in eating disorders. A patient may be talking perfectly normally about subjects that have very little emotional content (generally her preferred subject matter) but when subjects laden with emotional content are brought up, she begins to talk about her unacceptably fat body or how many calories are contained in her last meal. The body and the object become confused and the solution to her discomfort is to rid the body of the 'bad' content.

This loss of language to describe the internal world occurs when, in Segal's terminology, the subject and the object become blurred and symbols are experienced in a concrete way. Thus, language becomes impoverished and concrete and is unavailable for use when communicating with others and, importantly, with the self. Very interestingly, Segal suggests that it is when words are felt to be objects or actions that they are of limited use for the purpose of communication.

With limited language, and what there is being concrete, the patient has little possibility of being aware of her impulses and feelings that might have been the result of a meaningful emotional communication. Segal has described this impoverished state as there being splits between parts of the ego with no possibility of communication between them. The difficulty in the treatment of schizoid patients, Segal suggests, is this impoverishment of internal language that affects both communications with professionals and internal communication. They do not know what they are feeling, and, thus, cannot communicate what they do not know. Or, put another way, there are unknown unknowns.

Symbols as the basis for verbal thinking

Symbols are, thus, the basis of verbal thinking and words, when connected to the ongoing self state, are the building blocks of internal communication. As Segal says, 'Not all internal communication is verbal thinking, but all verbal thinking is an internal communication by means of symbols – words'.

In contrast, fully formed symbolic, nuanced thought and access to language-encoded memory result in emotionally in-touch thoughts, which are both symbolic and conceptual, leading to realistic and measured actions. In other words, the depressive position has been achieved. In particular, the result of the capacity to symbolise is to lessen anxiety and resolve conflict. An important factor is that this capacity can then be pressed into service to resolve earlier unresolved conflicts that previously had been experienced as concrete and primitive. Conflicts which are experienced in a concrete and primitive way generate anxiety which then adds to the vicious circle. In Segal's opinion, insufficient working through of early object relations creates instability in the system and can precipitate the move back to early paranoid–schizoid functioning. She describes the result of this instability as symbolic equations invading the ego. This shift in state might also be understood as – in response to a weakened ability to contain anxiety – the over-use of the 'body concrete' pathway to the amygdala rather than employing the symbolic emotional processing pathway. The resultant concrete thought processes are, thus, due to this changed mental state where all Segal's descriptions obtain.

Segal suggests that, in the depressive position, if the ego is strong enough it will be able to deal with anxieties. It will also be capable of dealing with earlier experiences that can be integrated into the ego via symbolisation. This process, she suggests, enriches the ego. In other words, the more frequently the symbolic emotional processing pathway is triggered, the more there will be access to symbolic and metaphoric use of language, memory, forward planning and reality testing. This access to 'richness' of language and thought, or access to the ongoing self-state, allows for deeper and more subtle responses to emotional challenges and strengthens the sense of self. Conversely, the more the 'body concrete' pathway is triggered, leading to concrete thought and solutions, the weaker the ego functions and the more fragmented and fragile the sense of self.

Chapter 5

Proposing a new model of the mind in eating disorders

Summary

Chapter 5 introduces a new model of the mind in eating disorders. It proposes a different way of thinking about eating disorders, seeing them in terms of mental function (how the ability of eating disorder sufferers to process their emotions may be fragile) rather than just the presence or absence of symptoms. As described in earlier chapters, we understand that emotions are either processed for meaning, by engaging symbolic and reality functions, or are denied access to these functions and are processed somatically by the body with no access to symbolic language (a discontinuous model of neural emotional processing).

The accepted model of eating disorders is whether there is the presence or absence of symptoms at specified levels. To have an eating disorder has always been about how many times a week the person vomits or binges or loses weight. This has changed little with the latest edition of the *Diagnostic and Statistical Manual of Mental Disorders* (DSM-5), which has merely introduced a loosening of the criteria and a broadening of the number of people who are included in the categories. The recommended treatment remains the same.

It perhaps needs to be stated here that while brain function is highly complex and incompletely understood, the following broad assertions and suggestions are derived from sound, well-received recent neurobiological research, which has been discussed more fully in the preceding chapters. For the purposes of this book, there is a level of acceptance of the general direction of research findings, while it is acknowledged that the neurobiological picture is far more nuanced than can be discussed in this work. In other words, we are describing systems rather than functions at the neuronal level. The neurobiological research is employed to support empirical findings.

In this chapter there are two diagrams to illustrate how the brains of eating disorder sufferers may function differently from the norm. The first diagram (Figure 5.1) plots symbolic functioning against emotional processing in language. Under non-anxiety conditions, it describes how people suffering from an eating disorder are relatively poor at understanding the meaning of, for example, metaphor, symbol and irony, and are less able to put their feelings into language (alexithymic). Conversely, it shows that those people who have greater symbolic capacity have more ability to process emotions via language.

The second diagram (Figure 5.2) describes the progression of an eating disorder. If our brains are already less able to access symbolic functions and we experience an emotional shock or trigger (this trigger may well be quite complex, in that we would probably have very mixed feelings about the experience), a danger signal is generated. This danger signal is generated by the amygdala (the 'receiving station' of information from inside and outside of the body), which results in the insula (the gateway to symbolic functions) closing access to the symbolic functions. The material is then returned unprocessed for symbolic meaning or tested against reality and finally expressed in un-thought-out behaviour, as symbolic activity has dropped to zero.

When this happens, eating disorder patients have changed state and are only able to think concretely about their bodies and how they are going to 'get rid of' the intolerable emotions and anxiety they are experiencing. Bingeing/vomiting, starving or over-exercising are attempts to lower the anxiety. When the anxiety is lowered, this allows some symbolic function to return. The problem is that there has been no chance to think about the problem that created the anxiety and while the eating disorder behaviour has reduced the anxiety, the person remains just as neurologically vulnerable as before (if not more so), as there has been no resolution of the emotional problem. Thus, the regained symbolic function is more fragile and vulnerable to complex emotional triggers than previously. It is suggested that this is the neurological result of the increasingly underused symbolic emotional processing pathway and the over-use of the 'body concrete' pathway (Hebb's Axiom (1949) – neurons that fire together wire together). The more a danger signal is attached, the more easily and frequently it will be attached to complex emotional material. With each eating disorder episode, the subject is left in a more vulnerable and unstable state as her store of workable emotional solutions is depleted and the use of the body solutions increases. Over time, the length of the periods spent in the symbolic state may decrease while those spent in the concrete state may increase. This is why it is so important for eating disorder sufferers to be referred to treatment as soon as possible so as to avoid the strengthening of the 'body concrete' pathway and the disuse of the emotional symbolic pathway that is, of course, harder to reverse.

Following these two diagrams of proposed mental function in eating disorders is a detailed discussion of the nature of possible triggers to this altered state of mind from symbolic to concrete thought. To illustrate what is meant by trigger material, examples of that material from several patients treated with ILET, a treatment that follows the logic of mental function, are described. (A description of this new treatment will be presented in Chapter 6.) Chapter 7 will describe in detail the ILET treatment and Chapter 8 describes and follows the treatment of 'Emily', the patient introduced at the beginning of the book.

Diagnosis of eating disorders

For the diagnosis of an eating disorder, the DSM-5 requires there to be certain symptoms present at certain intensities. This approach to diagnosis is in line with the psychiatric attitude of the importance of clusters of first-ranked symptoms. As has been stated above, up until DSM-5, when applied to eating disorders, only 20% of presenting eating disorders were diagnosed as having the full-blown syndrome. This, of course, left 80% in the EDNOS category. As Fairburn et al. (2007) have demonstrated, this group of patients responds equally well (less than 50% 'cure') to treatments designed for the fully expressed illness. Thus, Fairburn at that time ignored the problem of how to conceptualise the 80% of EDNOS patients by leaving the diagnostic criteria intact and suggested that the DSM-5 included a further category of binge eating disorder. He suggested, and it was accepted, that EDNOS patients should be treated the same as 'pure' eating disorder patients. This makes clinical sense but does not address the underlying neurological deficits shared by eating disorder sufferers in whatever category.

An alternative approach to the categorisation and diagnosis of eating disorders might be to address the underlying neurological difficulties. Patients might be better understood and helped if they were to be measured on their ability to attenuate anxiety by looking at their cortisol levels, rigidity of mind (set-shifting), creativity, central coherence, level of comprehension of theory of mind and ability to understand complex metaphor and irony. If this were done, the emphasis would shift from the observed behaviour to the very real deficits exhibited by this group. To this end a tool, 'The Ravello Profile', has been developed by Rose et al. (2011) as a global standard neuropsychological assessment for anorexia nervosa.

Diagrammatic representation of the proposed new model of the mind for eating disorders

Figure 5.1 shows a proposed new model of the mind in eating disorders. It describes all eating disorders, from EDNOS to the most severe life-threatening anorexia, and all points in between. It also offers a possible rationale for the progress of an eating disorder. As a result of the administration of a battery of tests of cognitive function (including testing for the presence of alexithymia, measures of frontal and verbal functions, measures of creativity, rigidity, verbal fluency, concepts of similarity, and verbal IQ), eating disorder subjects can be placed at a point on the two axes. Their position on the graph (see Figure 5.1) describes their level of ability to process emotions in language versus their symbolic functioning. This information permits the design of a treatment to repair the specific deficits expressed by the eating disorder population, and allows for a treatment to be tailored to the individual needs of the patient, rather than a 'one size fits all' package that only delivers a 'cure' for less than half of the patients treated.

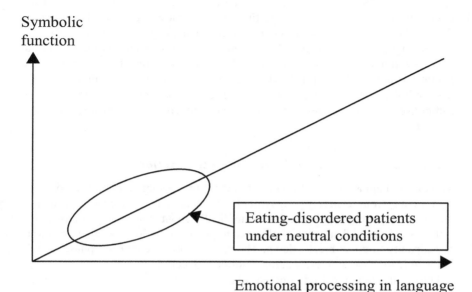

Symbolic
function

Emotional processing in language

Figure 5.1 Model of mental functioning in eating disorders: symbolic functioning against
emotional processing in language

As can be seen from Figure 5.1, generally the X (emotional processing in language) and Y (symbolic function) axes are positively correlated. The greater the
symbolic function, the greater is the ability to process emotions via language. It is
suggested that, under neutral conditions, the eating disorder population occupies a
low position on the graph within the shaded area. Thus, they are relatively poor at
understanding symbolic meanings of, for example, metaphor, symbol and irony,
and have poor emotional processing in language. The zero point on the graph
represents complete concrete function – that is, no ability to think symbolically
and no ability to process emotions in language. The zero point also describes
the concrete functioning typically found in the psychoses and, in particular,
schizophrenia.

It is suggested that because eating disorder patients function at the low end
of the symbolic scale, they are vulnerable to complex emotional stimuli that can
overwhelm their ability to process emotional material symbolically. Thus, this
subject group might be expected to process neutral stimuli adequately, but their
position on the graph would indicate that they do not have the ability to handle
demanding emotionally complex material that requires rapid checking of the self-
state and high symbolic language function.

Patients suffering from any form of an eating disorder can, at any one time,
be plotted as a point on the diagram. This may eliminate the need for a separate

category for EDNOS patients, as they can be placed on the same axes as 'true' eating disorders. However, after testing, we will know a great deal more about their abilities and deficits and can tailor a treatment programme accordingly.

It is suggested that patients do not remain as static points on the model but operate within parameters that are not stable entities and, under stress, can shift to another paradigm. This shift, it might be argued, can be in either direction along the symbolic–emotional processing axes. Thus, the patient is either more able to symbolise emotions in language or she will use concrete bodily expressions more frequently.

State change from symbolic to concrete function

The discontinuous model of neural emotional processing rests on the notion of state change from relatively poor symbolic function to absolute concrete function.

While the patient is able to think symbolically about emotionally neutral material, it is suggested that, when challenged to process emotionally salient material, her capacity to do so breaks down. The result is that she enters a phase of only being able to think concretely about emotional material.

During the hypothesised concrete phase, it is suggested that, because there may be no access to memory in language, poor frontal function and limited language ability, acted-out body behaviour might be employed to reduce the high level of anxiety. When this anxiety has been reduced sufficiently to return the mind to symbolic emotional function, it is suggested that the patient might settle at a decreased level of symbolic emotional capacity due to a lack of resolution of the emotional challenge. This may then leave the patient unable to address the reality of the emotional challenge and, thus, become increasingly stressed. This hypothesised new lower level of symbolic emotional capacity might then be more vulnerable to becoming destabilised. In addition, due to the lack of a reality solution to the current problem, the store of possible future solutions may become depleted, frontal function assessment of effectiveness of eating disorder behaviour as a solution to emotional challenges may be weakened, and the 'body concrete' pathway to the amygdala may be strengthened as the danger signal attached to the emotional material will have been applied to additional events and, thus, broadened. Trigger events, it is hypothesised, may then proliferate and the length of time spent in the symbolic state may decrease while that spent in the concrete state may increase.

Figure 5.2 describes the progression of an eating disorder. Owing to compromised symbolic functioning and under the pressure of a complex emotional trigger, it is hypothesised that a danger signal is attached to the material that causes the insula to return the material to the amygdala, causing symbolic ability to drop to zero that then creates a spike of anxiety.

It is hypothesised that at this point eating disorder patients have changed state and are only able to think in a concrete manner about their internal world. This, it is suggested, creates the conditions for concrete eating disorder behaviour as an

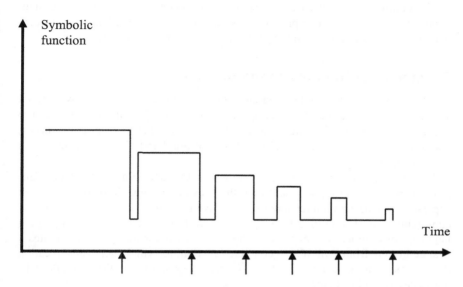

Figure 5.2 State change in eating disorder patients from symbolic to concrete processing following a complex emotional trigger

attempt to lower anxiety and deal with incomprehensible emotional information. This eating disorder behaviour may allow symbolic function to return. However, it is hypothesised that the regained symbolic function settles below the previous level, as a result of the neglect of symbolic emotional processing and the reinforcement of the danger signal attached to emotionally salient material. Settling at this lower level leaves the subject in a more vulnerable and unstable state, as the store of experiences of workable emotional solutions is depleted.

Owing to the change of state, the patient does not have the ability to symbolise and take a view as to the importance and relevance of the emotional challenge. This may leave the trigger material as perplexing as before the episode of eating disorder behaviour began. This, it is suggested, creates a raised background of anxiety and adds to the store of unresolved problems.

With the hypothesised increasingly compromised symbolic function, a reduced store of successful solutions to challenging emotional events and lessened reality checking, the patient becomes increasingly reactive to ever more minor triggers. The pattern, it is suggested, repeats with reducing symbolic function and shorter periods between state changes. This explains the typically observed progress of an untreated eating disorder.

It is suggested that the reduction in anxiety effected by eating disorder behaviour is brought about via acting out, in the concrete, of attempts at symbolic thought. Thus, a bad thought becomes something bad in the stomach to be evacuated. There is an attempt at problem solving but one that is not capable of being effective.

The culmination of the deficits in this developmental path, it is suggested, expresses itself in poor comprehension of complex emotional language. In particular, there is a failure to understand unusual metaphor and irony.

Trigger material for change of state

In Chapter 4, the process of how patients with an eating disorder may have arrived at their illness was traced from faulty maternal preoccupation, through insecure attachment styles, to right hemisphere deficits, poor interhemispheric transfer, poor emotional processing, deficits in theory of mind and, finally, difficulties in symbolisation.

The following section discusses the most recent work on how literal and figurative language is processed, and how the prevailing views have recently been superseded. This new understanding has paved the way for insights into how comprehension of figurative language may fail. It also examines the underlying language difficulties that may be at the heart of trigger material that creates a change in state from symbolic to concrete functioning, which then leads to eating disorder behaviour. A treatment based on repairing these specific symbolic deficits is described in Chapter 6.

When discussing trigger material, it is suggested that when there is a collapse from symbolic language to the concrete paradigm, there may be a signature residue of the attempted metaphoric/figurative understanding. This residue, it is suggested, contains within it clues to the nascent symbolic content of the attempted processing of the emotional stimuli. Expanding the collapsed metaphor, it is suggested, gives access to the hypothesised attempted symbolic processing of the emotional material and may allow the patient to catch and uncover her own thoughts.

The content of trigger material

The nature of trigger material, it is suggested, is of crucial importance in the understanding of how and why eating disorder patients react to a complex emotional stimulus.

The concept of theory of mind is essential in the understanding of communication as there is the need for other independent minds to be communicated with and influenced. It is insufficient for the receiver to understand only the literal content; the receiver needs to understand what the speaker is 'really saying' (Steen, 2007).

Our understanding of how our brains comprehend language has changed. Until recently the comprehension of figurative language has been described as 'indirect' or 'sequential'. By this is meant that the brain initially analyses passages for the literal meaning and if this makes no sense, it reprocesses the words in order to extract the figurative meaning. This view was based on a dichotomous model of laterality with the left hemisphere responsible for processing literal language and the right hemisphere for decoding figurative expressions. There is now a new understanding of how figurative language is processed – the 'coarse coding model'. This model predicts that the left hemisphere will be activated by any sentence that has a close semantic relationship but sentences that have a distant semantic relationship and are novel with multiple possible meanings activate the right hemisphere, regardless of whether the expression is intended metaphorically or literally (Schmidt et al., 2007).

Understanding irony requires both an association between the speaker's thoughts and those of another person and a sophisticated theory of mind. Being able to correctly attribute first-order beliefs (modeling what another person knows) is sufficient to understand simple metaphor but not irony. For that, a second-order theory of mind (modelling what another person knows about what a third person knows) is needed.

Conclusions regarding neurological processing of language

Recent work has opened up research into right hemisphere and left hemisphere processing of language meaning by focusing on the complexity of the stimulus. This approach links the early developmental environment with the development of theory of mind and processing of complex emotional stimuli. It suggests that in order to understand the nuances of complex communications that contain unusual metaphoric or ironic content, second-order theory of mind is required. Thus, damage in theory of mind subsequent to faulty maternal preoccupation, it is suggested, can detrimentally affect the ability to process emotional information that has multiple possible meanings.

Complex psychological triggers in eating disorders

The previous research has built up a picture of how eating disorder patients' neural development may have been impaired due to both constitutional and environmental factors. The majority of eating disorders begin in adolescence, when several developmental factors come into play. It is suggested that it is at this point that complex emotional triggers precipitate eating disorder behaviour.

First of these is the physiological maturation that accompanies puberty. Even though the onset of puberty is around the age of 7 or 8, the release of the gonadal hormones begins in the very early teens. At the same time, the frontal lobe connections pare down in much the same way as they do between the ages of 2 and 3, when infant connections give way to connections required during latency. At adolescence, neuronal connections required during latency fall away, and the adult brain does not settle down until the early twenties. When this paring down gets going, teenagers' abilities to peruse stimuli and correctly assess the environment deteriorate, and the hormonal swings create emotional havoc.

An eating disorder can arise if this turbulent time is overlaid on a poor ability to attenuate anxiety, a fragile sense of self, insecure attachment, impaired theory of mind, low emotional processing and poor ability to comprehend figurative language. Adolescence is anyway a risk time, as there are so many demands in terms of separation and individuation, the requirement to negotiate peer group relationships and pressures, as well as the need for teenagers to prove themselves academically and get ready to enter the world of adult pressures of work and relationships.

So much of what is swirling around this 'at risk' group of (mainly) young women will be incomprehensible to them if they are unable to understand complex metaphoric–ironic–figurative meaning.

While there is a preponderance of female to male suffers, there is, at present, no particular accepted understanding why eating disorders should be so skewed in favour of female sufferers. I would suggest that there might be several protective factors at play. Testosterone might play a part, in that boys tend to 'act out' as against girls 'acting in' on their bodies; boys are, on the whole, not expected to be emotionally literate and communicate with their peers over physical activities, or may settle disputes with a 'fight-or-flight' response. I have observed over many years that mothers who suffer from an eating disorder seem to experience an excess of postnatal depression on the birth of a boy child. An explanation might be (and it has been given to me by patients) that the mother feels that by being different from her the baby has already left her, and so she rejects him to protect herself from the loss. The birth of a boy is a possible 'norm violation' and it may be that the insula is involved.

The world of the young women sufferers will abound with emotional triggers that can easily overwhelm their emotional language processing ability. The danger signal attached to the complex emotional trigger will create the conditions for the employment of the 'fast and dirty' emotional processing pathway, leading to a bodily solution.

The trigger itself would have to be of a certain complexity, containing novel figurative material that requires rapid interhemispheric transfer. This transfer is between the ongoing self-state located in the right hemisphere and left hemisphere symbolic language processing skills that give access to stored memories.

Degradation of the figurative/metaphoric content of the emotional trigger as it collapses towards the concrete

The trigger material for an eating disorder event, it is suggested, contains valuable information. Also that when the processing of emotions breaks down, there is a signature residue of the trigger. Finding this residue will allow the stimulus thought to be resymbolised.

Buhl (2002) and Skarderud (2007) have described eating disordered individuals as experiencing an immediate equivalence between bodily and emotional experience, where metaphors are not understood as indirect figurative expressions but as a concrete reality, where the 'as if' of the metaphor becomes an 'is'. This may be a good description of how eating disorder patients are functioning when in the concrete state, but it does not describe them when they are not under conditions of emotionally triggered anxiety. Under neutral conditions they can, if to a limited degree, process non-salient emotions symbolically. However, when this limited capacity is overwhelmed by a complex emotional trigger, it is then that there is a collapse into the concrete state.

In the attempt to understand the emotional trigger symbolically, the mental apparatus, as it were, collapses under the resultant anxiety generated by the inability to comprehend the possible different meanings and complexity of the processing task confronting them. As a result, it is suggested that the 'fast and dirty' emotional processing pathway is triggered, cutting out access to the symbolic functions. At this point, only a concrete mode of thought is available. There has been an attempt at understanding the trigger material figuratively but the complexity of the demand, it is suggested, defeats the patient's capacities.

It is hypothesised that it is this attempt at processing that falls back or collapses. The resultant concrete state, it is suggested, contains elements of the symbolic attempts and it is this residue of the symbolic/metaphoric language that is to be found expressed in the bodily symptom and where the body becomes the symbol. At this point, the patient becomes totally unaware of the lost meaning and is trapped in the behaviour, or, as Skarderud describes it, the patients lack a 'conscious awareness of the metaphoric connections between their concrete symptoms and underlying emotions and sense of self'. He suggests that it is important to look for the metaphoric meaning of the behavioural and cognitive symptoms in order to understand how the patients are 'trapped in the concreteness of body symbolism'.

The critical moment of state change

This section discusses the hypothesised concept of a sudden and dramatic state change between symbolic and concrete function and suggests that this shift lies at the heart of the illness that expresses itself as an eating disorder. It is suggested that by focusing on the precise moment before the hypothesised state change, the content of the trigger material can be identified. It is suggested that it is then possible to help the patient to resymbolise and understand the complexities of the emotional task she faces.

Whereas similar conceptualisations about the development of an eating disorder (e.g., the work of Buhl, 2002, and Skarderud, 2007) describe the concrete state of functioning of eating disorder patients, they do not necessarily address moving in and out of the concrete state. This may be because these professionals have mainly concentrated on working with anorexic patients who tend to function a great deal of the time in the concrete state, although, with close attention, subtle state change can be detected. On the other hand, bulimic patients express quite marked state change, and at one moment can be describing events in their lives with adequate, if low-level, symbolic language and the next they will suddenly shift to the concrete with the content of their discourse relating to their bodies or food.

There is a general thrust in this area of research to help patients look for the metaphoric meaning of their behaviour. It is suggested that general approaches to increase symbolisation in eating disorders act as a scattergun and do not connect the mind and body in a direct manner.

The body of research quoted in this work supports the ILET approach to treatment that is designed to stimulate the use of the symbolic emotional processing pathway by discussing possible meanings of the trigger material.

Whereas Skarderud (2007) has suggested that the therapeutic enterprise can be conceptualised as focusing on the rehabilitation of the symbolic function, the ideas presented in this book concentrate on the moment of transformation between the symbolic and concrete states and to enlist the use of the symbolic emotional pathway to give immediate access to conceptual language function, memory in language and frontal reality-testing functions.

Examples of trigger material

Olivia

Olivia was 38 years old, married without children. She was referred by her general practitioner (GP) following diagnosis of bulimia, from which she had suffered since the age of fifteen, and for her loss of sex drive, which had led to there being no sexual contact within her marriage for the previous two years.

She was the elder of two sisters of working-class parents from Scotland whom she described as quiet and reticent. Her relationship with them was polite and dutiful but she found it difficult to describe her feelings towards them. She also found it difficult to explain why she had married her husband and put it down to his pursuit of her and the fact that all her friends were getting married. On taking a history, it emerged that she blamed herself and her illness for the parlous state of the marriage. She could make no sense of why she binged and vomited and despised herself for so doing and felt so bad about her body that she could not bear to have an intimate relationship with her husband.

During discussions around trigger moments, we discovered that it was usual for Olivia to binge and vomit after calling home. A particular trigger was identified if she had disagreed with her mother, who felt hurt and rejected. Olivia began to acknowledge that this made her feel very angry towards her mother but also very guilty for upsetting her. Olivia also felt guilty for the state of her marriage and said she was committed to trying to make it work. As Olivia became more aware of the trigger thoughts before bingeing and vomiting, which centred on not being listened to and taken seriously, she began to question and discuss her needs within her relationship with her husband. This change in the balance of the relationship created discord in her marriage.

Some ten sessions into the treatment, her bingeing and vomiting having been absent for the previous four weeks, Olivia brought to a session a feeling of puzzlement as to why she had binged and vomited on one occasion during the previous week. She was asked to describe the scene leading up to the change of state when she knew that she wanted to binge. She began by describing it as a typical evening, if somewhat fraught, that she felt was no different from the rest of the week when she had had no urge to binge and vomit. When asked to pinpoint the moment of state change she was only able to say it was when she was putting out the rubbish, a job she did every week at that time. As she was taken through each step of the activity, Olivia related and described in detail how she had to trundle the wheelie bin down a pathway by the side of the house, which was shared with a neighbour. She was able to identify the exact moment of state change when she began thinking about what food there was in the house to binge on. She was then asked to identify the last thought she had had just before the binge thought (which subsequently turned into a binge following the activity). She said that she had become aware of the noise that the bin was making on the bumpy path and worried that this might disturb her neighbour. Olivia was asked what it was about the noise of the bin that she thought would disturb her neighbour. She replied that it was very loud as the bin contained glass bottles. Asked why this short burst of not very disturbing noise should affect her neighbour who, since it was winter, most likely had the doors and windows closed, she replied in an embarrassed manner that the bin was full of wine bottles and she imagined that her neighbour would disapprove of the amount of alcohol she had drunk. Olivia was able to take back the projection of her own disquiet about the amount of alcohol she had been drinking. We addressed how she was dealing with the 'rubbish' in the marriage and she replied that it was by getting drunk to avoid her very painful feelings. She began to explore her angry and yet desolate feelings about her marriage and to acknowledge her feeling of not having 'chosen' him. She recognised that she had real reservations about the marriage that she had to face up to. This became a turning point in the therapy.

The point to note in this vignette was that the act of putting out the 'rubbish' from the marital home had allowed an associative reflection which momentarily provoked a metaphorical insight that the activity represented an avoidance of dealing with the problems (the rubbish) within the marriage and that she was using alcohol to avoid thinking about the very difficult state of her marriage. This fleeting metaphorical insight created acute anxiety and subsequently and instantaneously provoked the collapse of this thought into its concrete form. The concrete solution of bingeing and vomiting was a way of emptying her 'body mind'. By resymbolising the collapsed attempt at metaphorical understanding in the concrete thought left behind, she was able to access her difficult and anxiety provoking thoughts.

Olivia had poor emotional processing skills and very little memory store of successful emotional problem solving, due to her long history of bulimia. Thus, when presented with the complex task of addressing her needs within the marriage, or whether she wished to continue with the marriage, her compromised capacity to process the emotional demands collapsed under the pressure. A particular feature of the trigger was the ambivalent nature of Olivia's dilemma. She professed to want to work at and save her marriage but, due to her difficulty in acknowledging her negative feelings, she lacked the capacity to view and address the marital problems in a balanced way. The alcohol, which works by disinhibiting the frontal lobes, sets the scene for use of the concrete body pathway and, thus, allowed for impulsive concrete behaviour.

Sadia

Sadia, a young professional woman in her mid twenties, was referred for treatment. She had a ten-year history of anorexia and bulimia. During her teens, from around the age of 15 for two years, Sadia restricted and exercised. Her weight dropped significantly but never became dangerously low. The bulimia followed from the age of 17. At this time she settled into a pattern of restricting for a day or so, followed by bingeing and vomiting.

She was the daughter of her mother's first marriage and eldest of three children, with two younger half-brothers from her mother's second marriage. She had no contact with her birth father, who had left when she was a baby. Both brothers had been referred for psychological help in the past. Her mother's second marriage collapsed around the time of Sadia's first eating disorder symptoms. It was a very messy divorce, followed by her mother (who suffered from depression) deciding to move back to her country of origin with her sons. In order to finish her education, Sadia stayed in the UK and had to stay with her stepfather, who made inappropriate controlling emotional demands on her. Owing to her mother's state of health, contact with her mother was not as frequent as Sadia wanted. Subsequently, Sadia went to university, left her stepfather's house and forged a good career.

She presented for treatment suffering from depression and bulimia. In particular, she felt unable to deal with her stepfather's continual demands or her mother's depression. At the time of treatment, both parents and brothers were living abroad in different countries.

It was against this background that Sadia came to a session saying that she had just binged and vomited the previous night and had no understanding as to why this had happened (i.e., she was unaware of the trigger material). She had been given the ILET psycho-education and as a consequence her bulimic behaviour had reduced and she had understood and learned how to recover her insight and symbolic thinking. This episode, however, was beyond her ability to process.

When asked about the evening, she replied that she was just where she had wanted to be, having a quiet evening, planning to eat healthily with some pleasurable tasks to do. But somehow she found herself in the kitchen bingeing on 'bad' foods. When asked to identify the moment just before the thought of bingeing entered her mind, she was unable to recollect exactly. All aspects to her situation at home were explored but no one thing came to the fore as an 'aha' moment of emotional recognition. We then moved on to why she had chosen to be alone that evening; her reply was that she had had two invitations but had turned them both down. She was asked to recount her reasons for refusing the invitations; the first invitation was from a friend whom she knew less well. This invitation was easily refused and she did not feel at all conflicted by it. The second invitation was from a family of a friend she felt close to and the reason given for refusal was that 'the food was too rich'. Once Sadia had said this, her tone and conversation continued in a concrete manner, all about how the mother of this family always prepared rich food that she could not digest and would, therefore, make her feel fat and uncomfortable. The word 'rich' was focused on and explored. It was noted that it had both concrete and symbolic meanings. One metaphoric meaning was that the situation would be 'a bit rich', meaning that it could not be tolerated, as against the concrete meaning of the food being too oily and having too many calories in it. We explored her feelings around the invitation; about the nature of the family whose 'food' was too 'rich' and could not be 'stomached', it emerged that this family were very close and loving, and what would prove 'too rich to stomach' was seeing them all together and the support they were giving to one another. Once this insight had been reached, Sadia was able to explore her feelings about her own family that was cast to the four winds and about the conflict and drama that happened when they did get together.

The complex nature of the stimulus thought (and all its associations) had proved too much for Sadia to emotionally process through her symbolic functions and her emotions were hijacked and ended up being processed concretely as a concrete metaphor. The dire and distressing situation of Sadia's family, in contrast to the warm, close, loving family, plus the seemingly positive choice of staying alone, which accented her isolated situation, and all the challenges of how to deal with her demanding and unsupportive family overwhelmed her already compromised emotional-processing ability. Again, as with Olivia, above, Sadia had a poor sense of self, insecure attachment and limited store of successful emotional problem solving, creating fertile ground for emotional hijacking.

Theresa

Theresa was a 32-year-old recently married woman, who was referred by her psychiatrist for bulimia and rapid weight loss.

Her history was of a very unseparated relationship with her mother, who had recently forbidden her five children to keep contact with their father after he had been forced by the mother to leave the family home following a particularly serious argument. Theresa had sided with her mother in the family argument and chose not to see her father. One of her two brothers sided with father and went to live with him and, as a consequence, had been rejected by his mother.

It was shortly after the argument that Theresa began to develop symptoms. Her mother invited herself to stay with her and her husband and increasingly took over the household chores as Theresa succumbed to vomiting everything she ate. As her illness progressed, so her mother decided that she was going to stay with the young couple on a semi-permanent basis. It was at this point that Theresa came into therapy and was able to discover her own thoughts and wishes. However, as she regained her own mind, she found her mother's presence too stifling and so thanked her for her help but asked if she could return to her own home, as it was important for Theresa and her husband to have their own space. Her mother felt completely rejected and angry and left, cutting off all contact with Theresa, which initially felt devastating.

The work in therapy continued and concentrated on the triggers to her vomiting episodes which, unsurprisingly, featured difficulty in expressing any opinion that did not accord with that of others.

Theresa had been symptom-free for about two months when she reported, in therapy, that she did not understand why she had suddenly felt the urge to vomit the previous day. She had been eating in a familiar restaurant with close girlfriends, something she had not done since her bulimia began. Going to the restaurant and eating in public was a big step for her, but she had not anticipated any difficulties.

When asked to describe the moment just before she felt the urge to vomit, Theresa recalled that she was talking animatedly with her dinner companions. She remembered feeling proud of herself in that she was 'expressing her point of view' – something she had always had difficulty doing and which had had catastrophic consequences when she had asked her mother to leave. In fact, the exact words 'expressing my point of view' were the last words to go through her mind just before the urge to vomit. On being asked to survey the scene at this point of transition, she remembered looking up and seeing a woman looking at her. Theresa then had the thought that the woman was thinking 'who was Theresa to open her mouth and eat?' The metaphor of having the right to 'express a point of view' had collapsed into the woman 'pointing her view' (i.e., looking at Theresa), and then Theresa's projected injunction that she did not have the right to 'open her mouth' which, in the concrete, would be the orifice that was used to eat rather than speak to express her 'point of view', an activity which had precipitated the trauma of abrupt separation and rejection. At this juncture the therapy concentrated on why she felt unable to express a point of view, thus strengthening the symbolic pathway and finding an appropriate emotional solution. There was a wealth of material relating to how Theresa had experienced the danger of disagreement in her childhood and had made sure that her thoughts aligned with those of her mother, but following her marriage and her parent's separation, her ability to have her own mind came under severe pressure and created complex emotional triggers.

Amanda

Amanda was young professional woman of 26, referred by her psychiatrist for treatment of severe anorexia. Her highest weight had been 9 stone on a 5 foot 4 inch frame. She had reduced to 7 stone following university, and at referral was

5 stone 13 with a BMI of 14 (a healthy BMI is between 19 and 25). Usually, with such a low weight, a patient would not be treated in an outpatient setting but the referring psychiatrist was a long-time colleague whose judgement I trusted. She judged that the patient would be safe in an outpatient setting and would respond to the ILET approach, and it proved to be so.

Amanda began her eating disorder, relatively late, at the age of 18, after leaving home to attend university. On returning home in the first year, she alerted her mother to her difficulties with food but her mother did not respond to this communication. Amanda was conscious of a need to impress her difficulties upon her mother and began to restrict, but to no avail, as her mother (and father) did not respond in the way she had hoped. Amanda had been living with her boyfriend for a year, having begun the relationship when she weighed 7 stone. With the weight loss, her relationship became fraught and the communication between them deteriorated severely. It was the potential loss of this relationship that propelled her into treatment.

What concerned Amanda were the almost constant intrusive thoughts about calories and what was or was not a 'bad' food. However, she understood that she was underweight and wished to get well. She was aware that she had been trying to alert her mother to her difficulties by losing weight and so did not have all the characteristics that one might expect to see in someone of such low weight, in that she had insight into her eating disorder and was aware that she was underweight and needed help.

As per the ILET protocol, Amanda was taught about how her brain was built and functioning in the present. She was given the understanding of how the intrusive 'concrete' thoughts were, in fact, the sequelae of state change and to be noted as evidence that a complex emotional trigger thought had just occurred. Meanwhile, she had agreed a re-feeding schedule and was gaining on average 1lb a week. The triggers to state change were followed by either the desire to reduce her calorie intake or a general preoccupation with calorific content.

One such moment occurred when she was alone with her boyfriend. He was discussing a social event at work that he needed to attend. She noted that she suddenly began to think about what she could make for dinner that would be 'safe' for her to eat, that is, not the 'bad' calorific foods. When brought back to the moment just before she changed state and began thinking about food, she remembered that he was saying that he and another colleague were attending alone, as partners were not invited. However, she then remembered (the 'aha' moment) that she had seen the invitation on which was written 'plus one'.

As a consequence of identifying these moments of state change Amanda became aware of her thoughts and feelings and began to confront difficult emotional topics that had previously triggered eating disorder behaviour.

Maria

Maria was struggling with a difficult relationship with her parents, with whom she still lived at the age of 37. When referred for treatment, she was mainly eating one particular food that she felt 'cleansed' her 'insides' but even this needed to be vomited out. Nothing was allowed to stay inside. Her binges were on 'perfect, healthy' foods that she ate alone.

She had followed the ILET protocol and had begun to catch the moments before changing state. On this particular occasion, she found herself on the bus on the way home from her work suddenly craving to binge on porridge, not something that she usually binged on. As she had time before she could act, she decided to employ ILET. She began to muse about the meaning of porridge and first came up with the word Goldilocks. She noted that she was apprehensive about returning home and seeing her parents. She then perused the fairytale in her mind and linked it to her feelings about mother and father, who were either 'too hot' or 'too cold' and her feeling like a little girl, which both made her feel safe and frustrated her. Following this exercise, Maria noticed that the urge to binge had dissipated and that her feelings towards her parents seemed a little clearer. In a later session, Maria noted that she had begun a binge by first drinking too much coffee and then too much wine. Her associations to these drinks were that they were both 'grown-up' drinks, the last thought she remembered before indulging. This then led us back to thinking, was being 'grown-up' a function of what she drank, or was it about how she thought about and 'digested' her responsibilities to herself and her aging parents, to whom she rarely spoke but who supported her financially.

Georgina

The following vignette is interesting in that ILET had become a resource that Georgina was able to employ in anxiety-provoking situations that, in the past, would have triggered an eating disorder episode.

This is Georgina's account of how she experienced using the ILET method. At this point in her treatment she was no longer eating disordered, had married and had a child.

Her history is that she is one of four children. There was some evidence to suggest that her mother harboured some psychotic ideas, especially around food, only allowing very few 'safe' foods to be served and who, at times, was unable to feed the family at all. We were both aware that, due to her childhood, Georgina still experiences a high level of anxiety. The following is a report of her use of the ILET method when beset by extreme anxiety that in the past would have led to an eating disorder episode.

Georgina's report

> I'm walking towards the bus stop to catch my bus home. It has been another long day at work and I'm rushing to be on time to collect my child from nursery. I cross the road, there is the bus coming . . . I've got to run or I'll miss it! Now I have to cross again. Red light, never mind . . . try crossing anyway . . . OK, now run a bit more and I'm on the bus finally!

I should feel relieved but instead I'm feeling panicky. And actually, I think I am not well, yes I'm really not well . . . Not sure what it is exactly. I am probably going to faint. That's it; I'm going to die on bus X. Great! Okay, let's try calming down. Why do I feel like this? In the end I had a good day and I am looking forward to a nice evening with my child . . . So why on earth am I feeling like this? Where is the panic from?

It doesn't work. Trying to analyse the events in this way does not help. In fact, it makes the panic even more because if there is no obvious psychological reason to feel so bad, surely there must be a physical one. So, I am definitively unwell; I'm going to faint and very likely to die on this bloody bus.

Okay, let's try ILET. When did the panic actually start? Hmm . . . let's see . . . I was on the bus. No, actually a bit earlier . . . Running towards the bus? Crossing the road? Hum . . . oh! That's it, now I know when it was: it was even earlier when I left the office and started to walk very fast towards the bus. Yes, now I remember clearly: I had just left the office and as I turned the corner it all began. Now I can understand what the reason was: guilt. My thought was 'What am I doing at work 'til now instead of already on my way to the nursery?'

When I began to identify when the panic began and what I was thinking the moment before, that's what helped to relieve the anxiety. When I was able to identify what was the real reason for the anxiety I could start unpacking my thoughts and feelings. It is an exercise; it does not come easily or automatically. However, with practice, it seems to help in two ways: it disengages my mind from anxiety quite effectively, and it helps me to think about what the real problem is.

The more fundamental reason why this seems to help is because my mind is forced to concentrate on the exact moment when anxiety – or whatever was the feeling – kicked in. This has a major consequence, which is that my mind gets away from the anxiety pathway that generates even more anxiety and leads to concrete thinking. Instead, by focusing on the exact moment my mind changed away from its anxiety status I get a chance to think in a very different, more logical and abstract way.

These vignettes, I hope, illustrate the loss of, and the search for, the meaning in the trigger to state change. The patients delved into and explored the trigger thoughts that had previously overwhelmed their capacity to process complex emotions, thus gaining insight into emotional challenges and difficulties. The more they discovered their thoughts and feelings, tested them against reality and understood the emotional impact, the more they could begin to create a useful store of successful emotional solutions.

Chapter 6

Theory and practice

(For a step-by-step description of how ILET is delivered, see Appendix B.)

Summary

This chapter describes the theory and practice of the systematised application of the discontinuous neural emotional processing model of eating disorders –ILET – and lies at the heart of this book.

The key to this new treatment is to monitor and follow the shift in language, following an emotional danger signal, from symbolic/metaphoric to the concrete and then to return or re-inflate the language to its symbolic meaning, enabling the patient to 'bring to mind' in language the 'lost in the body' thoughts. Once restored to symbolic thinking, patients can be enabled to find alternative or flexible workable solutions to emotionally challenging problems that appear to the patient to be concrete bodily problems. This, in turn, helps patients to develop a strong sense of self and promotes symbolic emotional processing, which protects against any future emotional shocks resulting in eating disorder behaviour.

As I explained in the introduction, this new approach emerged from the many hours I have spent with my patients trying to understand this group of puzzling and confounding illnesses called eating disorders. Perhaps the most intriguing understanding that was gained was that, really, eating disorders have very little to do with food or bodies – even though that is how they are expressed. Rather, eating disorders are the result of the loss of symbolic and metaphoric language function that traps the eating disorder sufferer in the concrete world of the body and the number of calories she can or cannot consume or that has to be vomited out, purged with laxatives or just run off with the over-use of exercise. The eating disorder sufferer is trying to navigate her emotional responses to her world by manipulating her body. However, it is fairly clear that the external world remains stubbornly unchanged as a result of such behaviour. This state of affairs then compounds the problem. When acting on the body changes nothing in the real world, then the original emotional problem remains un-thought about and unsolved and usually gets worse. This, in turn, increases vulnerability to complex emotional triggers. Each time a body solution is enacted, as mentioned above, the 'concrete' brain pathway is strengthened, making it more likely to be triggered in the future, leading to an increase in eating disorder symptoms. Conversely, the less often the symbolic pathway is triggered, the weaker it becomes and is less easily triggered.

Explaining to patients how an eating disorder can come into being and how the brain responds to complex emotions often results in their saying that they feel relieved of the guilt and confusion that they have been carrying around. They had been trying to find the logic in a situation that defies logic. But by understanding the logic of how the brain is built, how it functions and by testing out the ILET theory that allows them to divine their thoughts and opinions, they were able to discover what they were thinking and feeling that was previously inaccessible to them. This knowledge has allowed them to be truly in control of their minds rather than battling to overcome overwhelmingly strong 'doing' impulses that defy face logic. The process of being in touch with their thoughts about their feelings gave them the opportunity to develop a unified sense of self and to be in the driving seat of their lives.

The ILET treatment is the product of both theoretical research and clinical practice and was developed on the treatment of a wide group of patients suffering from anorexia, bulimia and binge eating disorder in both inpatient and outpatient settings in the NHS and private sectors over thirty years of practice. It is the systematised application of the discontinuous neural emotional processing model of eating disorders, which means that emotions are either processed symbolically (tested against reality, access to memory in language, creative thinking, able to plan for the future) or concretely in the body (which includes any action acted out on the body: an eating disorder episode, self harm, drinking alcohol and exercise) and lies at the heart of this book. The model proposes that an emotional shock closes the access to symbolic frontal lobe functions, leaving the patient trapped in the concrete mode of thought until her anxiety reduces.

Communication between patient and therapist is paramount in treating any psychiatric illness but is perhaps even more crucial in eating disorders precisely because the patient is unable to focus on anything except her concrete bodily experience. Access to metaphor and irony, or indeed any symbolic language, has shut down. The therapist, on the other hand, naturally wishes to bring the patient into the symbolic world of emotional discourse, as it is clear that while the patient is preoccupied with her body, much of life and its challenges remain unattended. In traditional models of the mind, the therapist assumes that the patient can understand symbolic language and that is when communication fails. This is because, traditionally, practitioners and researchers have accepted a continuous model of the mind in that, if a patient is functioning in the concrete, she can be helped to gradually become more symbolic. In this way of thinking about mental functioning, there is no disjunction between concrete and symbolic thought, just a gradual increase from the concrete to the symbolic. The 'discontinuous model' follows how brains function when processing emotion. There are two pathways existing as separate pathways. In other words, an eating disorder patient is not a little concrete – they are *either* concrete *or* symbolic. When patients are in the concrete state, according to this model, they cannot just increase their symbolic capacity but must be reconnected to the symbolic pathway.

The ILET treatment closely follows the logic of the neural emotional processing pathways in that the aim is to identify the emotional shock or stimulus that precipitates the move from the symbolic to the concrete pathway. When this has been identified, the next stage is to detoxify the stimulus of the danger signal by examining, symbolising and metaphorising the material so that it becomes comprehensible to the patient. This model also predicts that the reduction of anxiety and the processing of the emotional material create the conditions for accessing and reconnecting to the symbolic emotional processing pathway.

As described above, eating disorder patients' symbolic language capacity functions at a lower than average level (see Figure 5.1) and their symbolic emotional processing capacities are vulnerable to being easily overwhelmed. When presented with a complex emotional trigger that requires high-level theory of mind and an ability to comprehend metaphor and irony, their emotional processing capacities frequently collapse. It has been suggested that the complex emotional challenge constitutes a danger signal, causing the insula to close access to the symbolic functions, whereupon the amygdala triggers the 'fight-or-flight' response. Thus, there is no access to the symbolic functions and no opportunity to peruse the emotional material; no reality testing, planning for the future, only access to concrete understanding and bodily experiences. The result is a collapse of the nascent metaphorical thought into its concrete equivalent. As has been discussed earlier, eating disorder patients have difficulty understanding the meaning of metaphoric and ironic material. Metaphorical thinking is an attempt to encompass the new, to give meaning to what is unknown in order to understand novel material and ideas. Eating disorder patients become trapped in the bodily expression of the failed metaphor with only concrete bodily solutions to sophisticated, complex emotional challenges that provoke troubling ambivalence.

The ILET treatment is aimed specifically at re-inflating the specific collapsed concrete metaphor, expressed bodily by the patient, with its symbolic meaning. This is done by identifying the trigger thought just prior to the change of mental state from symbolic to concrete function. This, it is suggested, allows patients to access their own thoughts and promotes the ability to process, in language, the failed metaphorical thought that then resides in the body or just simply in concrete form.

The key to this new treatment is to monitor and follow the shift in language from symbolic/metaphoric to the concrete and then to return or re-inflate the language to its symbolic meaning. This enables the patient to 'bring to mind' in language the 'lost in the body' thoughts. Once restored to symbolic thinking, patients can be enabled to find alternative or flexible workable solutions to emotionally challenging problems that appear to them to be concrete bodily problems. These ideas follow the neurobiological evidence on emotional processing. Under low stress conditions, the insula 'opens up' the pathway to the symbolic functions. When this happens patients have reported experiencing a sense of feeling particularly awake and alive. As the information from the body is integrated with emotional experience and intellectual function, patients feel a unified sense of self or an ongoing self-state. With access to conceptual thought allied to emotional meaning, the novel and complex stimuli can be understood and metaphors created to encompass the new challenge. When this pathway is shut down, the attempt to comprehend the internal and external environment, via symbolic understanding, collapses.

As metaphoric language reduces towards its concrete meaning, one is able to observe the attempt at, and failure to achieve, metaphoric thought. As Wright (1991) suggests, all language begins in the concrete, and metaphors are an attempt to 'stretch' language to encompass and express symbolic thought, which allows the unknown to be given meaning by the known.

The ILET approach proposes that there is a characteristic residue of the failed metaphor. It is suggested that through careful attention, the nascent symbolic/ metaphoric thought can be identified, and once this is identified the concrete metaphor can be re-inflated by the therapist in order to return to the patient her own lost thought. The aim of the treatment is to teach the patient to discover her own lost metaphoric thinking and, thus, restore symbolic functioning that allows for workable solutions to be found to demanding and complex emotional challenges.

The treatment guides the patient in working back to the moment when there is a change from general symbolic thinking to thoughts that become fixated on the body and food. The moment just prior to this cognitive shift is then identified. According to the theory behind the ILET treatment, this moment should contain a trigger that has had the effect of overwhelming the patient's symbolic functioning. According to the theory behind ILET, the nature of the trigger will contain complex metaphoric or ironic material as well as negative emotional material.

Identifying the trigger requires close examination of the language produced by the patient. What is being looked for are (a) 'dual-use words', that is, words that have both symbolic and concrete meanings and (b) general metaphoric sayings, for example, 'that takes the biscuit' or 'I can't stomach what he said'.

Initially the patient is seen for two extended stand-alone sessions. This is in order to introduce the patient to the ideas behind the treatment and to allow her to try out the method before agreeing to the therapy. This enables the patient to 'sign up' to the treatment and removes the greatest obstacle to treatment of this patient group, who notoriously consider their symptoms 'ego-syntonic' or, in other words, that their symptoms feel part of their sense of who they are, and are loath to give them up. When they trial the method and discover that it is their own thoughts that are being 'returned' to them and they are not having to 'take in' 'ego-dystonic' or, in other words, ideas that feel alien to who they are and that make no sense to them, they have reported that their anxiety reduces which, in turn, helps return them to symbolic function.

The ILET protocol

As with all first meetings with a new patient, we need to get to know one another and to decide if we get along and whether we feel we can work together. It is easy to forget how intimidating it is to come to a therapist when in need of help, especially when in the grip of an eating disorder that actually changes how we think. It is especially important that the therapist is comfortable with the treatment they have to offer. It is worrying that treatments to date offer a limited positive outcome and, as a result, engender pessimism in the professional about 'there being no cure for an eating disorder'. ILET follows the logic of neural emotional processing that describes how, when a pathway is neglected, it degrades and the behaviours known as eating disorders fade.

Part of the 'getting to know' one another is the invitation to the patient to ask as many questions as they wish about the therapist, his/her training, orientation and experience. In return, the therapist wishes to know as much about the patient as possible to ascertain whether the therapist has the suitable training and skills to help the patient and whether the patient's physical state is stable, as well as thinking about the addition of family or couple work. Ideally, both parties feel comfortable and it is a good match. Part of finding out whether the patient and therapist are a good match is the stand-alone nature of the first two sessions. We do not agree to work together until the patient has learned about the ILET theory and method. This usually takes two sessions, each lasting about two hours. It is not until part way through the second session that there is an agreement to work together. The patient is given the information and is given time between the two sessions to think about whether it makes sense to her and that she wants to have therapy. The therapist, by seeing how the patient responds to the ideas, can gauge if the patient is likely to do well and is motivated. A contraindication is that the patient is at too unstable a low weight and is not at all motivated to get well. This is usually the result of a late referral and the patient may well need an inpatient stay in order to arrest her decline.

If all is well, the therapist explains that it is necessary to take a very detailed history covering not only the presenting problem but going back in time to discover as much about her experiences as possible. This will include family relationships going back to the grandparent generation as well as school and education history and any work experiences. The focus will be on the patient's experience of what happened to her and not only the names and dates. Of course, medical history, present state of health and interventions in the past are also very important. Perhaps the best place to start is with what brought the patient to therapy in the first place. Was it of her own volition or did her family or GP suggest that she needs help? (A template for the protocol including, history-taking, and all explanations and handouts for the patient, can be found in Appendix B.)

Following the history-taking, it is then time to explain about ILET. We then go on to the psycho-education element of the protocol.

A good place to start, after finding out just how the patient came to ask for therapy and taking her history, is the 'story of the brain in eating disorders' and how it is built and shaped by internal and external factors. During the history-taking we will have spent some time asking about the family situation around the patient's birth: was her birth difficult or relatively straightforward? Did her mother have any post-natal depression that she had heard about? Was her birth planned or was she a 'surprise' baby? Did she have siblings and what was the birth order? Did her siblings have any difficulties? Were her parents under pressure around the time of her birth? Was there bereavement in the family around that time? Or was there a lack of family support or good support? Was she known to be a 'good' baby who ate and slept well or a 'difficult' baby who fretted and was the cause of much parental exhaustion? We then have a picture of the pressures or otherwise around her birth. It is then explained to the patient the importance to the baby's development of 'maternal preoccupation' and the need for a 'fit' between mother and child. Most births are, by definition, difficult, but it is not uncommon to discover a history of extra stresses. There is much adjustment for the parents, especially the mother, to make and if the mother is very anxious she may not be able to absorb her baby's primitive anxiety to the level that is needed by that baby. Some babies 'demand' the attention they need others do not, so the picture is one of how successful was the fit between mother and baby.

It is explained to the patient that there are a lot of boxes to tick for psychological difficulties to be expressed as an eating disorder. One of the problems that often arises is in the development of the right hemisphere where the 'music' of language is primed which later on carries the meaning of communication rather than just words. Mothers' right hemispheres 'talk' to their babies' right hemispheres in proto-language of sounds that communicate getting the baby ready for language in words and it is this delicate process that can be disrupted. A particular problem for eating disorder sufferers is their difficulty in putting their feelings into language (alexithymia) as well as being less able to figure out how other people are thinking (theory of mind). They are less able to 'self-soothe' or to attenuate or bring down their anxiety because they are less likely to be able to think through a problem and sufferers are more likely to have a fragile sense of self, since if we do not know what we feel, it is difficult to know who we are.

Eating disorder sufferers, it is explained, tend to perform lower than average on symbolic emotional tasks and the patient is talked through the possible reasons as to why she may have a reduced capacity to process emotions symbolically. This includes the explanation that, due to both constitutional and environmental factors, there may be weakness in her attenuation of anxiety (or self-soothing), alexithymia (difficulty putting feelings into words), possible insecure attachment (did she look to see if her mother would be upset by behaviour that at other times she would accept), and sub-optimal right hemisphere function leading to an inability to understand a complex, negative emotional field that contains novel metaphoric and ironic material.

If the patient is being treated as part of a trial, she will be shown Figure 5.1, and it is explained that as she is likely to be functioning at a lowered level of symbolic function, when a complex emotional shock occurs there can be a sudden loss of symbolic function (and change of neural pathway) resulting in concrete thinking and eating disorder behaviour.

It is interesting to note that patients treated with the ILET method find the concept of a change of state very compelling and revelatory. They have expressed that this understanding is the most helpful as, up until that point, they have felt convinced that their concrete thoughts were valid; previously, when experienced professionals had told them that these thoughts were invalid, they had experienced this information as quite maddening. For this patient group, their concrete thoughts have a similar power of reality as for patients with schizophrenia, in that frontal function is not engaged but, unlike with schizophrenia, the patient has the ability to reconnect to the frontal functions. Patients have recognised within themselves the shift in state and find it comforting that it has been described and understood.

Following on from the 'story of the brain in eating disorders' is a detailed discussion of triggers and trigger material. Particular attention is paid to the nature of the trigger material that has the capacity to overwhelm their symbolic emotional processing functions. It is explained that it is the complexity, rather than just the negative content, that is the defining characteristic of a trigger. At this point, the patient may be asked to describe the most recent eating disorder episode. She will be asked to identify the moment when she knew that she was going to binge, for instance, and is then helped to work backwards to identify the moment just before the change to thinking about food or her body. This moment is then explored in great detail, asking for all associations to the material produced. This exploration continues until the patient connects to an aspect of the material as emotionally relevant – the 'aha' moment. At this point, the trigger material is explored. The patient has then experienced how the treatment works and can 'buy in' to the treatment through knowledge of the process.

In the detailed protocol (in Appendix B), it places taking a history before giving an explanation of the story of the brain. As therapists become more familiar with the therapy, they may wish to reverse these two elements, except when ILET is being trialled. If the brain explanation is given first, it is then explained that it is necessary to take a detailed history of the patient and all the significant people in her life. This history should include the grandparental generation and the relationships between the family members. Particular attention is paid to the relationship between the patient's mother and her mother, the patient's grandmother, as it is frequently found that the middle generation (i.e., the patient's mother) has not received adequate mothering herself due to possible absence of her mother, depression, alcoholism, or if her mother had a narcissistic personality. When this proves to be the case, it is explained that it is possible that the patient's own mother was not in a position to provide optimal mothering. It is stressed that this is no fault of the mother, just as the eating disorder is the outcome of the confluence of constitutional and environmental factors. A full educational and work history is then recorded, along with a history of relationships with partners, if there have been any. This should provide a good background of how the patient has dealt with relationships and a guide to the level of emotional processing. All the usual physical history is taken, along with a history of weight fluctuations and the beginning and course of the eating disorder.

The path is traced from possible compromised maternal preoccupation, lack of regulation of anxiety, insecure attachment, paring down of frontal function in adolescence, poor emotional processing in language, finally culminating in the overwhelming of the ability to process complex emotional experience in language. The two pathways available for emotional processing are explained – the 'fight-or-flight' pathway – direct to the amygdala and the symbolic pathway which accesses reality testing, memory in language and the ability to think symbolically about emotions.

When the therapy forms part of a study, patients have been given a battery of tests of frontal, executive and symbolic function as well as a short-form measure of intelligence, and measures of eating disorder behaviour and alexithymia. These tests provide baseline measures of symbolic/reflective versus concrete function in order to test the efficacy of the treatment. The tests are repeated midway through and at the end of treatment. (See Appendix F for measures.)

Treatment process

If involved with a trial, the patient will be given a battery of tests (see Appendix G) or, if not, then for baseline measures the tests in Appendix F will be given pre-, mid- and post treatment. It is explained that people who go on to suffer from an eating disorder are already compromised in their ability to process emotions symbolically in language. It is demonstrated to them that there are certain functions that they perform less well, which leaves them vulnerable to being overwhelmed when confronted with challenging emotional experiences. It is quite useful to give patients feedback from the cognitive baseline tests to demonstrate the problem. It has been the case so far that during the baseline tests it becomes patently clear to most patients that they have difficulty performing the creative language tasks. Patients are also intrigued that it is known by the psychologist that they skip the metaphoric passages when they read a novel. Neither does this group of patients read much descriptive fiction anyway, preferring factual literature, as it is more comprehensible to them. Patients have often expressed relief when there is recognition of these difficulties, which, they are assured, are not related to intelligence. These patients can then become willing participants, or perhaps they are better described as partners, in the quest to discover their own minds rather than defensively believe the concrete 'reality' that their minds produce and which must be defended at all costs lest they feel mad.

Figure 5.2 is then presented to show the patient that, as her general symbolic ability is at a lower than average level, she is at risk of a sharp change of state when a complex emotional trigger overwhelms her emotional processing capacities. The progress of an eating disorder is explained and demonstrated via the diagram. With bulimic patients, it is explained that the sudden drop from symbolic to concrete function is expressed in the binge–vomit behaviour. For anorexic patients, there will be a subtler mental shift where the thoughts turn to food and its calorific content and what may or may not be eaten. For obese patients, there will just be the urge to binge. The bulimic response is more chaotic and may include sex, alcohol and drugs as part of the response, while the anorexic will be one of restraint and control of impulses. The obese response characteristically contains within it sadistic impulses that are anathema to the patient and need to be denied.

The concept of the borderline

The 'borderline' for our purposes, has certain features and qualities that might be described as overlapping with Freud's description of the unconscious (Freud, 1915). It might be hypothesised that, like Freud's 'royal road to the unconscious', it may be involved in our dream life (Solms & Turnbull, 2003). Let it just be said that this area of the mind can be described as not under the regulation of frontal functions. By reduced frontal function is meant that processes of symbolic thinking and reality testing are compromised. Thus, events or thoughts that might be the cause of anxiety are not checked out and worked over in the mind in relation to reality, but are abandoned in favour of discharging anxiety through action in the body.

In the borderline area, the thinking can be described as concrete, narcissistic and grandiose. Concrete thinking loses most of its possible meanings, as only one sliver of meaning is understood. An example of this might be the importance of weight as a number, but not as a subject being weighty or as responsibilities weighing heavily upon one. Narcissism, by its definition, implies that there is no regard for, or proper recognition of, the existence of the 'other'. Grandiosity means that there is over-inflation of the importance of the subject but also that all should be available to her by right. These aspects of borderline thinking have in common a failure to test thinking against objective reality.

These thought processes are simplistic and are expressed in black-and-white terms. Conflicting emotions seem to be particularly difficult to hold in mind for patients exhibiting this mode of thinking. There is a tendency to split their emotional world into good and bad and, in order to maintain or re-establish emotional equilibrium, to attribute negative attributes into the external world (projection).

Owing to compromised reality testing functions, patients experience the normal feelings of rage, greed, aggression and envy as intolerable and believe that these feelings make them a very bad and unacceptable and unlovable person. As a result, they frequently attempt to be perfect in order to deal with such impulses. If it is thought helpful (usually it is discussed some sessions into treatment), the patient is given this explanation so that she comes to understand that the primitive impulses she is experiencing are common to all eating disorder patients and do not define her individual personality. It is the experience of these primitive impulses that contributes to the 'bad' feelings that so plague eating disorder patients and which form part of the response to the trigger for state change. The intolerable feelings of badness, greed, envy, aggression, murderous rage and perceived self-ishness that are distilled into a bodily experience are the 'disgusting' feelings that have to be evacuated (vomited), diminished (starved), or drowned (binged).

When an explanation of aspects of thinking are 'borrowed' from psychotic thinking, the patient is able to create a structure to understand the chaotic, primitive world that she has come to inhabit. By recognising the different states of mind and their sequelae in thinking and behaviour, a structure is created, mediated by the intellectual functions, which acts as a containment for anxiety. This allows for the individual's intellectual understanding to function much as does the mother's mind in maternal preoccupation: making sense of the world and allowing prediction of the future based on learned experience.

Trigger events diary (TED)

In the next phase of the ILET treatment, the patient is given the TED in which she is to note binge or state change events and to describe the surrounding background environment to the state change. The patient is asked to describe these binge events in minute detail (this usually takes some training, as most people tend to take a broad sweep when describing an event, and the patient is prepared for accuracy to be achieved only after some sessions), paying particular attention to the moment her thoughts became body- or food-based. She is asked to think of this moment as if it were a photograph or a snapshot of a dream. Later, when she is familiar with the method, she can be asked to report all associations to the material as if it was a dream. In the early stages, this enquiry is done by the therapist.

The TED given to the patient asks for a recording of every eating disorder episode, stating the time and place and including the reason for the activity, who was present, and the patient's thoughts just prior to the moment of change to thinking about food or the body.

First treatment session

When the patient attends for the first treatment session, she will have filled in the TED, but before she and the therapist begin the hunt for the triggers, it is important that the patient has some time to talk about what had happened to her that week. It will soon become clear whether the week had been spent largely in the concrete (thinking about what she ate, vomited or ran etc.) or whether she had been able to navigate most of the week in the symbolic mode. Either way, it is important that the first 20 minutes allow a space that is entirely at the disposal of the patient, as there may have been difficult events that need addressing. This is particularly the case when there have been some changes in the patient, who might be expressing herself more forcefully in the family or with friends. That is why a family meeting needs to be arranged early in the therapy so that the family understands the process and can create a safe space for the growing self and opinions of their child (of what ever age).

After the de-brief, we then address how well the patient has been able to identify the most recent trigger moment. At this stage in the therapy, it is sufficient that she is able to identify the change of state and it is the job of the therapist to work back to the trigger thought. With each subsequent session, the task will increasingly fall to the patient, who is encouraged to do so by the therapist.

For patients with bulimia or suffering from obesity, the trigger events are relatively easy to identify, but with patients suffering from anorexia the triggers are harder to identify, as these patients often claim that they think about food all the time. However, with close questioning, it becomes clear that there are subtle state changes within the generally concrete functioning that stand out. This deconstruction of events requires the therapist to become attuned to the very subtle changes. Another technique for this group is to ask patients to associate to words that they have used to describe themselves.

How far the patient is able to work back by herself to the trigger moment (or the 'aha moment', as it is called) can be measured. This measure of the patient's progress can be added to the baseline measures of cognitive functioning taken at the start of treatment, midway, and at the end of treatment.

After the patient has attempted to identify the trigger moment, the therapist asks structured questions relating to the binge/starve episode following the format of the Emotional Events Questionnaire (EEQ). The aim of the EEQ is to teach the patient to work back and identify the concrete metaphors and to inflate them in the context of the trigger.

The EEQ is given to the patient, but is also a manual for the therapist. It guides the therapist to help the patient to engage the symbolic emotional processing pathway by utilising the intact intellectual functions, thus reducing anxiety and keeping it at the lowered level. The therapist takes an open, equal and enquiring stance alongside the patient in a spirit of mutual enquiry. Nothing is put into the patient that does not come from the patient's own mind and observations. Later, when the symbolic emotional processing is more stable, ideas about how people function or even low-level interpretations can be presented, but at this stage these foreign ideas might raise anxiety and, thus, increase the likelihood of symptomatic behaviour.

As explained above, it is wise to treat eating disorders early owing to the propensity for the symptoms to worsen as the concrete pathway is triggered more often and strengthened. The present situation is that due to the paucity of in- and outpatient treatment facilities, patients frequently do not find their way to treatment for on average of two years. Until recently, it was accepted practice that patients have to reach the diagnostic criteria for an eating disorder before they are considered for treatment, although now the advice is to treat any level of symptom as soon as it occurs. The typical outcome of the difficulty in accessing treatment is that a patient is often referred as an emergency when her life is threatened and she is less able to cooperate, making the clinician's work much more difficult and putting the patient at risk. It is suggested that this referral practice may unwittingly contribute to the high mortality rate seen in the field of eating disorders.

A general comment about ILET is that it is based on empirical research and that each task addressed and attitude taken has a rationale and the position taken by the therapist is clearly defined.

Chapter 7

The problem with CBT

Summary

In this chapter, the most widely used treatment for eating disorders, CBT, is compared and contrasted to the ILET treatment method in terms of delivery and theoretical underpinning. This is in order to explore and illuminate the stubborn inability of CBT to pass the 50% 'cure' rate in eating disorders and to put forward possible solutions to the theoretical gaps described in the CBT method which, it is suggested, are resolved by the ILET approach to the treatment of eating disorders.

The importance of theory

At present the most widely used treatment available for eating disorders is CBT; however, we know that a positive outcome is, at best, 50%. CBT tacitly accepts a continuous model of the mind but when there is acceptance of a discontinuous model (either/or) of neural emotional processing it illuminates the weakness in the CBT model and it is suggested that the lack of the discontinuous model may account for the difficulty in improving the 'cure' rate.

Unlike CBT, ILET offers a theoretical rationale based on neurobiology and psychoanalysis as to why the patient has developed an eating disorder and it describes a pathway out of the illness. There is some crossover between the methods employed by the two treatments but the differences are crucial. ILET addresses the underlying neurological competency that leads to the problem of concrete thought, whereas CBT addresses the behaviour through addressing negative thoughts, which are not the same thing as an altered mental state. Both treatments look for a trigger to the eating disorder behaviour, but CBT sees it as something to be avoided: for example, if bingeing usually happens in the kitchen then removal to the bathroom is suggested, whereas the theoretical research base that underpins ILET considers that the trigger holds the clues to the change of state from symbolic to concrete and needs careful attention in order that the state be reversed.

The popularity of CBT relies on its wide base of outcome studies but even so it does not seem able to break through the 50% 'cure' rate. The on/off nature of emotional processing, it can be argued, illuminates the weakness in the CBT (general learning theory) model and that the lack of the discontinuous neurobiological model may account for the difficulty in improving the 'cure' rate.

CBT is underpinned by a general theoretical model that posits that schemas and core beliefs are created during childhood. When these are activated, they supposedly trigger automatic thoughts that give rise to certain emotions that then govern behaviour. However, although it has been adapted for the treatment of bulimia by Fairburn (1981), CBT was not designed for the specific treatment of eating disorders and does not offer a specific theoretical rationale to explain the development of these illnesses. ILET theory can help us understand why CBT works well at times and why it might fail at others.

The neurobiological explanation of state change, which underlies ILET, can account for the behaviours and thought processes seen in eating disorders under the rubric of concrete emotional processing. Specifically, the theory which underlies ILET explains in detail how the brains of eating disorder sufferers are compromised prior to the expression of the eating disorder 'illness' behaviour, and offers a comprehensive explanation as to why a stimulus thought which is complex and negative overwhelms the compromised ability to process and comprehend the ironic and complex metaphoric emotional information which is seen in the normal complexity of emotional discourse.

ILET draws on the different disciplines of neuroscience, learning theory, psychoanalysis, attachment theory and linguistics to create a proposed unified theory of eating disorders. The freedom to move between, and to respect, these different disciplines enriches the understanding of the thinking underlying the illness behaviours that make up a diagnosis of an eating disorder.

The neurobiological underpinnings of ILET both explain how an eating disorder is created and offer an explanation for a treatment to 'cure' or correct the over-use of the concrete pathway in emotional processing. CBT, on the other hand, is restricted by the narrowness of learning theory that is used to explain the eating disorder. In fact, CBT does not claim to understand the genesis of an eating disorder other than in terms of faulty learning, which is a poor explanation of the illness behaviours grouped under the heading of eating disorders. It does not explain why some young women and fewer young men 'learn' to starve, binge and vomit or overeat and why others do not.

From a neurobiological point of view, once the underlying deficits have been understood, the treatment of these illnesses becomes relatively straightforward. It is perhaps the complexity of the cognitive–behavioural treatment and its relatively poor outcome that tells us that treating the myriad 'facts' of the illness has replaced the search for a unified theory. Because historically the different theoretical approaches to the treatment of mental illness have refused to engage in a dialogue, patients lose out on being the beneficiaries of the ignored fertile ground that such dialogue brings.

From a neurobiological perspective, all psychotherapy, whether behavioural or psychodynamic, works on the underlying plastic structure of the brain. The normal development of the brain passes through periods of paring down of the frontal lobes, where redundant pathways degrade and those required for the next stage of life are strengthened or created for the first time. This first happens between the ages of 2 and 3, when the infant connections become redundant, and then again in adolescence (Goldberg, 2001).

In adolescence, when eating disorders mainly manifest themselves, the typical 'body' mindedness and narcissism of this age group (as the frontal lobe connections are pared down through the latency connections becoming redundant) persists, as the 'fast and dirty' pathway is constantly pressed into service at the expense of the symbolic 'language' pathway to the executive functions.

With frontal functions becoming sub-optimal, the challenges of reality do not leave their mark on the frontal lobes – a process which normally results in the creation of the adult brain. It might be said that the 'cure' of an eating disorder is the bringing to a close the vagaries of the adolescent brain and the establishment of the adult brain.

CBT acts rather like a scattergun. There are certain aspects of the therapy that hit the mark in terms of promoting frontal maturation by confronting the sufferer with reality, be that via presenting certain foods to be eaten or by demonstrating that feared events do not happen. What it does not address is offering the sufferer an understanding of her lived experience, of how and why her brain functions as it does and an explanation of how to come out of the concrete state she finds herself in and the tools to do so.

How CBT works

At the heart of CBT lies the assertion that core beliefs drive cognitions and behaviour. A result of a core belief might be negative automatic thoughts that require challenging through Socratic argument in order to disprove the faulty core belief.

These negative automatic thoughts and core beliefs would be challenged by working with single dimensions. An example would be that with patients using any weight gain as evidence that they have become fat a therapist could present evidence from the BMI measurements to prove that the patient is still in the low range.

In some cases there would be work with two dimensions, addressing statements such as 'If I am thin then I will be attractive'; 'If I am thin then I will be happy'; and conversely 'If I am fat then I will be ugly'. These ideas are taken from Padesky (1994), who has described the technique of working with ideas that have become linked as the 'two-dimensional charting of continua'.

As an example of this, Waller et al. (2007) cited a patient whose core belief was that she did not feel worthwhile. She was asked to rate how worthwhile she felt on a scale of one to a hundred and asked to repeat this on a weekly basis. The patient was asked to think about other people she knew and to produce a list of worthwhile qualities and then asked if any of these qualities belonged to her. The therapist then used Socratic questioning to help the patient examine the evidence.

In order to help a patient produce new information (usually difficult with eating disorder patients) CBT therapists use behavioural experiments which test the patient's beliefs about themselves, other people and the world, construct and test different and more adaptive beliefs about themselves and the world, and add to, develop and verify their beliefs (Rouf et al., 2004).

These behavioural experiments have three aims: first, to help the patient understand how CBT works, that is, that beliefs have been learned and can be unlearned and that all beliefs can be tested and revised. Second, to help the patient reattribute beliefs: for example, the reason the patient might believe something is not because the world is the way it is but because she learned to see the world in that particular way due to her past experience. Third, to help patients change how they feel in particular situations: for instance, if a patient is terrified and feels out of control when she weighs herself, she will stop experiencing anxiety as a function of stopping believing that her weight will balloon out of control.

Waller suggests that behavioural experiments should always be linked to the case formulation in order that patients can test out the predictions that cause them anxiety and which derive from their assumptions and core beliefs.

Padesky (1994) uses the concept of prejudice as an analogy when working with eating disorder patients who find it hard (or impossible) to imagine that their thoughts and behaviours could be incorrect. The basis of the approach to working with such patients is that they hold a belief with such conviction that it is as if it were the truth, when it is patently not the truth. Socratic questioning is employed to test the patient's views of other people's prejudices.

This process is again very time-consuming but does attempt to address the problem in the patient's thinking by understanding that it is absolute, concrete and is not open to reality testing, but unfortunately the CBT approach does not conceptualise this thinking as a change of state.

CBT's starting point is to discern core beliefs and then to begin to divine the underlying assumptions and automatic thoughts, which are then challenged. ILET, on the other hand, understands the assumptions and so-called automatic thoughts to be the result of symbolic/metaphoric thinking that has collapsed into its concrete counterpart. Other than being re-inflated to their symbolic/metaphoric meaning, the concrete content of the thoughts is then ignored, obviating the need for charts and Socratic challenges to every thought.

This is a fundamental difference between CBT and ILET. CBT accepts the utterances of the patient to be a valid reflection of the patient's normal thought processes but holds these to be prejudices that can be shifted by argument. Because it does not use the concept of state change or employ the neurobiological understanding of the different pathways available in emotional processing, it necessarily needs to create an elaborate stratagem in order to help the patient unlearn 'faulty' beliefs. Every 'false' belief has to be addressed and countered. This has led to comments such as 'if I am fat then I will be ugly' being described as 'two-dimensional charting of continua' as against being understood as a concrete utterance of a patient who is unable to express feelings symbolically. These might be that she believes her self/body to be full of hateful thoughts and feelings which make her an 'ugly' unlovable person.

The most fundamental difference between the concepts that underlie the two approaches is the notion of state change. Without this concept, discussions between therapist and patient meander around concrete notions of the importance of calories and the significance of an inch of body fat. Socratic challenges to this 'faulty' thinking are both time-consuming and brittle in that the fundamental mode of thinking has not been recognised or changed. The patient may have been talked out of the particular belief, but she is still prone to believing that her concrete body experience is valid. This is a fundamental problem with CBT.

The second problem is the solution offered to the patient to replace the eating/binge/vomit behaviour. In CBT, it might be suggested that going for a walk or watching a film offers a solution to wanting to binge because, in that approach, the solution to a 'faulty' behaviour is replacing one behaviour by another unrelated to the emotional stimulus. When this happens, the opportunity to 'catch' the anxiety-provoking stimulus is lost and the patient is not helped to understand the very important symbolic meaning of her lost thought.

CBT understands eating disorder behaviour to be the result of faulty learning in childhood but does not specify how this comes about and what has to happen for faulty learning to take place. ILET differs in that it is based on neurobiological research into how and what is needed for the development of brain pathways involved in language, symbolisation, sense of self and self-agency to develop in the context of early maternal preoccupation. It describes what happens when certain neurological weaknesses occur that may culminate in the expression of an eating disorder. This difference in perspective is seen in how and what is emphasised when taking a history.

The main difference, after taking all the basic physiological history, is that CBT is very interested in the minutia around the symptoms, especially what foods are eaten or avoided; in what order they are eaten; if the patient eats marker foods such as carrots so that she knows that she has vomited everything up; how often the patient exercises and how she rates herself in terms of attractiveness. Family history covers general health issues but there is not much interest in the patient's experiences growing up; rather, there is more interest in the eating patterns of the household and any food-related issues, for instance whether certain foods were avoided in the household and if all foods were freely available or certain foods used as treats.

History-taking for the ILET method

First, as described in Chapter 6, the ILET approach also begins with taking a history. However, the content, besides looking at the patient's present situation, concentrates on the patient's early history, going back to the grandparent generation. There is an emphasis on understanding relationships in the family, between both the patient and family members and between the other members. Of particular interest is information about the patient's experience of being mothered and her mother's own experience with grandmother. This is to investigate the quality of the maternal preoccupation and the basis of the developing self. It is helpful to gain an impression as to how well the patient's mother coped with the task of containing her child's anxiety and whether she was under stress during this time. One might ask about support networks available to the mother or whether she suffered from postnatal depression. The relationship with the father is then explored from both the point of view of the parents and between the patient and her father, to discover whether strong bonds have been forged and whether he has been able to promote separation between the mother–child couple. The existence of siblings, their birth order and their relationship with the patient are also explored.

ILET history-taking is more in line with psychodynamic practice, looking into the quality of family and social relationships and with some exploration of the patient's inner world.

The history of the eating disorder is enquired into and also where it fits with the developmental–relationship history. All the technical information will be gathered: highest–lowest weight; eating pattern; absence or presence of bingeing; vomiting; laxative abuse; exercising; self-harm; obsessive–compulsive disorder; menstruation history; dental problems; any other psychiatric or psychological difficulties in the patient and any close relatives and any previous psychiatric or psychological treatments the patient experienced.

The assessment importantly includes listening for the quality of speech: whether it is highly symbolic and metaphoric or concrete in nature. There is also great interest around eating disorder behaviour: what situations usually trigger an episode and what is the quality of thinking and self-explanation concerning the behaviour.

The aim of the psycho-education is to demonstrate to the patient how her thinking has changed under the pressure of anxiety from complex symbolic thinking, which gives access to memory and frontal lobe planning functions, to concrete thinking. This is aimed at teaching the patient to understand that the thinned and concrete nature of her thinking is the result of the collapse of her symbolic/metaphoric ability to think. Owing to the change in pathway, the 'doing' content of these concrete thoughts should be disregarded other than as material to re-inflate with its symbolic meaning. These 'body thoughts', it is explained, can then be used as indicators of state change and as the starting point to find the symbolic meaning of the collapsed thought. The process of discovering the trigger thought is then engaged.

Point of departure between CBT and ILET

CBT acknowledges that emotional processing is involved in the understanding of eating disorders, but it fails to be specific about how and why emotional processing is difficult for this cohort of patients. The result of this lack of specificity is that while emotional difficulties might be addressed and tackled in a scattergun way (and, thus, promote the use of the symbolic emotional pathway), they are not allied to specific anxieties that trigger a binge/vomit/calorie/body/concrete event. It is suggested that the lack of close connection between the stimulus and the concrete response means that an opportunity for symbolic understanding and, thus, appropriate action and, finally, learning, is lost.

The Socratic debate which is the cornerstone of CBT treatment for the 'faulty' 'prejudiced' thoughts does bring reality home to this group of patients. However, stimulating the frontal lobes by encouraging the extraction of reality from the external world still allows the patient to regard her 'body thoughts' as valid *per se* and not disavowed as a class of thought which is present solely because anxiety has tripped the use of the 'fight-or-flight' pathway. CBT suggests that eating disorder patients have difficulty with negative emotions. But this does not, in my opinion, place enough emphasis on the complexity of the trigger or on the effects of the anxiety the trigger provokes.

ILET as an anxiety-reduction technique

Giving a structure to a patient through which to understand the workings of her mind and brain not only acts as an anxiety-reducing technique but also allows for a real sense of control over her internal world that up until then has been distorted by being trapped in concrete thinking. If patients have been trapped in the thought that emptying the contents of their stomachs is the solution to their emotional dilemma, and this belief is held in much the same way that someone suffering from a psychosis holds on to their paranoia, then being able to move away from the thought is easier than having to justify it in argument. Patients treated with the ILET method have expressed huge relief that their thinking is not 'mad' but a natural response to excessive anxiety and, thus, can be disregarded.

The active ingredient of ILET

ILET emphasises the importance of discovering the exact trigger thought that has collapsed into its concrete counterpart, as it is only by working on the patient's specific anxieties that they can be contained and 'detoxified', much in the way maternal preoccupation offers this service to the baby. It is this experience, it is suggested, that gives ILET its power to transform toxic anxiety into manageable thoughts that are then processed and acted on. This process also promotes the laying down of memory in language of successful solutions to emotionally challenging and overwhelming stimuli. These successful solutions are then available for future use.

ILET treatment promotes the maturation of the frontal lobes that marks the end of the neurological maturation of adolescence. CBT also works on the frontal lobes but, as has been described above, does so as a by-product of the treatment and not in a consciously targeted way.

Another technique (borrowed from psychoanalysis) used by ILET is enquiring about associations to the stimulus thought, much in the way dream material produces associations. It is an expected and common finding that when using the technique of exploring dream associations, patients report an 'aha' moment of emotional recognition. As in psychoanalysis, this emotionally important material is worked over and understood from a symbolic perspective. Concrete dream symbols are expanded to include possible symbolic meanings. It is through this process that 'unconscious' material can be explored.

In neurobiological language, experiences that are perceived through the non-dominant, mainly visuo-spatial, hemisphere (usually the right hemisphere) are enabled to cross the corpus callosum (the bundle of fibres that connects the two hemispheres), allowing for wordless experiences to be worked over in language. This process allows symbolic language to give greater depth of understanding to the material being worked over. Although there is some language function in the right hemisphere, it is concrete in nature and does not allow for sophisticated understanding. Once left hemisphere language function is engaged, memories can be laid down and drawn upon for future understanding of similar emotional challenges.

Traditionally, psychoanalytic patients are required to be symbolic in their thinking in order to benefit from the treatment. However, in recent times, patients regarded as borderline (in the psychoanalytic definition – concrete, narcissistic and grandiose) are now considered treatable but with a change in technique which aims to understand the concrete nature of the patients' inner world. Mentalisation therapy (Fonagy & Bateman, 2006) uses the technique of addressing empathy with the 'other' in order to address the underlying narcissistic personality structure.

ILET offers insight allied to the pertinent material that has created the anxiety which forces a change of pathway away from the concrete body area to the symbolic language area of the brain. It is the technique of redirecting the pathway in response to a specific stimulus that has the added benefit of strengthening the symbolic language pathway that differentiates ILET from CBT and mentalisation therapy.

The repetition by the therapist and patient (eventually of the patient alone) of the process to find the trigger thought is the active ingredient in ILET. This differs from CBT, which requires the therapist to engage in Socratic dialogue with the patient, who is still in thrall to the 'rightness' of her body thoughts and has no way of understanding her way of thinking as a change of state rather than faulty beliefs, each of which has to be challenged rather than understood as a class of thinking.

The importance of the neurobiological underpinnings of ILET

The neurobiological underpinnings of ILET both explain how an eating disorder is created and offer an explanation for a treatment to 'cure' or correct the over-use of the concrete pathway in emotional processing. CBT on the other hand is, in my opinion, restricted by the narrowness of the learning theory that is used to explain the eating disorder. In fact, CBT does not claim to understand the genesis of an eating disorder other than in terms of faulty learning and, by Fairburn, as a maintenance model where the genesis of an eating disorder is immaterial or at least not a subject for enquiry.

The neurobiological explanation of state change, which underlies ILET, can account for the behaviours and thought processes seen in eating disorders under the rubric of concrete emotional processing. Specifically, the theory and hypotheses that underlie ILET explain in detail how the brains of eating disorder sufferers are compromised prior to the expression of the eating disorder 'illness' behaviour. It offers a comprehensive explanation as to why a stimulus thought, which is complex and negative, overwhelms the compromised ability to process and comprehend the ironic and complex metaphoric information that is seen in the normal complexity of emotional discourse.

ILET draws on the different disciplines of neurobiology, learning theory, psychoanalysis, attachment theory and linguistics to create a unified theory of eating disorders. The freedom to move between, and to respect, these different disciplines enriches the understanding of the thinking underlying the illness behaviours that make up a diagnosis of an eating disorder.

Once the underlying deficits have been understood and supported by evidence, it is suggested that the treatment of these illnesses becomes elegant. It is perhaps the complexity of the cognitive–behavioural treatment and its relatively poor outcome that tells us that treating the myriad 'facts' of the illness has replaced the search for a unified theory. Because historically the different theoretical approaches to the treatment of mental illness refuse to engage in a dialogue, the patients lose out on being the beneficiaries of the ignored fertile ground that such dialogue brings.

From a neurobiological perspective, all psychotherapy, whether behavioural or psychodynamic, works on the underlying plastic structure of the brain. The normal development of the brain passes through periods of paring down of the frontal lobes where redundant pathways degrade and those required for the next stage of life are strengthened or created for the first time. In adolescence, when eating disorders mainly manifest themselves, the risk is run that the typical 'body' mindedness and narcissism of this age group perseverates as the 'fight-or-flight' pathway is constantly pressed into service at the expense of the symbolic language pathway. Thus, there is no challenge to the frontal lobes on which reality can leave its mark, finally resulting in the creation of the adult brain. It might be said that the 'cure' of an eating disorder is bringing to a close the vagaries of the adolescent brain and the establishment of the adult brain.

ILET treatment with 'Emily'

Summary

Chapter 8 follows the treatment of a patient, 'Emily', using ILET. The protocol is fully explained and, I hope, demonstrates how it happens in the consulting room.

Emily: *'I don't understand why – but I can't eat red vegetables.'*
Therapist: 'That's interesting – could you tell me the first word that comes into your head when I say "red vegetables"?'
Emily: 'Fear and – Oh my God! – sexuality.'

At this point she placed her hand over her mouth as she began to realise the meaning behind her profound fear of red vegetables. We thought together about the different attributes of red in the context of sexuality – what it would mean to be a grown woman and to have a woman's body, to menstruate and have sexual desires, to be capable of having a child – all this from fear of 'red vegetables'. And so we began the process of discovering meaning in her 'eating disorder', or perhaps it is better described as understanding the meaning located in certain foods or parts of the body – the 'concrete symbol' – in place of her complex feelings about her self and her world of relationships.

Let me introduce 'Emily'. Emily has generously agreed to allow her treatment with ILET to form a chapter in this book in order for this new and different method to be more widely known about. Of course, all identifying details have been changed but I hope that the essence of this way of approaching eating disorders remains.

As per the protocol, the first two sessions introduced the concepts of ILET as well as taking a detailed history.

Emily was a 22-year-old university student who came to me after having met a patient I had treated some years previously. At the time of assessment, Emily was living with her parents and three older siblings.

When I first saw Emily she cut a sad figure. She had not had a period for three years and had a BMI of just under 16. Her appearance was unkempt and she seemed lost. She had been referred to her local hospital by her GP and was being seen occasionally by a nurse at the eating disorder unit.

Emily spent a great deal of time walking and ruminating, going into shops but not buying anything. She also swam and pushed herself to her limit. Thinking about food occupied her mind most of the time and she would go out to buy the perfect food each morning, according to what her desire dictated. Food was consumed, usually when she was alone, in the kitchen and if it was consumed in front of the family it usually had to be different from the food eaten by the family and then only eaten in small amounts so as not to be seen as greedy. By the evening Emily was usually starving hungry – a state she needed to be in before allowing herself to eat.

I always ask about my patient's mother's family history, as frequently this illuminates the quality of early mothering my patient has received. When asked about her relationship with her mother, Emily described a longed for but intolerable level of closeness. She described her mother as having experienced an overly close relationship with her own psychologically unwell mother and Emily felt that her mother seemed to want and need the same closeness in her relationship to her. Emily's mother had also suffered from anorexia and bulimia as a teenager and had become very severely physically ill. While Emily expressed sympathy for her mother's difficult childhood, she also felt ragingly angry with her at the same time. These mixed feelings caused Emily distress and confusion, as she felt very dependent on her mother and enjoyed their shared activities but felt that she could not cope with her mum's overwhelming level of anxiety. Emily described her relationship with her father as both open and yet at times experienced as remote.

Emily described the atmosphere in the house as very tense and she felt guilt that it was her behaviour that was responsible for the tension.

In the assessment, Emily described an emotionally painful incident in her childhood when she had felt that her mother had not been able to hear her concerns and instead had become angry with Emily.

Just prior to developing her eating disorder, Emily took a gap year, went travelling and lost weight to the point that other people began to comment. When it came to university, she had been unsure which to choose, and, due to external circumstances, had to attend the only one available. During her first year, her eating disorder increased in severity and, due to Emily's inability to make up her own mind, she followed her mother's advice to change university. She regretted it deeply, which seemed to fuel her eating disorder even more. Emily described a similar constellation to when she was a child and felt that her wishes and feelings had not been asked for or taken into account.

We can see that the ingredients for an eating disorder were all there: a mother who has had poor mothering herself, had suffered an eating disorder in her youth, operating in an unseparated way and who was highly anxious. There was a lack of a containing maternal mind to hold Emily's anxiety plus a raised level of background anxiety in the family. Emily described poor emotional processing skills (some difficulties with relationships when young as well as in the present) and had good intellectual skills that were favoured over more emotional intuitive skills. She wished to have a healthy relationship with her mother but was only offered a fused relationship with a highly anxious mother and a father who did not intervene in the difficulties between Emily and her mother when there was an explosive difference of opinion.

On being given all the information about ILET and the neuroscience underlying the method, Emily found the psycho-education element very illuminating and said that it made a great deal of sense to her. She said that she felt very excited and hopeful for the first time, as when attending the hospital eating disorder unit she had been told that the chance of being free of her eating disorder, even with treatment, was low and that she would always have it in some form all her life. I explained to Emily that there was a difference between being prone to anxiety and various other underlying characteristics and their being expressed as an eating disorder. It was explained that instead of responding to every emotional trigger with a change of state and eating disorder behaviour, after treatment it would take an overwhelming emotional trigger to effect the same result. Also, ILET would give her the tools to recognise that a trigger had occurred when she changed state, allowing her to pre-empt the eating disorder behaviour. In other words, she might in the future have a vulnerability to responding to triggers by going 'concrete' but she would be able to reverse the process.

At the end of the first assessment session, Emily was asked to consider all the information she had been given. I also asked her to take note of any change of state just before she began to think and obsess about a particular food in the intervening time between the first and second assessment sessions. If she was able, she was asked to write down where she was and what was happening around her. She agreed to do this, but I assured her that if it proved difficult it was not a problem and we would go through it together when we met for the second assessment session. I also asked her to consider if she felt comfortable working with me and that she absolutely had a choice of both treatment approach and therapist. If she felt that the therapy that I offered was not for her, I would be happy to find her another therapist, as it is very important that she is settled in her own mind that this is the approach she feels comfortable with. I asked her to spend some time before deciding. She agreed to think about it but said that having spoken to someone who had been treated by me and based on her own experience of the first assessment session, she was inclined to go forward.

Second assessment session

Emily came into the second assessment session in a remarkably different and quite concrete state to the day before. She was agitated and distraught. I was a little surprised, given how hopeful she had been. Her demeanour was markedly different from other patients' responses, as they usually felt less anxious. I was curious as to what might have happened. It turned out (sometime later in the session) that after returning home from the previous session, Emily told her family that for the first time she felt hopeful that she could be free from her eating disorder. It seemed that the prospect of Emily getting well was both a welcome relief and also a catalyst to allow her parents the freedom to express their own difficulties, which had been put aside while Emily was very ill. A very explosive argument between her parents had ensued. However, this information was delivered to me not by Emily coming into the session and talking about it in a straightforward way, but as a preoccupation with her overwhelming need to find the exactly right sandwich for lunch.

Faced with this 'concrete sandwich' state of mind, I began the session where Emily was – in the concrete. ILET always stays close to what the patient says, as it posits that the meaning of the symbolic thought lurks in the concrete language. ILET understands that concrete thought is trying to convey a message to the patient but, unfortunately, without access to the symbolic language area of the brain, she would be unable to translate it into its symbolic meaning and thereby understand what she is trying to tell herself. With this in mind, I began by asking her what it was about the sandwich that was so important. She spoke of her guilt at spending on a ready-made sandwich when she had no money, but if she did buy it, she could see where the cheese was placed so that she could buy the same ingredients and place them in the exact same position. I wondered why things needed to be in the exact same place and what would happen if things got out of place. She replied that she did not know what would happen except that it would be disastrous. I then asked when she began to think about the sandwich. She replied that it was last night. Exactly when last night? She thought for a moment and said that it was after she had been talking with her father. So I asked what the conversation with her father was about. She began to describe the conversation about being excited and hopeful that she would overcome her eating disorder but she then suddenly remembered that during the conversation a heated argument between her parents had broken out and there were threats of ending the marriage. This was her 'aha' moment of emotional recognition. Emily became quite emotional and spoke of her feelings of abandonment and the fear of her home disappearing. Her shift to symbolic speech was dramatic and what had been a free-floating anxiety that had coalesced around food and was expressed in concrete thought and speech became an emotionally appropriate response to the shocking and disturbing events.

At this point in the session, the work was to connect the concrete utterances, about searching for the perfect sandwich and guilt over spending money in order for Emily to give herself what she desperately wanted, with the revelatory emotional insight and understanding. Thus, I suggested that the 'making sure that everything was in place in the sandwich' could be understood as her wish to keep the family members and home in place. Emily's reaction was astonishment and recognition – she wondered how she could have 'forgotten' about what had been said and was really shocked that all she could think about was the sandwich when something so momentous had happened. This was an important moment, when it had become startlingly clear what was happening to her with the state change from symbolic to concrete and the subsequent change in language and focus. She had understood that there was meaning in her symptoms.

As a response to the connecting of the symptom and an emotional insight, Emily brought up something she had been puzzling over – she wanted to make sense of her aversion to eating red vegetables. She said, 'I know it is mad but I feel compelled to avoid them and I just can't make sense of it.' As per the ILET protocol for anorexia nervosa, I asked her to associate to the colour red – her first reply was 'fear' and then 'sexuality' – she put her hand to her mouth and said 'Oh my God' as we expanded her concrete language about the colour of foods that could not be eaten. We played with the associations and spoke about her fear of being a grown up sexual woman – menstrual blood, danger, opening up to someone else. All this from red vegetables! Emily now understood how ILET worked and said that she definitely wanted to work both with the method and with me as her therapist.

As a result of the session, Emily resolved to talk to her parents about the possibility of divorce and the impact on herself and the family. This would, of course, require her to be in the symbolic mode and was quite an ask, having only just agreed to twice a week therapy and not due to begin therapy proper until the following week. I was a bit concerned about whether she could manage such a task but trusted her determination to do so.

Beginning therapy

When we did meet the following week, a quite different Emily came into the session. She was more composed and immediately talked of having spoken to her father. This was not to say that it had been an easy task for her, but she had tackled it. She asked to speak to him and began by asking for reassurances about what would happen to her, where would she live, given that she was so dependent as she had yet to finish university. He reassured her that there would always be a place for her with him as well as with her mother. Emily was also able to ask him why he had argued so volubly with her mother when she was just beginning her therapy – didn't he realise that this was very destabilising for her? He replied that he thought the fact that he was just so relieved by her news and felt that she was being taken care of had something to do with it but he apologised for causing her added distress.

The atmosphere in the consulting room became quite sad as we spoke about what it means to accept that our parents are not perfect. Emily was able to acknowledge the difficulties in her parent's marriage and began to take a view of them from a separated position. However, this was still very early in her therapy and there were many times during her therapy that she experienced anxiety that triggered a concrete state. When this happened in the consulting room, we were able to catch the state shift and began the search for the trigger thought in order to resymbolise the concrete contents. In this instance, it was the task of realising, as we must all do during adolescence, that our parents are not perfect but must be accepted for who they are – warts and all. However, this was a particularly difficult task when Emily's ability to think about her emotions symbolically was only just emerging.

When, like Emily had been in this session, a patient is able to be in the symbolic mode, I usually ask about how their eating has gone. ILET predicts that when the symbolic pathway is functioning the concrete response is not accessed. So

I asked about how she had felt when eating breakfast that morning. She replied with astonishment that she hardly remembered eating it but she knew she had – it had become just breakfast instead of the exquisite experience of eating the perfect food in the perfect conditions. Again she found it reassuring that these pockets of normality were beginning to emerge and began to understand that desperately searching for the perfect thing, be that food or an essay mark, would not change the stubbornly imperfect world.

Because Emily's BMI was low, she suffered from obsessions and had difficult family pressures, we made the decision not to put a limit on the number of sessions but to reassess around session 20.

The next few sessions concentrated on recognition of a change of state and focused on locating the trigger event both in and out of the consulting room. This process was entirely collaborative and driven by curiosity on Emily's part in wanting to understand the reason behind her rituals and obsessions. She expressed relief that she wasn't 'mad' and that she felt she was beginning to build her own mind. As she began to be aware of her thoughts and opinions, Emily's meltdowns and arguments between herself and her mother unsurprisingly and unfortunately increased. Emily had reduced the amount of time she spent in the concrete and, thus, spent more time in the symbolic, which led to her expressing more of her needs at home with her family. I was aware that this was quite quick and we had not yet arranged a family meeting to help the family understand the process and to create space to nurture their daughter's growing opinions.

One evening, Emily addressed the issue of being listened to and heard by her parents – to her parents. The main concern expressed by Emily was the issue of boundaries and she asked her mother to both knock before coming into her room and to leave it when requested. She also asked her mother to ask for her opinion and wishes rather than to assume her wants and needs. Of her father she requested that he be more involved, as she found her mum's anxiety too difficult to deal with especially as she was trying to focus on addressing her own eating disorder in therapy. Owing to her mother's very difficult and painful upbringing, which it seems had resulted in the need to be close to Emily in the same way she had been close to her own mother, Emily's mother felt very rejected and, it seems, was unable to express her feelings other than to become extremely distressed, which lasted for many hours. This changed the focus of the family from listening to Emily's needs to trying to comfort Emily's mother.

Emily's dilemma was the same as that of many girls suffering an eating disorder experience; needing a mum to absorb her anxieties and help her to grow her individual self and mind and a dad who can intervene in the relationship between mother and daughter if it goes awry. Unfortunately, she discovered that her mum and dad, even though unintentionally, were unavailable to fulfil that need.

As described above, our task is to bring our patients to reality, which includes seeing parents for who they are, faults and all, and to somehow come to an acceptance of them and to find what nourishment they can, if not entirely from parents, then from others in their lives. However, when bingeing and vomiting or starving or exercising interrupts our thoughts and concerns about relationships or difficult emotional situations, we are not only unable to resolve these challenges but we are not even aware that they exist. The opposite is true as well. The more time spent in the symbolic state, the more solutions can be found to these difficult emotional problems. This was the case with Emily and her family. As Emily increased the time spent thinking symbolically so she made more emotional demands on her family. However, her family continued to act as before.

Emily's therapy illuminated a particular dilemma that when delivering ILET, we need to be aware that, because ILET can effect change quite quickly, families may not have time to adjust to the normality they seek. As a result of the pressure on her family of Emily's increasing sense of self and opinions, we quickly arranged a family meeting so that the whole family could hear about how ILET works and the need for other members of the family to adjust their expectations and responses. In a sense, all ILET is designed to do is to allow the eating disorder sufferer to get to know her own mind and then help her think through what she wants to do in response to these new understandings.

The family session became a turning point in the therapy after Emily had insisted that her mother hear what she was trying to tell her about how she had felt as a child; her mother eventually seemed to understand the situation from Emily's perspective, stopped trying to justify her actions and apologised. This became an important and valued moment between mother and daughter. It was clear that Emily's mother wished to be a good mother to her daughter but was handicapped by having great difficulty in understanding emotional situations from Emily's point of view. It became clear that Emily's father, a reticent man, found the demand on him to participate in the emotional life of the family quite difficult. However, he understood that he needed to help his wife and daughter by intervening when there were difficulties between them.

Emily found the session extremely helpful and it had a dramatic effect on her level of anxiety. She wrote the following message:

> I wanted to feed back that I don't think the session could have been more helpful. Knowing people are becoming aware of their role made me feel secure for the first time in a long time this evening. I hope today will have been taken on board as I feel both less responsible and less willing to blame. It is very freeing. I do however have reservations about spending time with mum as I am concerned that she doesn't quite get her responsibility and I don't yet know how appropriately skilled I am in stopping her in her tracks to help her listen to me or take account of my emotions. It is an ancient dynamic we have and one I find difficult to always be aware of. I suppose practice is key. Thanks again. I didn't anticipate the session encouraging such emotional relief on my part and I am very appreciative.

An example of how Emily was able to begin to connect her preoccupation with food and her emotional life followed on from difficult events of the week before.

Emily: 'It was a very difficult week, very hard.'
Therapist: 'In what sense?'
Emily: 'I spent a lot of it very concrete and it was just a huge mish-mash of stuff.'
Therapist: 'Do you recognise any of the moments that sent you concrete?'
Emily: 'I flipped in and out – a good point was Sunday evening. Sunday as a day was okay, I had breakfast, lunch and dinner and although I had a lot of anxiety before dinner, because it was the Sunday roast, I managed my way through it and I ate almost the same thing as everyone else except rather than roasted potatoes I had boiled potatoes. That was good, part of that was me – I couldn't decide whether to have chicken or fish. For ethical reasons I'm a pescatarian and so I sat down and really thought about it: is there something I should feel bad about? I absolutely wanted the chicken. I had to sit down and think: is there anything that I feel bad about? Have I done anything wrong? Is it me feeling like a bad person, that I can't have the chicken? Because on the other scale of things I'm also aware that I'm in recovery and that not having barriers is important. I was thinking about a huge argument I had had with my mum the night before and had been feeling bad about it. Once I had addressed that the chicken was okay.'

Much of Emily's preoccupation with food centred around eating with the family or friends. When it came to eating with the family, it was not surprising that Emily found it very difficult. Unfortunately, the family situation remained very tense and so the pressure was on Emily to make changes. Emily dearly wanted to be able to eat with her family but there were many different 'concrete' reasons why this was proving very difficult. Emily's food had to 'match' in terms of colour and consistency and if the food provided by whomever in the family was cooking that day did not meet the required criteria, then Emily would have to cook for herself. One such incident happened when Emily rejected the food that was offered but still wanted to eat with her family, but as she had left it too late she had to cook when the family were already eating. This left her standing and cooking while the family were at the kitchen table. Emily came into the following session upset that she did not achieve her aim of a family meal. I noted that, given the work we were doing on relationships with family members, being in the room together was an improvement.

I was curious about how the incident had come about and asked Emily to talk me through the evening. She said that it was her father who was cooking and in fact had cooked what she had requested, but when she arrived for the evening meal and examined it, she found that there were too many colours mixed together and she became more anxious. I asked what it was about the colours that made it impossible to eat. She explained that something red had been introduced but it was not just about the colour red, it was they way that it was all mixed up so she could not separate it. We thought about having 'mixed feelings' about eating with the family and all the 'mixed feelings' she had about the family and how difficult it was for her to negotiate her way through all the love and the anger she had towards her parents. We then looked at what her behaviour meant. First of all she wanted to be with the family but did not have a way of processing all her very mixed feelings. She wanted to be nurtured and intuitively fed just what she wanted and that included the family staying together to help her heal. But the actual family was in turmoil in that mum and dad were hardly speaking. So her behaviour of feeding herself, because no one else could give her what she needed, happened with her standing up away from the table but still being in the room. I suggested that this vignette accurately mirrored her feelings – she was trying to get closer to her family but still harboured very mixed feelings of neediness, anger and guilt which prevented her from sitting down and joining them.

Emily also expressed distress that she was unable to meet with friends due to her preoccupation with the mechanics of eating. There was an incident when she was supposed to go out with old schoolfriends but Emily became very anxious about the choice of restaurant and was concerned that if she didn't choose it she would not be able to eat as, at the time, she was only eating what her 'body' was telling her to eat. If there were nothing on the menu she wanted to eat then she would be so hungry that she would cry and she didn't want to be the centre of attention. I was rather struck by her not wanting to be the 'centre of attention' (which turned out to be the trigger thought) so I asked her to tell me about the people she would be meeting. She was easily able to describe them and the quality of the interactions between the group. She seemed less anxious than when describing the food situation. It turned out that the girls were quite a competitive and intelligent group who all tried to be witty and knowledgeable about politics and there seemed to Emily to be a competition for who was the wittiest. This evidently raised her anxiety and, thus, triggered her concrete preoccupation with food. The connection was drawn between being the centre of attention for being the brightest and wittiest and the centre of attention for crying because she could not eat the food and was not in control of the venue. It was put to Emily that she understood that she could make her self the centre of attention quite easily but she did not want to be so for pathological reasons. She would not be able to compete in the witty stakes if she was so concerned with the contents of her stomach. In other words, she 'could not stomach' losing the competition. This led on to a discussion about what it meant to be 'good enough' and not 'the best', not 'perfect'. So again we began the session in the concrete and 'translated' the anxieties that were expressed in food into their symbolic meaning.

As Emily's therapy continued, she became more practised in noting state change and attempting and often succeeding in finding the symbolic meaning. However, the ebb and flow of the therapy tended to mirror the state of tension in the family. Emily acknowledged that she was the lightening conductor for the marital stresses and also that her illness was a major stressor, which insight pro- voked in her a great deal of guilt. She also noted that when she began to improve in mood and ability to eat, there seemed to be more arguments in the family. We understood her parents' reaction to Emily's increasing health as possibly her par- ents having the space to try to resolve their own difficulties rather than focusing on, and worrying about, Emily.

By this point we had been meeting twice weekly and, as agreed, at session 20 we reviewed her progress and outlined her aims for future sessions. Emily recognised the shift in her thinking away from food and her body and found the process to be very exciting, if at times very daunting. Her focus was to reduce further her loss of control when faced with anxiety-provoking social events but also to address her fears about returning to university. She expressed her deep commitment to our shared work and spoke about how important our relationship was to her that was allowing her to discover herself.

Emily's eating and weight had stabilised and she was eating a weight main- taining diet, but at a low weight. We discussed how increasing her weight might happen and as I was to go on leave during the summer, we decided that it might be a good opportunity for her to attend the day clinic at her local eating disorder unit. From the ILET point of view, there is no conflict with addressing weight issues using CBT and I was fully supportive of Emily joining the day programme. Addressing nutritional needs is an important element of recovery, as, while there is meaning to be discovered in the symptoms, it is necessary to 'eat what is on one's plate'. In Emily's case, it meant that she had to accept that there was no 'perfect' food that, if consumed, would put her emotional world to rights. Under the supervision of the day unit, Emily was faced with, and ate, an increasingly wide variety of ordinary foods with, at times, greater or lesser success. She had the benefit of being in a group of young women who could support each other. During this time we continued our sessions via Skype and by understanding the meaning of her difficulties with different foods, she was better able to try them.

Face-to-face therapy sessions resumed and Emily's understanding of the fam- ily dynamics and her reaction to them increased. She continued to notice changes of state and searched for the triggers which were then worked on in therapy as well as when she was by herself.

The family situation remained unresolved and so the tensions in the home and around mealtimes continued. To add to the home pressures, Emily had to organise returning to university but received discouraging news by email. I knew some- thing very difficult had happened as Emily's reaction was similar to the beginning of therapy. She communicated it in a similar way as she had to her parents' dis- tressing argument. The entire session consisted of talk about whether she should have a wrap or a sandwich for lunch and the pros and cons of each. There was little sense to be made of it other than my suggesting that something important and disturbing must have happened which involved pros and cons and she didn't seem to know what to do. We carefully worked back to identify the trigger to this 'sandwich' state. She remembered the email she had received from the university and she immediately changed back to the symbolic state. The remainder of the session was conducted entirely in the symbolic as we spoke about the changed realities facing her at university. This broadened into a discussion about the realities of the unknowns that Brexit would bring that could well hamper her dream of living and working in Europe. Again Emily was quite shocked that this problem had not occurred to her and brought the realisation that, in her concrete state of mind, she had lost the ability to keep an eye on reality. In this way, her adolescent brain was experiencing and responding to the reality shocks that it needed to develop into an adult brain.

As Emily became more practised in finding the triggers to state change, she became more adventurous, which of course brought new pressures. She decided that finding a job would solve her dilemma about never having enough money and feeling financially dependent on her parents, particularly her father.

She began to face the realities of getting herself prepared to study, contacting her lecturers and addressing her need to take care of her body.

At this point, Emily was moving into a more symbolic way of thinking and talking which highlighted her mother's concreteness of thought and language. Emily reported that it seemed her mother's eating disorder had revived, as her mother always made sure that she ate less than Emily. Emily felt sympathy for her mother because as Emily began to vacate the 'eating disorder' space in the family, she observed her mother seemingly stepping into it. Her parents' relationship had become increasingly tempestuous but Emily was able to take a view, step back, and let them resolve it as best they could. She became quite sad as she came to terms with her family's lack of perfection. She began to look towards the future and plan for how she was going to pick up on her studies, get used to the emotional rough and tumble of university and contemplate flirting with young men.

Emily's time at the day clinic came to an end just before she returned to university. We would also shortly be making the transition back to using Skype. In our penultimate face-to-face session she felt naturally distressed, given all the transitions she was making; leaving home and not knowing if things would stay the same in the family or not, not 'seeing' me, leaving the day clinic and having to be 'grown up' about taking care of herself at university. So we set about unpacking all her very complex feelings.

Emily, of course, harboured mixed feelings towards the unit that worked so hard to help her face the practicalities of eating and putting on weight that was felt to be a mixed blessing. Even though she was pleased to be of 'normal' weight, she felt very worried about taking over responsibility for her food. Emily expressed these mixed feelings on her last morning at the unit. Emily had prepared thoughtful gifts for both staff and patients but somehow had not left herself sufficient time to wrap them up beautifully as she had intended. She began to get very anxious in the unit and had to return home to eat as she found it impossible to eat with the others. She felt dreadful, as if she had let herself down after making such good progress. We understood the 'not leaving herself enough time to finish wrapping the gifts' to stand for her ambivalence towards leaving. She wanted to leave, but while she was very grateful indeed for the care of the staff, she naturally had had very angry feelings towards them for being the people who confronted the issue of increasing her weight. She was going to miss the other girls and the staff but she was glad to be getting on with her life. She was sad that there did not seem to be a space to discuss her mixed feelings at the unit leading up to, and on, her last day and that she had left by acting out rather than with a mutual understanding of her ambivalent feelings. She felt it was very helpful to have a chance to understand what had happened.

While we were going to continue twice-weekly Skype calls, Emily would be facing many new challenges. We would be meeting face to face when she returned home at the end of term. Our last regular face-to-face session was a chance for Emily to express her feelings about our therapy together. She spoke about her fear of just losing control and continuously bingeing when she was at university. We understood this to be an expression of her emotional neediness. She would be leaving her family, had just left the day unit, and now our contact would be different. She was able to speak about worrying that she was making too many demands on me, and my time. I was able to reassure her of the bounds of our work together and that she was entitled to my therapeutic time and to trust that I would create safe boundaries to contain her fears of either abandonment or intrusion.

Recovering from anorexia, especially when there are underlying obsessions, is no easy task. It is yet more difficult if there are intractable family problems and developmental issues such as those that left Emily with high levels of anxiety and little ability to self-soothe. Add to this the travails of adolescence, where the frontal lobes pare down, giving uncertain access to symbolic language function, and you end up with many threads that need to be unwound and repaired. However, Emily fully understood and was involved in the process, so the task became shared and, as a consequence, more manageable. Knowing what is happening in the brain created a structure that made sense to her and helped contain her anxiety.

Sometimes we can effect some change in how a family functions, sometimes very little, but whatever was to happen, Emily had to find a way of discovering what she was trying to communicate to herself via her 'concrete symbols', create her sense of self and use the tools she had been given to help reduce her anxiety to manageable levels in the future.

Chapter 9

Conclusions

This book is the culmination of my years working in the field of eating disorders and thinking about the counter-intuitive nature of this group of illnesses. There lies a perversity at their heart. The eating disorder (particularly anorexia) comes to stand for the self but as the illness progresses the self is destroyed. A rationale given (again in anorexia) is that the sufferers want to be more attractive and love-able, but the reality is that they become skin and bone and their world narrows to become preoccupied with their bodies and calories. They wish to be entirely independent but are unable to feed themselves and so become utterly dependent. Bulimia is a hidden illness where the sufferer tries to engage with the world but can only respond to its demands by bingeing and then vomiting, gradually losing more and more contact with her emotional world and her ability to define who she is. Those who suffer from binge eating disorder express the wish to lose weight but respond to the emotional demands of their world by filling up every space in order not to experience painful emotions.

These conundrums preoccupied me and so began a search for an explanation or possibly even a unified theory that might account for all the observed phenomena.

I began to study for a PhD and formally tackle my intuition that by melding research and theory from disparate theoretical disciplines of neuroscience, psychoanalysis, developmental psychology and linguistics, a greater understanding of the origin, process and possible cure of these illnesses could be gained.

The result of this research was to provide a theoretical explanation for the observed efficacy of the ILET treatment – the development of a discontinuous model of neural emotional processing in eating disorders. This model also offers a possible explanation as to why other continuous models are relatively unsuccessful and predicts a curative process.

There is a growing body of neuroscience literature relating to eating disorders but a much larger and well-accepted body of knowledge in the field of neurobiology relating to emotional processing, maternal preoccupation, attachment, alexithymia, language function and hemispheric interaction. The entirety of this body of knowledge, when directly applied to eating disorders, illuminates and offers explanations for observed phenomena and underpins a new treatment stance.

In order to place these ideas in context, the book began with an explanation of the psychoanalytic understanding of eating disorders and a discussion about the development of the self and possible disturbances in this process. The case was made that there is a growing body of literature pointing to underlying cognitive deficits in eating disorder sufferers that may account for some of the difficulties experienced by this group.

This was followed by the literature on emotional processing integrated with research on alexithymia and brain function. Interhemispheric communication and the role of the right hemisphere in verbal communication and self-regulation were described as well as the central involvement of the right hemisphere in the analysis of information from the body. This introduced the topic of the role of the insula in processing bodily based information as well as, crucially, acting as a junction box for information coming from the amygdala, which either opens the pathway to the symbolic functions or returns the information unexamined to the amygdala.

Metaphorical thinking and eating disorders was viewed from a neurobiological perspective, and this discussion was followed by a description of the psychoanalytic approach to the concept of symbolisation.

Following the review of the literature, a case was made for there being a conceptual gap in thinking about eating disorders and a need for a new model of the mind which would naturally lead to a new treatment approach.

It is generally accepted that there is a lack of a unified theory of eating disorders. This book set out to describe such a unified theory by describing how eating disorder patients might be vulnerable to triggering brain pathways that, under stress, fail to reach the symbolic language emotional processing functions. Instead, there is a return to the area of the brain that controls the body responses to anxiety, the amygdala, where there is no access to verbal symbolisation, just concrete language and acted out behaviour. As described above, this process can be conceptualised as a discontinuous model of neural emotional processing where the patient either is able to emotionally symbolise in language and has access to symbolic language, reality testing, memory in language, creativity and planning functions or is only able to function in a bodily concrete paradigm leading to impaired intra- and interpsychic functioning.

The next chapter was concerned with filling the conceptual gap and attempted to integrate the neuroscientific research with the psychoanalytic body of thought in order to illustrate the interdependence of the two approaches and the interplay that can enrich both approaches and deepen our understanding.

It began by looking at the development of symbolisation from a neuropsychoanalytic perspective. The interplay between the early environment and the child's neurobiological makeup, it was suggested, leaves the child vulnerable, owing to instability in processing complex emotional internal states through language.

The development of 'the self' was discussed from both the psychoanalytic and neuroscientific perspectives by tracing the maturation and functions of the right hemisphere that underlie the requirements for a successful maternal preoccupation for both mother and child, which then influences successful attachment. Genetic factors that might influence the maturation of babies' brains were discussed.

Early right hemisphere function was then discussed as a precursor to the development of verbal communication. This was taken further, and right hemisphere language functions, importantly among other attributes, were described as responsible for understanding metaphor. The right hemisphere also serves to retrieve past emotional experiences, particularly negative ones, which are then available to be incorporated into the reasoning process.

This led on to a discussion of the two pathways of the emotional processing system, which are seminal to the ideas presented in this book. This area of neurobiological research is well established and provides the underpinning of the notion of state change that underlies the ILET treatment. The amygdala, which receives information from the external and internal environments but has no access to symbolic language, sends this information to the insula, a junction box that either sends the information to the symbolic functions for processing in language or back down to the amygdala with an added danger signal. The amygdala then initiates the release of signals to the body that are experienced as anxiety. The trigger for this process is, in this formulation, the inability to handle complex negative ironic and/or complex metaphorical material.

Interhemispheric communication and its relationship with low emotional intelligence, alexithymia and the imaginal functions was then discussed and it was suggested that this is an area of deficit for the eating disorder population. It is suggested that with low emotional intelligence there are reduced amounts of REM sleep and associated deficits in the processing of 'procedural-implicit' memory (i.e. a 'doing' without consciously thinking).

Two reasons are given as to why states of emotional arousal evoked by the amygdala remain unregulated. (1) A reduction in unconscious inhibitory feedback from the prefrontal cortex to the amygdala due to an impoverished representational world which limits the ability of the prefrontal cortex to make a detailed cognitive appraisal of the complex emotional stimuli. (2) Limited ability to represent and, therefore, contain emotions in language, which then reduces the ability to use fantasy to imagine different solutions to emotional problems.

Finally, the work of the psychoanalysts Hannah Segal and Melanie Klein was integrated and underpinned by neurobiological research on emotional processing and the development of symbolic thinking, and its implications for the treatment of eating disorders were set out.

A new model of the mind in eating disorders was introduced, suggesting that eating disorders can helpfully be reclassified according to cognitive and neurological function rather than the presence or absence of symptoms at specified levels. This was explained using two diagrams (Figures 5.1 and 5.2) of mental function in eating disorders. A detailed discussion of the nature of triggers that provoke state change were illustrated with examples from patients treated with ILET.

The logic behind the new ILET treatment was discussed and was followed by a discussion of the nature of typical trigger material that provokes state change from symbolic to concrete thought which then leads to eating-disordered behaviour and is based on recent research on how literal and figurative language is processed.

This new understanding, it was suggested, has paved the way for insights into how comprehension of figurative language can fail, in that deficits in the developmental process are expressed in poor comprehension of complex emotional stimuli and language, in particular unusual metaphor and irony.

The next section introduced the concept of the degradation of the figurative/metaphoric content of language of the emotional trigger as it collapses towards the concrete. It is this collapse, it is posited, which stimulates concrete action. The patient becomes trapped in concrete thought and the only solutions available are concrete ones allied to the body.

This collapse leads to the crucial and critical moment of state change, the sudden and dramatic change between symbolic and concrete function. It was suggested that by focusing on the precise moment before state change, the content of the degraded trigger material can be identified, making it possible to help the patient resymbolise and understand the complexities of the emotional task or stimulus which has overwhelmed her ability to process emotions in language. To illustrate this process, examples of trigger material were given from patients treated with ILET.

Following on from the description of trigger material, the ILET treatment was described in detail, including a discussion of the analytic concept of the borderline with its features of concrete thinking, narcissism and grandiosity and its place in the psycho-education of patients – an essential element of the ILET treatment approach.

Patients would be asked to keep a TED that entailed keeping a detailed record of binge events and the description of the environment and thoughts just prior to the change of state from 'normal symbolic thought' to preoccupation with thinking about food or the body. The TED is then used as a base for the EEQ, which has seven items or steps that explore the trigger material.

In order to illuminate the properties of the ILET approach, there followed a comparison between the conceptual frameworks and practice of ILET and CBT, to examine how the two approaches address the underlying deficits traced in the previous chapters.

The importance of the neurobiological underpinnings of the ILET approach was explored in order to suggest and offer an explanation as to why it might provide a better outcome than 'maintenance models', which offer no explanation as to the genesis of the illness. This encompassed a discussion of the point of departure between the two treatment approaches in order to illuminate the areas of CBT that do not address the core issues and deficits in the neurological functioning of this patient group. The CBT approach was described as meandering into unnecessarily complicated and labyrinthine byways to address the assumed thinking behind the observed behaviour. The complication in this treatment model, it was suggested, is the result of its being based on a continuous model of emotional mental function.

The most important and crucial difference between the two approaches was introduced – the concept of state change, based on a discontinuous model of neural emotional processing. It was also suggested that CBT does not place enough emphasis on the complexity of the trigger material. In CBT, the trigger is just prior to the eating behaviour, and in ILET it is the precursor to state change and the eating-disordered behaviour might occur hours or even days later. CBT acknowledges that there is a trigger event, but it is seen simply as a negative event rather than as consisting of complex emotional material.

This led on to a discussion of the hypothesised active ingredient of ILET and the importance of finding the exact trigger thought that provokes state change that has collapsed into its concrete form. It was suggested that it is the accuracy in pinpointing the thought that allows the patient and therapist to work on the specific anxiety of the patient that had overwhelmed her ability to process her emotions. The hypothesis was put forward that these anxieties can be contained and 'detoxified', much in the way maternal preoccupation offers this service to the baby. Subsequently, these anxieties are transformed into manageable symbolic/metaphoric thoughts (and, therefore, stimulate the use of the symbolic language functions), which are then processed and acted upon. It is further hypothesised that this process also promotes the laying down of memory in language of successful solutions to emotionally challenging problems and overwhelming stimuli, which are then available for future use.

As suggested by the meeting on the future of psychoanalysis, this lies in neuroscience. It could equally be stated that all psychological treatments, of whatever persuasion, could benefit from this understanding.

This book has emphasised the need for a neurobiological underpinning in the design of future treatments. If therapies follow the logic of how the brain functions, it theoretically increases the power of the therapy to effect change. The neurobiological basis of the ILET treatment model allows testable hypotheses to be generated. It also offers an explanation as to how an eating disorder is created and contains within it the possibility of a cure.

Perhaps the most vexing question is: 'Why do the neurological deficits and environmental stressors described above result in an eating disorder rather than another manifestation of disturbance or none?' While there may be no clear answer at present, this opens up the subject as to what may be the active components that predispose someone to an eating disorder and trigger it. This book has tried to give a theoretical explanation, but it remains to be seen whether this can be translated into clinical evidence that can account for both the illness and the factors that protect against the expression of it, and also why certain features are present or not. An interesting line of enquiry might be which factors, either environmental or constitutional and in what proportion, underlie a particular illness expression.

Postscript

What's your gut feeling about this book?

Here's mine: this is an extraordinary book. Barbara Pearlman writes from the hard-earned perspective of a clinician and therapist with rich experience of treating and helping clients with eating disorders. Unlike quite a lot of us who like to pontificate and posit theory from the comfort of our academic ivory towers, Barbara brings all her experience of practice in the psychoanalytic tradition in extremely careful observation and description based on the hundreds of patients she has treated.

From this unique perspective, she draws together an impressive literature spanning developmental neurobiology, neuropsychoanalysis, Kleinian theory and the latest eating disorder treatment outcome data. In this regard alone, the book offers an impressive distillation of some very diverse theory and research findings.

However, this book goes much further than presenting a novel intersection of theory and practice. I think it represents the first serious attempt to develop a neuroscientifically based treatment for people with eating disorders. The neurobiological basis for eating disorders has been explored by many researchers (and comprehensively reviewed in this volume), yet practitioners have understandably been cautious about the utility of all this neuroscience, since researchers have had little to say about how their findings might actually help them to help their clients recover.

ILET covers all the major bases of contemporary eating disorders neuroscience and incorporates this knowledge into the treatment model. This includes right hemisphere dysfunction. Put simply, emotional processing in the brain is asymmetric (generally, all the good 'approach' stuff goes to the left side and all the bad 'escape' stuff goes to the right in healthy right-handed people – and snails, for that matter (Craig, 2005)). ILET accounts for the propensity of people with eating disorders to back away from the very bedrock of Maslow's hierarchy – nutrition.

The book also touches on the self–non-self distinction that has become the focus of recent theoretical advances (Moncrieff-Boyd et al., 2014): as Barbara puts it,

> If these [developmental] needs are on the whole met then the child will be in a good position to be able to attenuate or bring down their own anxiety

(self-soothe), develop a strong sense of self (know what they think and feel and recognise the boundary between themselves and others) and become emotionally literate in order to understand what they themselves and other people are meaning.

In reviewing the psychoanalytical literature on maternal preoccupation, Barbara steers a very careful line in avoiding 'mother blaming'. As she suggests, we only have to revisit the literature on 'refrigerator mothers' in autism to remind ourselves where that approach can lead . . . Nevertheless, it is important that we understand and support mothers who have lived with the experience of an eating disorder in their early parenting (and especially feeding).

We have tried to be very clear about the importance of not blaming parents in the title of our first paper exploring the insula hypothesis: 'The fault is not in her parents . . .' In the context of services for children and adolescents, I commend the inspirational approach of Dr Julie O'Toole and her colleagues at the Kartini Clinic in Portland, Oregon, whose 'strapline' is: 'parents do not cause eating disorders; but they are central to successful treatment'. Equally, Professors Janet Treasure and Ulrike Schmidt have led on creative approaches to support those who care for someone with an eating disorder – potentially one of the toughest roles imaginable for a parent or partner.

On the other side of the equation, as Barbara points out, 'it may also be that the child may have neurobiological deficits that militate against joining in the "dance" [between mother and child]'. Our noradrenergic dysregulation hypothesis locates this predisposing risk factor firmly in early (probably random plus epigenetic) factors in foetal brain development that makes this child or young adult more vulnerable than another to discovering that disordered eating is a powerfully reinforcing way to help themselves manage profoundly difficult feelings: when I restrict I feel a little less worse and when I eat I feel terrible.

Barbara suggests that a problem with the psychoanalytic approach to eating disorders is that it does not necessarily take into consideration aspects of brain function. She makes the point that, as a neurologist first, Freud anticipated a future time when his 'artificial structure of hypothesis' would be superseded by advances in physiology and chemistry. Although there have been staunch critics of neuropsychoanalysis, recent work on mentalising fits neatly with the ILET model; and in this regard the current model is in the 'good company' of Winnicott, Fonagy, Target, and Skardarud.

Crucially, this novel amalgam of existing theory leads naturally to a coherent, trainable and parsimonious treatment approach: to monitor and follow the shift in language from symbolic/metaphoric to the concrete and then to return or re-inflate the language to its symbolic meaning. In Chapter 5, Barbara offers a rich description of examples of this shift in several clients that really helps to bring the therapeutic techniques to life. Chapter 8, by exploring in depth the work with her client 'Emily', elegantly translates her theoretical thesis into a sympathetic and detailed account of clinical practice.

As the book concludes: 'The neurobiological basis of the ILET treatment model allows testable hypotheses to be generated. It also offers an explanation as to how an eating disorder is created and contains within it the possibility of a cure'. This impressive work linking the clinical insights of many hundreds of hours of offering therapy with a coherent summary of the latest neuroscience offers the real possibility of a profound shift in how we understand and help people who are struggling with such beguiling, difficult to treat disorders.

Dr Ian Frampton
Senior Lecturer in Developmental Neuropsychology
Centre for Clinical Neuropsychology Research
University of Exeter

Appendices

Appendix A

Glossary of abbreviated terms

ADHD	attention deficit hyperactivity disorder
ALT	alternate uses test
BDI	Beck depression inventory
BED	binge eating disorder
BMI	body mass index
CAT	cognitive analytic therapy
CBT	cognitive behavioural therapy
DSM-IV	*Diagnostic and Statistical Manual of Mental Disorders*
DSM-V	*Diagnostic and Statistical Manual of Mental Disorders*
EDI	eating disorder inventory
EDNOS	eating disorder otherwise not specified
EEQ	Emotional Events Questionnaire
FAS	verbal fluency task
ILET	internal language enhancement therapy
IPT	interpersonal behaviour therapy
LEAS	levels of emotional awareness scale
MEDE	management of eating disorders evidence report
NART	National Adult Reading Test
PTSD	post-traumatic stress disorder
REM	rapid eye movement
TAS	Toronto Alexithymia Scale
TED	trigger events diary

The ILET protocol

Summary

This is a detailed description of how ILET is carried out in the consulting room. I shall try to make the description as easy to follow as possible in order that professionals, sufferers and their families may gain some understanding of, and familiarity with, this new way of thinking about and treating eating disorders and, if they wish, take their interest further.

Phase 1: introduction and assessment

Helping the patient to access therapy

I think it is easy to forget just how difficult it is, when one is in turmoil, to go into a consulting room to talk to a therapist, a complete stranger, about personal issues. In eating disorders, it is even more complicated, as the ability to communicate is directly affected by the illness. Whereas professionals and family see a devastating illness that could, and does in a significant minority of cases, lead to the death of the sufferer or severe life limiting physical damage, the sufferer herself sees a solution to intolerable feelings of disgust and self-loathing. Thus, the scene is set for confrontation between patient and therapist. The patient needs to avoid the reality of her physical condition and hold tight to the unifying structure of her illness. She instinctively wants to retreat from therapy and this leaves the professional holding the anxiety, frustration and concern for the safety of the patient.

When an eating disorder is neglected and gets a grip, it may feel to the sufferer that she cannot let go of her eating disorder solutions because they have come to define who she is and she fears complete disintegration if she were to lose them, as they have become a substitute for a sense of self. That is why it is important that the patient is given the theory and research behind the ILET method in order that she can begin to understand why she is thinking the way that she does and to question it, rather than just unquestioningly believing that the feelings she experiences in her body reflect reality. The patient is reassured that she is neither 'mad' nor 'bad' but simply that her thinking has changed when her brain does not allow access to symbolic thought. The brain does not recognise that it has changed state and that her thinking is now concrete in nature – so it is perfectly understandable, if not entirely helpful, that she fervently believes that losing weight or bingeing and vomiting is the answer to the anxiety that she feels about her body.

As discussed in previous chapters, when patients are less able or unable to understand symbolic language, metaphor or irony and respond to complex emotional information by becoming concrete in their thinking, talking to them about difficult emotional subjects or about food and their bodies is fairly guaranteed to raise anxiety and halt communication between patient and therapist. The therapist being entirely open, equal and curious alongside the patient in the quest to find a way out of this troubling condition reduces the patient's anxiety, and when anxiety is reduced there is less chance of being triggered into the concrete state that results in eating disorder behaviour. So, in ILET, we do not act as if we 'know' what the patient thinks or ought to think and just deny the reality of her experience and we do not interpret the 'real' meaning of what she is saying. On the other hand, we do not ignore the meaning held in the symptom and neither do we concentrate solely on the eating disorder symptoms.

It is made clear that the therapist does not know the hidden meaning of what the patient is trying to say but we explain that we have a method by which she can come to understand what it is that she is trying to say to herself. The aim is to 'translate' the meaning held in the 'concrete symbol' back to the patient and not to 'interpret' the meaning so held. For example, when Amanda (see Chapter 5) worked back to the 'aha' moment of remembering the invitation with plus one on it, she was able to get in touch with the painful recognition that her boyfriend was choosing to exclude her. This led to the understanding that she must address the difficulties in her relationship. She was able (with the help of the therapist) to trace the spike in anxiety that she experienced when her boyfriend lied to her, which prompted her to remember the invitation. She now had all the ingredients to come to her own conclusions about what she was thinking but, just as importantly, she was building confidence in her own mind.

The four elements of ILET

There are four elements to ILET: the stance of the therapist; taking a detailed history; psycho-education and focus on the trigger thought before state change.

The stance of the therapist – open, equal and curious

The importance of the therapist taking an open, equal and curious stance, alongside the person who has come to them for help, cannot be overemphasised. But what is meant by 'an open, equal and curious stance'? The process is open because there is no hidden agenda; everything that we put before the patient is entirely transparent.

When a patient is referred or refers herself, there is usually a phone conversation. During the phone call the potential patient is told that she and the therapist will initially meet for two assessment sessions of two hours' duration, usually a week apart. It is explained that during the process of taking a history and her being given an explanation of how ILET works, she and the therapist will have the opportunity to get to know each other. The patient is encouraged to ask about the method and also to feel free to question the therapist about his/her qualifications and professional experience. It is explained that at the end of the first assessment session, she will be given a written summary of what she has heard so that she can think about the method and whether it makes sense to her and whether she feels comfortable working with the therapist. She will also experience the method so that she can make an informed decision as to whether she wishes to work in this way. It is explained that it will be around two-thirds of the way through the second assessment session, when she will have understood and experienced how ILET works and the therapist will have had time to think about whether ILET is the correct therapy for the patient at this time, that the decision will be made whether to work together using these new ideas. Thus, the patient comes to the first assessment session with a pretty good idea of what is going to happen. Again, this helps reduce the patient's anxiety at going into a room with a total stranger to discuss her very ambivalent feelings towards her illness.

The first assessment session is open in that it provides a roadmap for ILET where the reason for, and content of, the sessions is described along with the eventual aim of developing the adult brain that preferences symbolic function over concrete acted-out solutions to difficult emotional challenges. It is equal because it is made clear from the earliest moment that patient and therapist meet that this will be a collaborative endeavour. The therapist does not know what the patient is thinking any more than the patient does. But the job of the therapist is to be the holder of technical information – the how to – in order to give back to the patient the ability to discover and understand the contents of her own mind. She is given information about how the brain is built and how an eating disorder can come into being. This is to give the patient equal knowledge – from research to technique, all is available to the patient as it is to the therapist. In particular, the patient is told that therapy will only begin when she has had enough time to think about the method and consider whether it makes sense to her. It is only then that a contract to begin therapy is agreed. The therapist must also take time after the first session to consider whether the treatment is suitable for that particular patient, when and whether other members of the family need to be included in the therapy and in what capacity. Thus, when the patient and therapist make their decision, they have both thought about and signed up to the therapy.

The 'curious' element follows on from understanding that the contents (i.e., the meaning of the patient's thoughts) are held in the concrete symbol and it is by expanding the metaphoric and symbolic meaning of the concrete symbol which allows the patient access to her mind and the chance to build her sense of self. Both the patient and therapist need to take a curious stance, wondering what a certain situation might be about, the language and imagery that the patient chose that might hold a clue to the content of her occluded thoughts. It borrows some Freudian ideas. Freud said that being a psychoanalyst is rather like being a detective, and both patient and therapist do become sleuths, trying to decipher the meaning held in the concrete symbol. It is rather like discovering the meaning held in the symbols when we dream. Thus Emily (opening paragraph of Chapter 8) understood that her fear of red vegetables must mean something and we soon discovered her fear of sexuality as we followed her treatment session by session.

Taking a history

The second essential element in ILET is explaining to the patient that we will need to go into her history in detail. This is because we need to understand how she experienced her childhood and any significant events that occurred, her network of relationships and the history of the wider family. This history will give us the context of our patient's life and the influences on her and may well give us an idea of the triggers that provoke state change. It is quite exhaustive and, depending on the time available, might well need an extended session. An experienced ILET therapist can usually complete the history and explanatory tasks within two extended sessions but it might be that the decision to work together is not taken until all the necessary information has been either gathered or given. All of these explanations and history taking make up phase 1 of the ILET treatment. The history taking also includes questions about other areas of their lives, in particular, health and education.

A good place to start taking a history is to find out how the patient came to be in the consulting room. Did she come of her own volition or did her family and/ or GP insist on the referral? It is, of course, preferable if it were she who decided that she needs help but agreement to come is also a reasonable place to start. It is usually quite illuminating to discover how the patient came to therapy. If it is by word of mouth, she is usually primed to work with these new ideas and when that happens things can go quite smoothly. I often find that patients who have been through other therapies arrive feeling quite despondent, particularly if they have tried CBT and the symptoms return, as they feel that they have reached the end of the road and frequently feel that it is they who have failed and not the therapy. Given that CBT is successful in, at best, only 50% of cases, it is understandable that these patients may have lost hope. If this is the case, then it is very important to reassure the patient that an eating disorder can fade and not, as they might have been led to believe, that it can never be cured. It is also helpful to explain that, while they probably have an ongoing vulnerability to emotional stress that can trigger an eating disorder episode, treatment will strengthen the brain pathways that will protect them from reacting to the stress with eating disorder thinking and, subsequently, behaviour. It also provides them with the tools to deal with possible, but occasional, significant emotional shocks that act as triggers to these episodes.

ILET history template

When we take a history for ILET, we will have already discovered what brought the patient to therapy. This will have probably touched on family relations and difficulty in communication, which, as we know, may well raise the patient's anxiety level. Therefore, the history taking needs to return to more emotionally neutral territory. For that reason, the first topic to tackle when taking the history, after taking contact and medical supervision details, is a comprehensive educational history. This is followed by a work history and career aspirations and whether (depending on the patient's age) they have been achieved. We then move on to questions of general health, including when menstruation began. Following this, we turn to the history of the eating disorder. This will usually raise anxiety levels, so should be asked about in a very neutral way. First, we need her current weight followed by the highest and lowest weights and the rough dates these occurred and note the patient's height in order to work out the BMI. We then note the date the eating disorder started and the symptoms, and includes frequency, duration and, in the case of bulimia, what the patient binges on in what quantities. We are interested in whether there is any particular pattern to the binges – are they in the morning or evening? Are there any rituals that go with the bingeing? We are very interested in what is happening just prior to the binge, so the trigger events diary that will be given to the patient with the hand-outs at the end of the second assessment session will gather this information. We need to get an idea about how much the patient restricts, whether she uses laxatives or exercise to reduce weight, and note any remissions between episodes. It is useful to establish a baseline over the previous three months. To do this, we need to discover what percentage of the day the patient spends thinking about her body and food. This provides a baseline of how much of the day she spends in the concrete state. Has she had previous treatment for her eating disorder and if so when? What type of treatment and for how long? At this point we might ask what was her experience of the treatment – what was helpful and what was not and why.

The next set of questions relates to the family and relationships between family members both in the nuclear family and with grandparents and any other significant people in the patient's life. We ask whether the parents are alive and if they live together or are separated. There is particular interest in the maternal grandmother and her relationship with the patient's mother. This is to try to ascertain the quality of maternal preoccupation through the generations. We need to get quite a detailed picture of how the family interacts and find out who is close to whom and how the family functions. At this point, we should bear in mind that if it sounds as if the family is in crisis, then it may be politic to invite the whole family to help allay their anxiety and fears and to support them in creating a space for their daughter to develop her nascent mind. As was discussed in the introduction, it is often the case that families rally round their unwell child, who is unable to reality test and keep herself alive, in order to take over her thought processes. The family needs to feel confident enough to let go of their primitive protection towards their child and encourage independent thought. Because ILET tends to work rather quickly (when the frontal symbolic pathway is opened the patient experiences a plethora of thoughts and feelings) this can challenge the families'/parental/partner's protective stance and destabilise the family system. For this reason, it is important to include a family meeting soon after the patient has chosen to begin therapy. The family meeting also allows them to understand how ILET works and, as with their daughter, all information is open to them and it is an opportunity to ask questions and express their concerns and anxieties.

Psycho-education

The third element of the ILET approach is psycho-education and by this is meant an explanation of how the developing brain can develop fragility in certain functions that leaves the child and, later, the adolescent at risk of developing an eating disorder. How the psycho-education is delivered is again governed by the open, equal and curious stance. The patient is given a written explanation about how brains develop; how an eating disorder can develop and the outline of a new treatment, ILET. She is then talked through its contents, allowing time and opportunity for questions, and it is suggested that she takes it away with her. She is also given copies of Figures 1.1, 5.1 and 5.2, and has these explained to her.

The following explanation is given to the patient and, after it has been read through together with the patient, is taken away by her after the session.

'At the end of the written piece is a small amount about the technique we are using and how it will help you to get out of your current way of thinking (concrete), by opening up the disused (symbolic) pathway – and this is how we go about it.

'What we are aiming to do is to strengthen the "symbolic" pathway, which allows us to think about our feelings rather than to react to "discomfort" by acting on our bodies.

'The more we use a pathway the stronger it becomes and the reverse is true – the less we use a pathway the weaker it becomes. As we have seen, when a danger signal is attached to difficult emotions, the insula "junction box" activates the body reaction and stops us thinking about the problem (refer to Figure 1.1). The problem is then 'solved' by bingeing/vomiting/laxatives/exercise/restricting and you are none the wiser as to what has upset you nor have you found a workable solution to the problem. All that has happened is that you are more likely to use the body solution to an emotional problem next time, as you have strengthened the body pathway and weakened the thinking pathway.

'The adding of the "danger" signal happens without our conscious awareness and so it takes a bit of work to discover exactly what it was that triggered the change in our thinking. A sign of the change is that we use language differently; we lose the symbolic meaning of words. For example: instead of thinking that we 'have a lot on our plate this week that we cannot stomach' meaning we have a lot of difficult things to do that we will find very onerous (symbolic thinking) – we literally think that there is too much food on the plate that we cannot put into our stomachs (concrete thinking). When we comprehend that our understanding of language has changed, we can decide to re-symbolise it and then understand what it was that we were trying to tell ourselves.

'We are now going to look for a trigger that made you change state from symbolic to concrete so that you can get an idea of how this treatment works. Can you give me an example of a recent binge/restriction?'

At this juncture in the assessment, the therapist introduces the seven steps of the EEQ that guides the patient through the process of discovering the trigger thought just prior to changing state from symbolic to concrete thought.

The patient is then introduced to the eating disorder trigger events diary and asked to note down when she first knew she was going to binge/restrict and when she actually binged or restricted, plus noting what was happening to her at these precise moments. The therapist guides the patient through this process in the assessment session so that the patient experiences looking for and discovering the 'aha' moment of emotional recognition. The patient is then asked to think about or write down any eating disorder events that might occur during the coming week and to describe what she was doing and why she was doing that activity and who else was involved. In order that the patient doesn't feel that she has failed, she is told that at this stage it is the therapist's job to lead her back to the trigger thought and to expand it by adding symbol and metaphor to the thought.

Focus on the trigger thought before state change

The fourth element of ILET is the focus on the trigger thought just before state change which lies at the heart of the method. By the end of the first assessment session, the patient will have been introduced to the concept and practice of discovering and expanding the trigger thought. When the therapist and patient meet for the second assessment session, the patient will have had time to experience the effect of ILET and will also have decided whether she wishes to work with the therapist. A frequent response from the patient is usually one of surprise and elevated mood. Owing to the reconnection to the symbolic pathway during the first assessment session and the on–off nature of either symbolic or concrete thought, the patient may have experienced an extended period of symbolic thought. When this happens, eating disorder behaviour doesn't happen, or happens much less frequently than previously. Thus, patients feel attached to the process and are inclined to commit to ILET. It is explained why this reduction in eating disorder behaviour has happened and that if they commence ILET treatment they must expect that symptoms will fluctuate for a while, as we would be dealing with difficult emotional material that will fade only gradually as the symbolic pathway is strengthened.

The trigger thought

The content of the trigger thought, as has been explained in previous chapters, is required to have a complexity to it and it is this complexity that overwhelms the compromised brains of people who go on to develop an eating disorder. The trigger needs to have both positive and negative elements to it and it may well contain metaphorical or ironic material creating ambivalent responses in the recipient. Finding the trigger thought is where the detective work comes in. We need first to teach the patient to recognise when she has changed state. This will take time to accomplish, but for the purposes of the assessment needs to be done at the end of the first extended session. It is important to give the patient an experience of the ILET method before making a commitment to the therapy.

Trigger events diary

The patient is given the trigger events diary (TED) in which she is to note binge or state change events and to describe the surrounding background environment to the state change. The patient is asked to describe these binge events in minute detail (this usually takes some training, as most people tend to take a broad sweep when describing an event, and the patient is prepared for accuracy to be achieved only after some sessions), paying particular attention to the moment her thoughts became body-or food-based. She is asked to think of this moment as if it were a photograph or a snapshot of a dream. Later, when she is familiar with the method, she can be asked to report all associations to the material as if it was a dream. In the early stages, this enquiry is done by the therapist.

The TED given to the patient asks for a recording of every eating disorder episode, stating the time and place and including the reason for the activity, who was present, and the patient's thoughts just prior to the moment of change to thinking about food or the body. She will take the TED away with her to be completed in the intervening time between assessment sessions 1 and 2.

Thus, the patient's decision to work with this method is an informed one. It might well prove anxiety reducing and illuminating for the patient. Experience suggests that the acceptance of, and commitment to, the therapy is enhanced when this happens.

Following assessment and an agreement to work together, discovering the trigger thought and the 'aha' moment of emotional recognition becomes the central focus of the work. This is when the therapist and patient become detectives, as they together add symbol and metaphor, in other words, meaning to the concrete thought. And by this method it allows the sufferer to begin to discover their complex, ambivalent and uncomfortable thoughts rather than express them through the body.

The length of the therapy really depends on the situation of the patient. In cases of bulimia, if the illness began in late teens or later and the personality is relatively well formed, then 20 sessions may well be sufficient. If the patient has anorexia, especially if it is early onset and the patient is now in her late teens or early twenties, or there is a long history, then the number of sessions is dictated by need. The frequency of sessions is again dictated by the severity of the illness, but the protocol suggests that at the beginning of therapy the patient does best if seen twice a week. This both helps to reduce anxiety and encourages adherence to the practice of recognising state change and discovery and expansion of the trigger thought. Particularly at the beginning of therapy, before the symbolic pathway is reinforced and preferred over the concrete, the support of the therapist is vital. Although ILET has been designed as an outpatient programme, it would fit very well into a day or inpatient programme.

The agreement to work together brings to a close the first phase of ILET.

Phase 2: growing recognition of state change from the symbolic to the concrete mode of thought.

In phase 2, each of the sessions takes the same form.

At the beginning of the session, the patient is invited to give feedback of the week's events for around 15–20 minutes. This allows the patient to bring what she feels to be important in order that a significant event is not missed.

Following the week's debrief, the therapist and patient discuss the contents of the diary, looking for eating disorder events. Once an event has been chosen for deeper discussion, the steps 1–7 of the EEQ are worked through. This is in order that the patient begins to become aware of the sequence of an emotional challenge, followed by the change to the concrete state, which would then usually be followed by eating disorder behaviour. As the patient becomes aware of her concrete use of language at times of emotional stress, she can begin to expand the language to explore its fuller meanings. This will naturally help to increase her awareness and understanding of the trigger thought. The longer-term aim is to equip the patient with the tools to monitor her state change and to reverse the process by finding the trigger thought and/or event and becoming her own interpreter.

Phase 3: examining the past and addressing the future – saying goodbye

Phase 3 concentrates on using the newly acquired skill to process emotions symbolically. Once able to fully recognise the depth and the breadth of their emotional responses, patients have the opportunity to look at past relationships and to try to understand them from this new emotional perspective. Most probably there will still be moments of state change but that is to be expected and dealt with as previously. Quite often patients have to mourn past relationships that do not survive the change in the patient. Frequently, these past relationships are based on some aspect of the illness and when the dependency in the relationship gets out of kilter the previous satisfactions that each party gained no longer exist. This can be a difficult time, especially if the old relationships fall away before they have had a chance to be replaced by new, healthier ones. Looking towards the future also means previewing the end of therapy. Owing to the 'waking up' of the frontal functions, which allows the patient to fully experience her emotions and feelings, she will leave the therapy as a more mature adult (no matter what age she was when she began) and will ideally feel attached to the process and to the therapist. So it is that the relationship between the patient and the therapist comes more to the fore. The patient's relationship with her family will, one hopes, have changed for the better and deepened. As the patient's brain matures from its adolescent state into that of an adult, so there will be more acceptance of everyone's flaws, including the patient's, her family, friends and, of course, her therapist. As she has begun to know herself better and is able to plan for the future and reality-test her choices, we come to the issue of separation. Once she can rely on her own mind, separation is not the terrifying thing it once was. Perfection has had to give way to 'good enough' and the trials and tribulations that await in the future are real enough and have to be tackled in reality and not fantasy. Psychodynamic therapists in particular are quite familiar with this stage in therapy, when patient and therapist look at and discuss their relationship, but inherent in this approach is the story of what has happened to the brain as well as to feelings and behaviour.

Follow up

The number of follow-up sessions depends on the duration of therapy and need. Normally there would be three follow-up sessions monthly followed by a further three two months apart.

History template

Contact information

Name:
Address:
Tel no: home: mobile:
Email address:
GP: name, address and tel no:
Age:
DoB:
Referrer:
Occupation:
Previous treatment and dates:
Status:
If married: husband's age and occupation
Children: sex and ages
Parents' status: (alive/married/divorced)
Siblings: sex and ages
Who lives at home?

Ask what brought the patient to therapy now. What was the stimulus? Did she initiate the contact? Who made the referral? Was she pushed by others or pulled by her symptoms? How does she feel about coming to therapy? This will give the therapist an idea of how ready the patient is to begin therapy.

State early in the session that 'this session is about getting to know each other and you getting to understand how I work. You will get an opportunity to see whether this way of thinking makes sense to you. We will meet for two sessions and at the end of the second session we will decide if we will work together using ILET'.

Taking a history

Educational history
Work and career aspirations and whether they have been achieved

Eating disorder history
Current weight
Highest/lowest
Height
BMI
Date eating disorder started
Symptoms
Frequency
Duration
What they binge on – quantities
Any particular pattern – eve/am – rituals that go with it?
Restricting
Laxatives
Exercise
Any remissions in between
Go back over the previous three months to establish a baseline of eating disorder
history
How much (%) of the day do they spend thinking about their bodies/food

Family relationships
Enquire if the parents are alive, what is /was the quality of the parent's relationship whether they live/lived together or are separated?
Enquire into the relationship between the patient and each of the main people in
her family:

Father
Mother
Grandfather
Grandmother
Husband/Partner
Siblings
Each of their children

Information for patients

The brain, eating disorders and ILET

An eating disorder, one might think, has something to do with food or at least body shape; however, research into how the brain deals with emotions suggests the thinking about calories and shape of the body that is typical of eating disorders is a result of changes in the brain pathways that we use for dealing with our emotions.

The way that we process our emotions is through thinking about our feelings in symbolic language: for example, 'My boss makes me feel very stupid when he patronises me and I cannot stomach it and feel fit to burst with anger'. But when our feelings make us very anxious (worrying that we have upset our boss and may be fired and not be able to pay our bills), this symbolic pathway is shut down and we are no longer able to think about our feelings in symbolic language. The only brain pathway that is available to us is the body pathway and the only language available to us is concrete language: for example, the emotions about the boss's behaviour become instead about the body: 'I feel the need to eat and eat until I feel that I will burst so I must vomit out the food'. When this happens, we feel and locate the 'difficult' feelings in the body as discomfort, with the result that we try to do something about getting rid of the uncomfortable body 'feeling' by bingeing, starving, vomiting and purging. This, of course, does not solve the uncomfortable feelings about the boss and so, when the situation with the boss repeats itself, there is the same increase in anxiety and the same use of the 'concrete' body pathway. When this cycle happens, the body pathway becomes more easily triggered and the symbolic thinking pathway loses strength, which explains why eating disorders tend to get worse over time.

So, rather than treatment for an eating disorder addressing either food or body preoccupations, if we reverse the over-use of the 'body' emotional brain pathway, people with an eating disorder can return to 'normal' symbolic thinking about their emotions rather than 'feeling' their emotions in their bodies. When this happens, the need to find a 'body' solution to an emotional problem fades.

The two pathways for processing emotions

We have two different pathways for dealing with our emotions: the 'thinking' pathway and the 'action' pathway. What normally happens is that when we experience an event that provokes an emotional reaction, the brain decides whether it is something we have the luxury to take our time to think about. If the brain decides that the situation is life threatening, it shuts down the thinking pathway in favour of the action pathway. The difference between these two pathways is that the thinking pathway allows access to what is called the 'executive functions' – we can take stock, look at potential merits and problems and imagine different solutions before taking considered action. This kind of thinking is called 'symbolic' thinking. The action pathway only allows for 'concrete' thinking where the difficult and uncomfortable feelings are experienced as something horrible inside the body. The logical action, if the problem is experienced in the body, is to do something to the body to 'get rid' of the discomfort, which leads to the behaviours typical of eating disorders. If the problem feels as if there is something horrible inside the body, then the logical 'concrete' solution is to get it out by vomiting or starving or punishing the body in some way.

Why one pathway rather than the other?

When we are highly anxious, our brains can react as if there is danger in the environment and they will shut down that part of the brain that thinks in a symbolic way about the problem at hand (in metaphoric language – 'I've got a lot on my plate this week and I cannot manage to do it all'). Instead, the brain opens the pathway to action by the body and releases adrenalin, ready either to stand and fight or to run away. So, if we are faced with a dangerous situation – say a snake – we cannot afford to hang around and wonder what kind of snake we are facing; we just run. To do this, our bodies are primed for action and not thought. Our thinking in this situation of having too much to do becomes concrete ('there is too much food on my plate and I cannot put it into my stomach').

Who gets an eating disorder?

Research tells us that, on the whole, people who go on to have an eating disorder have difficulty in putting their emotions into language. They often find difficult emotional situations and relationships quite overwhelming and become very anxious.

When we feel very anxious, the brain shuts down our higher functions that, in normal circumstances, allow us to plan for the future (leave enough time to get to our destination), check reality (can we really get to two parties in one night on opposite sides of London?) and remember things we have learned, so that we do not keep repeating the same mistakes.

Quite a lot of boxes need to be ticked for an eating disorder to develop. It might be helpful to understand how our brains are built and develop so that we can understand where things can go awry and what we can do to put ourselves back on track.

How brains develop

When we are first born we are completely helpless – we do not know where our arms and legs are, and we cannot see further than about 10 inches. Our cries are undifferentiated and it is up to our mothers to try to decipher what it is we are communicating. Mothers have to guess and find out what their babies need. On the whole, mothers get it right more times than they get it wrong. However, if the mother is under stress (she might have been bereaved or abandoned or is mentally unwell following the birth or maybe just feels a failure if she does not understand her baby's cry first time or is just very anxious), she might be unable to do this. This happens quite frequently and does not, on its own, cause an eating disorder. What does happen is that the baby fits to the mother, rather than the mother to the baby. Thus, the baby's sense of herself is a bit weakened as she waits for things to occur that are not consequences of her seeking to communicate her needs. This might seem very subtle – and it is – but it can be the beginning of feeling out of control of what happens to oneself and perhaps lead to an automatic response of allowing others to think about one's needs rather than doing it for oneself. Such problems in this period of 'maternal preoccupation' can result in difficulties in bringing down one's anxiety (self-soothing) and also in 'mentalising' (thinking about one's feelings in language).

People who go on to have an eating disorder often have difficulties in other areas. There is evidence that difficulties in executive functioning (planning, reality testing, imagining different solutions to problems and memory in language) may lead to misinterpretation of other people's intentions, which, in turn, will affect the understanding of one's own and other people's minds.

Allowing others to think for us does not present too much of a problem when we are children, but once we hit adolescence (the age when the majority of eating disorders start to show themselves), if we cannot make emotional sense of our environment, we run into a lot of difficulties. During this important time of our lives we have to come to terms with our sexuality, choose what we want to study and what we want to become, negotiate friendships and develop a social life. Quite a tall order. All this happens against a background of changes in the brain that hamper these developmental tasks.

The adolescent brain

At around 2 years of age, the frontal lobes (where the executive functions live) pare down the connections that are needed in the brain during infancy. We no longer need these connections but they disappear randomly and result in the typical two-year-old tantrums. When we get to adolescence the same thing happens to the brain. We become monosyllabic teenagers who seemingly are unable to plan, assess risk or express our feelings in language.

Those young people who already have weakened executive function, once they hit adolescence, find themselves really at a loss to understand their emotional environment. They have relied on the minds of others and have tremendous difficulty in discovering their own minds. If we do not know what we feel, it is very difficult to know who we are, or what our opinions are.

It is at this point that anxiety becomes abnormally raised, shutting down the weakened emotional pathway to the (executive) planning, creative, reality testing and symbolic language part of the brain and opening up the body pathway. The more we use a pathway the stronger it becomes; conversely, the unused pathways weaken.

How to open up the symbolic pathway and reduce the use of the body pathway

When the brain processes emotions, it uses either the pathway to the executive functions or the one that goes back to the body. So, if we make ourselves think in symbolic language about what is emotionally troubling us, we cannot also feel the problem as being in our bodies. If we identify the event that is upsetting us and think about it, we will not have the urge to eat/starve/binge/vomit, etc.

Just before feeling a 'body' or 'concrete' reaction, the brain will have already assessed the environment for danger. If we look at the diagram [Figure 1.1] we see something called the amygdala, which functions as a receiving station below our conscious awareness. It picks up information from both inside and outside of the body, looking for danger in order that we survive. As explained above, during adolescence the ability to understand the emotional world diminishes. For some young people, the emotional world becomes so anxiety provoking that difficult mixed and negative emotions are labelled a danger signal. This makes the amygdala tell the insula (the gateway that decides in which direction the information will go) that there is a danger. As a consequence, the insula shuts down access to the symbolic functions, resulting in a lost opportunity to understand and learn from solving an emotional problem. This leaves the person in a weakened position and yet more prone to find emotional problems anxiety provoking. And every time we use a pathway we strengthen it, meaning that the eating disorder will worsen. When we do not know what we think, we also weaken our sense of ourselves. When we know what we think, then we get a clearer understanding of our own minds.

A new treatment – internal language enhancement therapy (ILET)

Following the logic of the neurobiology of emotional processing, if we identify and return to the trigger thought that made us go 'body' and think about the meaning it has to us – even if that is uncomfortable – we open up the symbolic pathway. At first it will be the therapist who helps you identify the trigger and starts the process of thinking about the material, but the aim of ILET treatment is to teach the method so that you can discover your own mind.

Emotional Events Questionnaire (EEQ)

This questionnaire is to be filled in by the professional, from the responses given by the patient.

Item 1
When was most recent binge episode?

Item 2
Was there a moment when you became aware that a binge was inevitable and if so when was this?

Item 3
Please describe exactly what was happening at that moment:

Where you were
Who you were with
What you were doing
How you came to be doing that activity
If there was an alternative activity you chose not to do
Who said what to whom?
   Prompt expansion of these thoughts, for example why did you say that to that person? What is your relationship to this person? How come you decided to accept this invitation and not that one? What are the characteristics of this person? This process will take quite some time until all aspects are pretty well exhausted.

Item 4
What was the last thing that went though your mind just before you knew that it was inevitable that you were going to binge?
   Write down verbatim the patient's response. The therapist should identify adjectives that relate to food or a bodily state, for example, rich, full, empty, heavy. Identify both the concrete and metaphoric meanings of these words (called dual meaning words), for example, (a) food is both rich in calories that make you fat and a situation can be 'a bit rich', that is, too difficult to take into the mind; (b) a stomach may be too full and therefore there is the wish to empty it, or one

might be full of feelings that one might wish to empty out of one's mind; (c) one might have an empty feeling in the stomach and therefore the response would be to fill up the stomach or insides, or one might feel one's life to be empty and lonely, or someone made an empty promise. One might feel too heavy or someone might be weighed down with cares.

Item 5
Following the identification of these adjectives, construct appropriate metaphors by looking at the content of the patient's description of events. If, for example, the patient seems to be carrying a heavy burden for the family and is fed up and complains that eating one biscuit turns into a binge, an appropriate metaphor might be 'that took the biscuit – that was the last straw'. If the patient wants to get rid of the weight of responsibility she might want to be as light as a feather. Or perhaps if she is too full of angry bad feelings she might be at bursting point rather than literally bursting with food.

Item 6
The focus of the next section is to explore the entirety of the patient's thoughts about the episode described just prior to the wish to binge, paying particular attention to the metaphoric meanings of the identified adjectives: for example, a feeling of emotional emptiness or an angry feeling full to bursting and very uncomfortable, rather than concentrating on the concrete food or body descriptions of needing to starve or purge to get rid of the feeling of being uncomfortably full. The feeling of being faced with unacceptable demands, turned into a concrete concern about the calorie content of food, becomes 'that's a bit rich'. The unacceptability of another's behaviour rather than the unacceptability of the contents of the stomach becomes 'I couldn't stomach that'. The inability to tolerate a situation, which leads to a binge, becomes 'I am fed up to the back teeth'.

Item 7
This next section will, as the therapy continues, form an increasingly greater percentage of the remainder of the sessions and may well form the basis of continuing therapy should it be considered necessary. (This will hold true for many patients treated for eating disorders, as only relatively straightforward cases can manage with only 20 sessions. These cases are more likely to be found among patients who are now classified as EDNOS.)

When the therapist and patient can easily identify the triggers to state change, the therapist should encourage the exploration and expansion of the trigger material. The aim is to continually expand the understanding of the trigger material in relation to the emotional relationships in the background of the patient's life.

This requires the therapist to systematically re-metaphorise the concrete terms produced by the patient in the light of the material. The therapist needs to stay very close to the detail of the utterances as, as the sessions progress, the triggers become less obvious and can be easily missed by both parties. Sometimes, if there is no obvious trigger, the material should be re-visited until the state change can be identified. Patients suffering from anorexia often require a modified version of the EEQ. As these patients spend a great deal of the time in the concrete state, it is useful to ask them to say the first word that comes to mind, for example, 'fat' (if that is what they abhor) and start expanding on their response.

At all times, the aim of the treatment is to reduce the patient's anxiety and, therefore, if the material is very distressing, there needs to be an acknowledgement that she is finding it difficult to think about this particular material. This technique is often sufficient to contain the anxiety and is again an element of maternal preoccupation where feelings are accurately identified and reflected.

Item 8
Repeat this exercise for a recent binge episode for the remaining number of sessions or until the patient begins to automatically take over the process of identifying and thinking through emotional triggers.

Baseline measures pre- and post-treatment

In order to gain a good baseline measure of pre-morbid IQ, the National Adult Reading Test (NART) is administered. This ensures that the concrete utterances of an eating disorder patient are not a function of low IQ. The NART requires the subject to try to pronounce words that do not follow the usual rules of pronunciation. Higher scores correlate with higher mental functioning. This ability does not decline much with age

The alternate uses test is a test of executive capacity requiring creative ability. The subject is presented with a series of objects for which she is asked to find as many unusual uses as possible in a limited time. 'Old' or usual uses reflect largely automatic retrieval processes from long-term memory (with executive capacity having some role), while production of 'new' uses requires much greater executive capacity.

The similarities test asks the subject to suggest a similarity between two objects or ideas with the pairs requiring increasing conceptual/symbolic understanding.

The Eating Disorder Inventory (EDI-3) is a forced-choice inventory assessing several behavioural and psychological traits common in two eating disorders, bulimia and anorexia nervosa. The EDI-3 is a self-report measure and is used as a screening device and outcome measure.

The TAS produces measures of difficulty in identifying and communicating feelings, difficulty in distinguishing between feelings and bodily sensations, impaired symbolisation, as evidenced by paucity of fantasies and other imaginative activity and a preference for focusing on external events rather than inner experiences.

The verbal fluency task (FAS) produces a measure of both frontal and temporal lobe efficiency. Subjects have to say as many words as possible from a category in a given time (usually 60 seconds). This category can be semantic, such as animals or fruits, or phonemic, such as words that begin with a certain letter. The most common performance measure is the total number of words. Other analyses, such as number of repetitions, number and length of clusters of words from the same semantic or phonetic subcategory, or number of switches to other categories, can be carried out. Impairments in the function of these areas of the brain typically produce a reduction in the number of items generated.

The Gorham Proverb Test is a test of abstract against concrete reasoning. It places the quality of responses into one of five categories. A score of unrelated is given to responses that have no apparent connection to the proverb; rejection is scored when a subject refuses to attempt an interpretation; related is scored if the response is based on the words of the proverb but ignores the proverb's abstract meaning; abstract/inadequate is scored when interpretations of the proverb are abstract but inappropriate interpretations of the proverb's abstract meaning, and a score of abstract/adequate is given to interpretations that convey the proverb's abstract meaning (see Appendix B for examples of proverbs and their level of syntactic complexity).

The EEQ is a seven-step treatment programme that teaches the patient to identify the shock that precipitates the shift to the concrete trajectory and to re-symbolise the trigger thought (see Appendix D).

Measures for randomised clinical trials of ILET versus treatment as usual, CBT and/or IPT

The specific measures are:

EDI-3
The EDI-3 assesses several behavioural and psychological traits common in two eating disorders, bulimia and anorexia nervosa. The EDI-3 is a self-report measure and is used as a screening device, outcome measure, or part of typological research. It does not purport to be a diagnostic test for anorexia nervosa or bulimia.

TAS
The TAS was chosen because it provides a measure of

1   Difficulty in identifying and communicating feelings.
2   Difficulty in distinguishing between feelings and bodily sensations.
3   Impaired symbolisation, as evidenced by paucity of fantasies and other imaginative activity.
4   Preference for focusing on external events rather than inner experiences (Taylor & Bagby, 1988).

The Ravello Profile
The Profile incorporates well-established tests of thinking processes and visuospatial function, including tests of executive function and local versus global processing.

The information gleaned from the study is then passed back to the Ravello Profile to add to the database of eating disorder patients' cognitive profiles in order to determine the significance of the abnormalities identified to date.

The neuropsychological domains have been chosen on the basis of empirical findings and theoretical rationale. The specific tests have been chosen on the basis of psychometric properties. In addition to the neuropsychological battery, there is a measure of BMI, eating disorder psychopathology, and common co-morbid disorders including depression, anxiety and obsessive–compulsive disorder.

Ravello Profile tests
1   Rey Copy and Immediate Recall
2   Verbal Fluency Test
3   Wechsler Vocabulary Test
4   Rey Delayed Recall
5   Wechsler Matrix Reasoning Test and Vocabulary Test
6   Colour Word Interference Test
7   Trail Making Test
8   Brixton Spatial Anticipation Test
9   Hayling Sentence Completion Test
10 Tower of London Test

Beck Depression Inventory II (BDI-II)
The BDI-II is a multiple-choice self-report inventory for measuring the severity of depression. It is designed for individuals aged 13 or over and is composed of items relating to symptoms of depression, for example, hopelessness and irritability, as well as cognitions such as feelings of being punished and guilt. It also enquires about physical symptoms such as fatigue, lack of interest in sex and weight loss.

Measures of concrete/abstract thinking
Similarities.
    This test asks the subject to suggest a similarity between two objects or ideas with the pairs requiring increasing conceptual/symbolic understanding.

Gorham Proverb Test
This is a test of abstract as against concrete reasoning.

Examples of proverbs in Gorham Proverb Test
Some examples of the proverbs that can be used and have been rated with differing levels of familiarity, abstractness and syntactic complexity:-

Proverb	Familiarity	Abstractness	Syntactic complexity
Blood is thicker than water	high	high	high
The squeaky wheel gets the oil	high	high	low
The early bird catches the worm	high	low	low
The hot coal burns the cold one blackens	low	high	high
The bread of strangers can be very hard	low	high	low
The rich never lack relatives	low	low	high
Wild colts make good horses	low	low	high

NVIVO 8

The NVIVO 8 tool (Gibbs, 2002) allows for an overview of the most common topics or utterances that occur in a transcript. The topic that is under study, such as frequently occurring words related to the body or food, can then be put into 'free' nodes that are then collapsed into a tree node (e.g., concrete discourse). This allows for matrix coding which permits qualitative exploration of how many times the tree node 'concrete discourse' and eating disorder symptoms, for example, bingeing and vomiting, occur in the same passage.

Alternate uses test

This is a test of executive capacity requiring creative ability. The subjects are presented with a series of objects for which they are asked to find as many unusual uses as possible in a limited time.

'Old' or usual uses reflects largely automatic retrieval processes from long-term memory (with executive capacity having some role), while production of 'new' uses requires much greater executive capacity.

Measure of galvanic skin response

Measuring galvanic skin response during a session will reflect an affective process that precedes and guides cognition (Wagar & Dixon, 2006) and may actually impair logical decision making (Shiv et al., 2005).

NART

The NART is a good baseline measure of IQ, ensuring that the concrete utterances of a patient are not a function of low IQ. The NART requires the subject to try to pronounce words that do not follow the usual rules of pronunciation. Higher scores correlate with higher mental functioning. This ability does not decline much with age.

References

Amanzio, M, Geminiani, G., Leotta, D. & Cappa, S. (2008). 'Metaphor comprehension in Alzheimer's disease: novelty matters'. *Brain & Language*, 107(1): 1–10.

Ambwani, S., Berenson, K.R., Simms, L., Li, A., Corfield, F., & Treasure, J. (2016). 'Seeing things differently: an experimental investigation of social cognition and interpersonal behavior in anorexia nervosa'. *International Journal of Eating Disorders*, 49(5): 499–506.

American Psychiatric Association (2013). *Diagnostic and Statistical Manual of Mental Disorders*, 5th edn (DSM-5). Washington, DC: American Psychiatric Association.

Andrade, V.M. (2005). 'Affect and the therapeutic action of psychoanalysis'. *International Journal of Psychoanalysis*, 86: 677–97.

Apfel, R.J. & Sifneos, P.E. (1979). 'Alexithymia: Concept and measurement'. *Psychotherapy Psychosomatics*, 32: 180–90.

Arnsten, A.F. & Li, B.-M. (2005). 'Neurobiology of executive functions: Catecholamine influences on prefrontal cortical functions'. *Biological Psychiatry*, 57: 1,377–1384. DOI: 10.1016/jbiopsych.2004.08.019.

Aron, A.R., Durston, S., Eagle, D.M., Logan, G.D., Stinear, C.M. & Stuphorn, V. (2007). 'Converging evidence for a fronto-basal-ganglia network for inhibitory control of action and cognition'. *Journal of Neuroscience*, 27(44): 11,860–64.

Aron, A.R., Herz, D.M., Brown, P., Forstmann, B.U. & Zaghloul, K. (2016). 'Fronto-subthalamic circuits for control of action and cognition'. *Journal of Neuroscience*, 36 11,489–95. DOI: 10.org/10.1523/JNEUROSCI.2348-16.

Baddeley, A. (1992). 'Is Working Memory Working? The Fifteenth Bartlett Lecture'. *Quarterly Journal of Educational Psychology*, 44A(1): 1–31.

Bagby, R.M., Joffe, R.T., Parker, J.D.A., & D. Schuller (1993). 'The validity of the DSM III R personality disorder clusters'. *Journal of Personality Disorders*, 7: 320–28.

Bailer, U., de Zwaan, M., Leisch, F., Strnad, A., Lennkh, C., El-Giamal, N., Hornik, K. & Kasper, S. (2004). 'Guided self-help versus cognitive–behavioural group therapy in the treatment of bulimia nervosa'. *International Journal of Eating Disorders*, 35(4): 522–37.

Banich, M.T. (1995a). 'Interhemispheric interaction: Mechanisms of unified processing'. In F.L. Kitterle (ed.), *Hemispheric Communication: Mechanisms and Models*, Lawrence Erlbaum: Hillsdale, NJ, pp. 271–300.

Banich, M.T. (1995b). 'Interhemispheric processing: Theoretical and empirical considerations'. In R. Davidson & K. Hugdahl (eds.), *Brain Asymmetry*. MIT Press: Cambridge, MA, pp. 427–450.

Bar-On, R. (1997). *The Bar-On Emotional Quotient Inventory (EQ-i): A Test of Emotional Intelligence*. Multi-Health Systems: Toronto, Canada.

Barth, F.D. (1988). 'The treatment of bulimia from a self psychological perspective'. *Clinical Social Work Journal*, 16: 270–81.

Bateman, A. & Fonagy, P. (2004). *Psychotherapy for Borderline Personality Disorder: Mentalization-based Treatment*. Oxford University Press: Oxford.

Bateman, A. & Fonagy, P. (2010). 'Mentalization based treatment for borderline personality disorder'. *World Psychiatry*, 9(1): 11–15.

Bates, E. (1979). 'In the beginning, before the word: Review of S. Harnad, H. Steklis, & T. Lancaster, "Origins of language and speech".' *Contemporary Psychology*, 24(3): 169–17.

Bauermann, T.M., Parker, J.D.A. & Smith, C. (1999a). 'Alexithymia, sleep and dreams: Some preliminary findings'. *Sleep*, 22(Suppl. 1): 253–4.

Bauermann, T.M., Parker, J.D.A. & Smith, C. (1999b). 'Alexithymia and sleep: A preliminary study on dream reports and sleep architecture'. *Sleep Research Online*, 1: 270.

Beckendam, C.C. (1997). 'Dimensions of emotional intelligence: attachment, affect regulation, alexithymia and empathy'. Doctoral dissertation, The Fielding Institute, Santa Barbara, CA.

Bion, W.R. (1962). *Learning from Experience*. Basic Books: New York.

Blakemore, S.J. & Mills, K.L. (2014). 'Is adolescence a sensitive period for sociocultural processing?' *Annual Review of Psychology*, 65: 187–207.

Blanz, J.B., Detzner, U., Lay, B., Rose, F. & Schmidt, M.H. (1997). 'The intellectual functioning of adolescents with anorexia nervosa and bulimia nervosa'. *European Journal of Child & Adolescent Psychiatry*, 6: 129–35.

Blass, R.B. & Carmeli, Z. (2007). 'The case against neuropsychoanalysis. On fallacies underlying psychoanalysis' latest scientific trend and its negative impact on psychoanalytic discourse'. *International Journal of Psychoanalysis*, 88(1): 19–40.

Blowers, L.C., Loxton, N.J., Grady-Flesser, M., Occhipinti, S. & Dawe, S. (2003). 'The relationship between sociocultural pressure to be thin and body dissatisfaction in preadolescent girls'. *Eating Disorders*, 4(3): 229–44.

Borod, J.C., Pick, L.H., Hall, S., Sliwinski, M., Madigan, N., Obler, L.K., Welkowitz, J., Canino, E., Erhan, H.M., Goral, M., Morrison, C. & Tabert, M. (2000). 'Relationships among facial, prosodic, and lexical channels of emotional perceptual processing'. *Cognition and Emotion*, 14: 193–211.

Bourke, M.P., Taylor, G.J., & Crisp, A.H. (1985). 'Symbolic functioning in anorexia nervosa'. *Journal of Psychiatric Research*, 19: 237–78.

Bourke, M.P., Taylor, G.J., Parker, J.D.A., & Bagby, R.M. (1992). 'Alexithymia in women with anorexia nervosa. a preliminary investigation'. *British Journal of Psychiatry*, 161: 240–3.

Bourne, V.J. & Todd, B.K. (2004). 'When left means right: an explanation of the left cradling bias in terms of right hemisphere specializations'. *Developmental Science*, 7(1): 19–24.

Bowlby, J. (1999). *Attachment. Attachment and Loss* Vol. 1 (2nd edn). Basic Books: New York.

Brazelton, T.B. (1982). *On Becoming a Family: Growth of Attachment*. Delacourte Press: New York.

Britton, R. (1998). *Belief and Imagination*. Routledge & Kegan Paul: London.

Bruch, H. (1973). *Eating Disorders: Obesity, Anorexia Nervosa and the Person Within*. Basic Books: New York.

Bruch, H. (1982). 'Anorexia nervosa: Therapy and theory'. *American Journal of Psychiatry*, 139(1): 531–8.

Bryan, K.L., & Hale, J.B. (2001). 'Differential effects of left and right cerebral vascular accidents on language competency'. *Journal of the International Neuropsychological Society*, 7(6): 655–64.

Buhl, C. (2002). 'Eating disorders as manifestations of developmental disorders: Language and the capacity for abstract thinking in psychotherapy of eating disorders'. *European Eating Disorders Review*, 10: 138–45.

Bulik, C.M., Sullivan, P.F., Carter, F.A., McIntosh, V.V. & Joyce, P.R. (1998). 'The role of exposure with response prevention in the cognitive–behavioural therapy for bulimia nervosa'. *Psychological Medicine*, 28(3): 611–23.

Campbell, D. & Enckell, H. (2005). 'Metaphor and the violent act'. *International Journal of Psychoanalysis*, 86: 801–823.

Cardi, V., Corfield, F., Leppanen, J., Rhind, C., Deriziotis, S., Hadjimichalis, A. et al. (2015). 'Emotional processing, recognition, empathy and evoked facial expression in eating disorders: An experimental study to map deficits in social cognition'. *PLoS One*. DOI: 10.1371/journal.pone.,0133827.

Chessick, R. (1984/85). 'Clinical notes toward the understanding and intensive psychotherapy of adult eating disorders'. *Annual of Psychoanalysis*, 12/13: 301–22.

Chiron, C., Jambaque, J., Nabbout, R., Lounes, R., Syrota, A. & Oulac, O. (1997). 'The right brain hemisphere is dominant in human infants'. *Brain*, 120: 1,057–65.

Christakou, A., Brammer, M., Giampietro, V. & Rubia, K. (2009). 'Right ventromedial and dorsolateral prefrontal cortices mediate adaptive decisions under ambiguity by integrating choice utility and outcome evaluation'. *Journal of Neuroscience*, 29(35): 11,020–28.

Christman, S.D. (1994), 'The many sides of the two sides of the brain'. *Brain & Cognition*, 26: 91–8.

Concise Oxford English Dictionary (2011). Main edition 12. Oxford University Press.

Connan, F., Campbell, I.C., Katzman, M., Lightman, S.L. & Treasure, J. (2003). 'A neurodevelopmental model for anorexia nervosa'. *Physiology & Behaviour*, 79: 13–24.

Cooper, P.J. & Steere, J.A. (1995). 'Comparison of two psychological treatments for bulimia nervosa: Implications for models of maintenance'. *Behaviour Research & Therapy*, 33: 875–85.

Corcos, M., Guilbaud, O., Speranza, M., Paterniti, S., Loas, G., Stephan, P. & Jeammet, P. (2000). 'Alexithymia and depression in eating disorders'. *Psychiatry Research*, 93: 263–6.

Cozolino, L. (2002). *The Neuroscience of Psychotherapy: Building and Rebuilding the Human Brain*. Norton: New York.

Craig, A.D. (1996). 'An ascending general homeostatic afferent pathway originating in lamina I'. *Progress in Brain Research*, 107: 225–42.

Craig, A.D. (2004). 'Human feelings: why are some more aware than others?' *Trends in Cognitive Science*, 8, 239–41.

Craig, A.D. (2005). 'Forebrain emotional asymmetry: a neuroanatomical basis?' *Trends in Cognitive Science*, 9(12): 566–71.

Craig, A.D. (2009). 'How do you feel – now? The anterior insula and human awareness'. *Nature*, 10(1): 59–70.

Craig, A.D. (2011). 'Significance of the insula for the evolution of human awareness of feelings from the body'. *Annals of the New York Academy of Sciences*, 1225: 72–82.

DaCosta, M. & Halmi, K.A. (1992). 'Classification of anorexia nervosa: Question of subtypes'. *International Journal of Eating Disorders*, 11: 305–14.

Damasio, A.R. (1994). *Descartes' Error*. Grosset Putnam: New York.

Davies, H. & Tchanturia, K. (2005). 'Cognitive remediation therapy as an intervention for acute anorexia nervosa: a case report'. *European Eating Disorders Review*. DOI: 10.1002/erv.655.

Davies, M., Stankov, L. & Roberts, R.D. (1998). 'Emotional intelligence: in search of an elusive construct'. *Journal of Personality & Social Psycholology*, 75: 989–1,015.

Decety, J. & Chaminade, T. (2003). 'When the self represents the other: A new cognitive neuroscience view on psychological identification'. *Consciousness and Cognition*, 12: 577–96.

De Groot, J. & Rodin G. (1998). 'Coming alive: the psychotherapeutic treatment of patients with eating disorders'. *Canadian Journal of Psychiatry*, 43: 359–66.

Devinsky, O. (2000). 'Right cerebral hemisphere dominance for a sense of corporeal and emotional self'. *Epilepsy & Behavior*, 1: 60–73.

Dolan, R.J., Mitchell, J. & Wakeling, A. (1988). 'Structural brain changes in patients with anorexia nervosa'. *Psychological Medicine*, 18: 349–53.

Dunn, J., Brown, J. & Beardsall, L. (1991). 'Family talk about feeling states and children's later understanding of others' emotions'. *Developmental Psychology*, 27: 448–55.

Emde, R.D. (1988). 'Development terminable and interminable. I. Innate and motivational factors from infancy'. *International Journal of Psychoanalysis*, 69: 23–42.

Enckell, H. (2002). 'Metaphor and the psychodynamic functions of the mind'. Doctoral dissertation. Department of Psychiatry, University of Kuopio, Finland.

Eviatar, Z. & Just, M.A. (1999). 'Brain correlates of discourse processing: An fMRI investigation of irony and conventional metaphor comprehension'. *Journal of Neuro-psychiatry & Clinical Neuroscience*, 11: 470–4.

Faigel, H.C. (1975). 'Learning disabilities in adolescence'. *The Practitioner*, 214: 181–91.

Fairburn, C.G. (1981). 'A cognitive behavioural approach to the management of bulimia'. *Psychological Medicine*, 11: 707–11.

Fairburn, C.G. & Cooper, Z. (2011). 'Eating disorders, DSM-5 and clinical reality'. *British Journal of Psychiatry*, 198(1) 8–10.

Fairburn, C.G., Bailey-Straebler, S., Basden, S., Doll, H. A., Jones, R., Murphy, R., O'Connor, M.E. & Cooper, Z. (2015).'A transdiagnostic comparison of enhanced cognitive behaviour therapy (CBT-E) and interpersonal psychotherapy in the treatment of eating disorders'. *Behaviour Research and Therapy*, 70: 64–71. DOI: 10.1016/j.brat.2015.04.010.

Fairburn, C.G., Cooper, Z., Bohn, K., O'Connor, M., Doll, H. & Palmer, R. (2007). 'The severity and status of eating disorder NOS: Implications for DSM-V'. *Behavior Research & Therapy*, 45(8): 1705–1715.

Fairburn, C.G., Cooper, Z., Doll, H.A., O'Connor, M.E., Palmer, R.L. & Dalle Grave, R. (2013). 'Enhanced cognitive behaviour therapy for adults with anorexia nervosa: a UK–Italy study'. *Behaviour Research and Therapy*, 51: R2–R8.

Fairburn, C. G., Cowen, P. J. & Harrison, P (1999). 'Twin studies and the etiology of eating disorders'. *International Journal of Eating Disorders*, 26(4): 349–358.

Fairburn, C.G., Hay, P.J. & Welch, S.L. (1993). 'Binge eating and bulimia nervosa: Distribution and determinants'. In C.G. Fairburn & G.T. Wilson (eds.), *Binge Eating: Nature, Assessment, and Treatment*. Guilford Press: New York, pp. 123–43.

Fairburn, C.G., Jones, R., Peveler, R., Carr, S.J., Solomon, R.A., O'Conner, M., Burton, J. & Hope, R.A. (1991). 'Three psychological treatments for bulimia nervosa: A comparative trial'. *Archives of General Psychiatry*, 48: 463–69.

Fairburn, C.G., Jones, R., Peveler, R., Hope, T. & O'Connor, M. (1993). 'Predictors of 12 month outcome in bulimia nervosa and the influence of attitudes to shape and weight'. *Journal of Consulting & Clinical Psychology*, 61: 696–98.

Fairburn, C.G., Welch, S.L., Doll, H., Davies, B. & O'Connor, M. (1997). 'Risk factors for bulimia nervosa. A community-based case control study'. *Archives of General Psychiatry*, 54(6): 509–517.

Ferraro, F. R., Wonderlich, S. & Jocic, Z. (1997). 'Performance variability as a new theoretical mechanism regarding eating disorders and cognitive processing'. *Journal of Clinical Psychology*, 53: 117–21.

Fink, G.R., Markowitsch, H.J., Reinkemeier, M., Bruckbauer, T., Kessler, J. & Heiss, W.-D. (1996). 'Cerebral representation of one's own past: Neural networks involved in autobiographical memory'. *Journal of Neuroscience*, 16: 4,275–82.2.

Fonagy, P. & Bateman, A. (2006). 'Mechanisms of change in mentalisation based therapy with BPD'. *Journal of Clinical Psychology*, 62: 411–30.

Fonagy, P. & Target, M. (1996). 'Playing with reality: I. Theory of mind and the normal development of psychic reality'. *International Journal of Psychoanalysis*, 77: 217–33.

Fonagy, P. & Target, M. (1997), 'Attachment and reflective function: their role in self-organization', *Developmental Psychopathology*, 9: 679–700.

Fonagy, P., Gergely, G., Jurist, E.L. & Target, M. (2002). *Affect Regulation, Mentalization and the Development of the Self.* Other Press: New York.

Fossati, P. (2012). 'Neural correlates of emotion processing: from emotional to social brain'. *European Neuropsychopharmacology*, 22: S487–91.

Fotopoulou, A. & Tsakiris, M. (2017). 'Mentalizing homeostasis: the social origins of interoceptive inference', *Neuropsychoanalysis*. DOI: 10.1080/15294145.2017.1294031, published online 28 Feb.

Fox, M.A. & Mahoney, W.J. (1998). *Children With School Problems: A Physician's Manual.* Canadian Pediatrics Society: Ottawa.

Frampton, I. & Rose, M. (2013). 'Eating disorders and the brain'. In B. Lask & R. Bryant-Waugh (eds.), *Eating Disorders in Childhood and Adolescence.* Wiley: London, pp. 125–47.

Frank, G.K. (2015). 'Recent advances in neuroimaging to model eating disorder neurobiology'. *Current Psychiatry Reports*, 17(4): 1–9. DOI: 10.1007/s11920–015–0559-z.

Freedman, N. (1985). 'The concept of transformation in psychoanalysis'. *Psychoanalytic Psychology*, 2: 317–39.

Freud, S. (1915). 'The unconscious'. *The Standard Edition of the Complete Psychological Works of Sigmund Freud, Volume 14.* Hogarth Press: London.

Freud, S. (1920). *Beyond the Pleasure Principle. The Standard Edition of the Complete Psychological Works of Sigmund Freud, Volume 18.* Hogarth Press: London.

Freud, S. (1926). *Inhibitions, Symptoms and Anxiety. The Standard Edition of the Complete Psychological Works of Sigmund Freud, Volume 20.* Hogarth Press, London.

Freud, S. (1927). *The Ego and the Id. The Standard Edition of the Complete Psychological Works of Sigmund Freud, Volume 12.* Hogarth Press, London.

Freud, S. (1939). *Moses and Monotheism. The Standard Edition of the Complete Psychological Works of Sigmund Freud, Volume 238.* Hogarth Press: London.

Gardner, H. (1983). *Frames of Mind: The Theory of Multiple Intelligences. Basic Books*: New York.

Garrett, A.S., Lock, J., Datta, N., Beenhaker, J., Kesler, S.R. & Reiss, A.L. (2014). 'Predicting clinical outcome using brain activation associated with set-shifting and central coherence skills in anorexia nervosa'. *Journal of Psychiatric Research*, 57: 26–33.

Gazzaniga, M. S. (1992). *Nature's Mind: The Biological Roots of Thinking, Emotions, Sexuality, Language, and Intelligence*. Basic Books: New York.

Gazzaniga, M.S. (1995). 'Consciousness and the cerebral hemispheres,'. In M.S. Gazzaniga (ed.), *The Cognitive Neurosciences*. MIT Press, Cambridge MA, pp. 1,391–400.

Geist, R.A. (1985). *Self Psychological Reflections on the Origins of Eating Disorders*. Guilford Press: New York.

Gergely, G. & Watson, J.S. (1996). 'The social biofeedback theory of parental affect-mirroring: The development of emotional self-awareness and self-control in infancy'. *International Journal of Psychoanalysis*, 77: 1,191–212.

Gillberg, I. C., Gillberg, C., Rastam, M. & Johansson, M. (1996). 'The cognitive profile of anorexia nervosa: A comparative study including a community-based sample'. *Comprehensive Psychiatry*, 37: 23–30.

Giora, R. (2007). 'Is metaphor special?' *Brain and Language*, 100(2): 111–14.

Goldberg, E. (2001). *The Executive Brain: Frontal Lobes and the Civilized Mind*. Oxford University Press: New York.

Goldman-Rakic, P.S. (1996). 'Regional and cellular fractionation of working memory'. *Proceedings of the National Academy of Sciences*, 93: 13,473–13,480.

Goodsitt, A. (1997). 'Eating disorders: A self-psychological perspective'. In D.M. Garner & P.E. Garfinkel (eds), *Handbook of Treatment for Eating Disorders*. Guilford Press: New York, pp. 205–228.

Gorham, D.R. (1956). 'A proverbs test for clinical and experimental use'. *Psychological Report Monograph*, 2: 1–2.

Grunwald, M., Ettrich, C., Assmann, B., Dahne, A., Krause, W., Busse, F. & Gertz, H.J. (2001). 'Deficits in haptic perception and right parietal theta power changes in patients with anorexia nervosa before and after weight gain'. *International Journal of Eating Disorders*, 29: 417–28.

Hamsher, K. de S., Halmi, K.A. & Benton, A.L. (1981). 'Prediction of outcome in anorexia nervosa from neuropsychological status'. *Psychiatry Research*, 4: 79–88.

Happaney, K., Zelazo, P.D. & Stuss, D.T. (2004). 'Development of orbitofrontal function: Current themes and future directions'. *Brain and Cognition*, 55: 1–10.

Harlow, H.F., Harlow, M.K., Dodsworth, R.O. & Arling, G.L. (1966). 'Maternal behavior of rhesus monkeys deprived of mothering and peer associations in infancy'. *Proceedings of the American Philosophical Society*, 110: 58–66.

Heatherton, T.F. & Baumeister, R.F. (1991). 'Binge eating as escape from self-awareness'. *Psychology Bulletin*, 110: 86–108.

Hebb, D.O. (1949). *The Organization of Behavior*. New York: Wiley.

Heilbrun, A.B. & Worobow, A.L. (1991). 'Attention and disordered eating behaviour: I. Disattention to satiety cues as a risk factor in the development of bulimia'. *Journal of Clinical Psychology*, 47: 3–9.

Heilman, K.M. (1997). 'The neurobiology of emotional experience'. *Journal of Neuropsychiatry & Clinical Neuroscience*, 9: 439–448.

Herholz, K. (1996). 'Neuroimaging in anorexia nervosa'. *Psychiatry Research*, 62: 105–110.

Hoppe, K.D. (1977). 'Split brains and psychoanalysis'. *Psychoanalytic Quarterly*, 46: 220–244.

Hoppe, K.D. & Bogen, J.E. (1977). 'Alexithymia in twelve commissurotomized patients'. *Psychotherapy & Psychosomatics*, 28: 148–55.

Hsu, L.K. (1995). 'Outcome of bulimia nervosa'. In K.D. Brownell & C.G. Fairburn (eds.), *Eating Disorders and Obesity*. Guildford Press: New York, pp. 238–246.

Hugdahl, K. (2002). 'Functional brain asymmetry and attentional modulation in young and stabilised schizophrenic patients: a dichotic listening study'. *Psychiatry Research*, 109(3): 281–7.

Huntington, D.D. & Bender, W.N. (1993). 'Adolescents with learning disabilities at risk: Emotional well-being, depression and suicide'. *Journal of Learning Disability*, 26: 159–66.

Jansen, A., Elgersma, H., Nederkoorn, C. & Smeets, T. (2002). 'What makes treatment of bulimia nervosa successful?' Paper presented at the European Association for Cognitive and Behaviour Therapies Congress, 18–21 September, Maastricht.

Johnson, C.L., Sansone, R. & Chewning, M. (1992). 'Good reasons why young women would develop anorexia nervosa: The adaptive context'. *Pediatric Annals*, 21: 732–7.

Jones, E. (1916). 'The theory of symbolism'. *British Journal of Psychology*. DOI: 10.1111/j.2044-8295.1918.tb00221.x.

Juarascio A.S., Manasse, S.M., Espel, H.M., Kerrigan, S.G., Forman, E.M. (2015). 'Could training executive function improve treatment outcomes for eating disorders?' *Appetite*, 90: 187–93.

Kanzer, M. (1966). 'The motor sphere of the transference'. *Psychoanalytic Quarterly*, 35: 522–39.

Kitayama, O. (1987). 'Metaphorization – making terms'. *International Journal of Psychoanalysis*, 68: 499–509.

Katzman, D.K., Christensen, B., Young, A.R. & Zipursky, R.B. (2001). 'Starving the brain: Structural abnormalities and cognitive impairment in adolescents with anorexia nervosa'. *Seminars in Clinical Neuropsychiatry*, 6: 146–52.

Katzman, D.K., Zipursky, R.B., Lambe, E.K. & Mikulis, D.J. (1997). 'A longitudinal magnetic resonance imaging study of brain changes in adolescents with anorexia nervosa'. *Archives of Pediatric & Adolescent Medicine*, 151: 793–7.

Keel, P.K. & Mitchell, J.E. (1997). 'Outcome in bulimia nervosa'. *American Journal of Psychiatry*, 154: 313–21.

Kensinger, E.A. & Schacter, D.L. (2006). 'Processing emotional pictures and words: effects of valence and arousal'. *Cognitive, Affective, & Behavioral Neuroscience*, 6: 110–26.

Kihlstrom, J.F. (1987). 'The cognitive unconscious'. *Science*, 237: 1,445–52.

Killen, J.D., Taylor, C.B., Hayward, C., Wilson, D., Haydel, K. & Hammer, L. (1994). 'Pursuit of thinness and onset of eating disorder symptoms in a community sample of adolescent girls: A three-year prospective analysis'. *International Journal of Eating Disorders*, 16: 227–38.

Killingmo, B. (1989). 'Conflict and deficit: Implications for technique'o *International Journal of Psychoanalysis*, 70: 196–206.

Kingston, K., Szmukler, G., Andrewes, D., Tress, B. & Desmond, P. (1996). 'Neuropsychological and structural brain changes in anorexia nervosa before and after refeeding'. *Psychological Medicine*, 26: 15–28.

Kircher, T.T., Leube, D.T., Erb, M., Grodd, W. & Rapp, A.M. (2007). 'Neural correlates of metaphor processing in schizophrenia'. *NeuroImage*, 34: 281–9.

Klein, M. (1930). 'On the importance of symbol formation in the development of the ego.' *Contributions to Psycho-Analysis*, 1: 921–45.

Kosslyn, S. M. & Koenig, O. (1992). *Wet Mind: The New Cognitive Neuroscience*. Free Press: New York.

Krause, K.W. (2008). 'Mapping metaphor: this is your brain on figurative language'. *The Humanist*, July/Aug.

Krieg, J.-C., Lauer, C., Leinsinger, G., Pahl, J., Schreiber, W. & Pirke, K.-M. (1989). 'Brain morphology and regional cerebral blood flow in anorexia nervosa'. *Biological Psychiatry*, 25(1): 41–8.

Krystal, H. (1979). 'Alexithymia and psychotherapy'. *American Journal of Psychotherapy*, 33: 17–31.

Krystal, H. (1988). *Integration and Self-Healing: Affect, Trauma, and Alexithymia*. Analytic Press: Hillsdale, NJ.

Lacey, J.H. (1983). 'Bulimia nervosa, binge eating, and psychogenic vomiting: a controlled treatment study and long term outcome'. *British Medical Journal*, 286(6378): 1,609–13.

Lake, A.J., Staiger, P.K. & Glowinski, H. (2000). 'Effect of Western culture on womenre attitudes to eating and perceptions of body shape'. *International Journal of Eating Disorders*, 27(1): 83–9.

Lakoff, G. & Johnson, M. (1980). *Metaphors We Live By*. University of Chicago Press.

Lakoff, G. & Johnson, M. (1999). *Philosophy in the Flesh. The Embodied Mind and its Challenge to Western Thought*. Basic Books: New York.

Lakoff, G. & Turner, M. (1989). *More than Cool Reason: A Field Guide to Poetic Metaphor*. University of Chicago Press.

Lane, R.D., Reiman, E.M., Axelrod, B., Lang-Sheng, Y., Holmes, A. & Schwartz, G.E. (1998). 'Neural correlates of levels of emotional awareness: Evidence of an interaction between emotion and attention in the anterior cingulate cortex'. *Journal of Cognitive Neuroscience*, 10: 525–35.

Lane, R., Sechrest, L., Reidel, R., Weldon, V., Kaszniak, A. & Schwartz, G. (1996). 'Impaired verbal and nonverbal emotion recognition in alexithymia'. *Psychosomatic Medicine*, 58: 203–10.

Lankenau, H., Swigar, E., Bhimani, S., Luchins, D. & Quinlan, D.M. (1985). 'Cranial CT scans in eating disorder patients and controls'. *Comprehensive Psychiatry*, 26: 136–47.

Laplanche, J. (1981). *Problematiques III: La Sublimation*. Presses Universitaires de France: Paris.

Laplanche, J. & Pontalis, J.B. (1973). *The Language of Psycho-Analysis*. Hogarth: London.

Lask, B., Waugh, R. & Gordon, I. (1997). 'Childhood-onset anorexia nervosa is a serious illness'. *Annals of the New York Academy of Sciences*, 817: 120–26.

Lauer, C. J., Gorzewski, B., Gerlinghoff, M., Backmund, H. & Zihl, J. (1999). 'Neuropsychological assessments before and after treatment in patients with anorexia nervosa and bulimia nervosa'. *Journal of Psychiatric Research*, 33(2): 129–38.

LeDoux, J.E. (1986). 'Sensory systems and emotions: A model of affective processing'. *Integral Psychiatry*, 4 237–48.

LeDoux, J.E. (1989). 'Cognitive–emotional interactions in the brain'. *Cognition & Emotion*, 3: 267–89.

LeDoux, J.E. (1996). *The Emotional Brain*. Simon and Schuster: New York.

LeDoux, J.E. (2003). 'The emotional brain, fear, and the amygdala'. *Cellular and Molecular Neurobiology*, 23(4/5): 727–38.

Lehoux, P.M., Steiger, H. & Jabalpurlawa, S. (2000). 'State/trait distinctions in bulimic syndromes'. *International Journal of Eating Disorders*, 27: 36–42.

Lena, S.M. (1987). 'Early diagnosis and management of anorexia nervosa'. *Paediatric Medicine*, 2: 59–65.

Lena, S.M., Fiocco, A.J. & Leyenaar, J.K. (2004). 'The role of cognitive deficits in the development of eating disorders'. *Neuropsychology Review*, 14(2): 99–113.

Levin, R. (1990). 'Psychoanalytic theories on the function of dreaming: A review of the empirical dream research'. In J. Masling (ed.), *Empirical Studies of Psychoanalytic Theories, Vol. 3*. Analytic Press: Hillsdale, NJ, pp. 1–53.

Levitan, H. (1989). 'Failure of the defensive functions of the ego in psychosomatic patients', In S. Cheren (ed.), *Psychosomatic Medicine: Theory, Physiology, and Practice, Vol. 1*, International Universities Press, Madison, CT, pp. 135–57.

Lidz, R.W. & Lidz, T. (1952). 'Family studies and a theory of schizophrenia'. In *The American Handbook of Psychiatry, Vol. 1*. Basic Books: New York, pp. 322–324.

Linehan, M.M. (1993). *Cognitive Behavioural Treatment of Borderline Personality Disorder*. Guilford Press: New York.

Lissner, L., Odell, P.M., D'Agostino, R.B., Stokes, J. III, Krieger, B.E., Belanger, A.J. & Brownell, K. (1991). 'Variability of body weight and health outcomes in the Framington population'. *New England Journal of Medicine*, 324(1): 839–844.

Little, S.S. (1993). 'Nonverbal learning disabilities and socioemotional functioning: A review of recent literature'. *Journal of Learning Disability*, 26: 653–665.

Lledo, E.P. & Waller, G. (2000). 'Bulimic psychopathology and impulsive behaviors among nonclinical women'. *International Journal of Eating Disorders*, 29: 71–5.

Macquet, P., Péters, J.-M., Aerts, J., Delfiore, G., Degueldre, C., Luxen, A. & Franck, G. (1996). 'Functional neuroanatomy of human rapid-eye-movement sleep and dreaming'. *Nature*, 383: 163–6.

Mahler, M., Pine F. & Bergman A. (1975). *The Psychological Birth of the Human Infant: Symbiosis and Individuation*. Basic Books: New York.

Mancia, M. (ed.) (2006). *Psychoanalysis and Neuroscience*. Springer Verlag: New York.

Mansour, S., Rozenblat, V., Fuller-Tyszkiewicz, M., Paganini, C., Treasure, J., Krug, I. (2016). 'Emotions mediate the relationship between autistic traits and disordered eating: A new autistic–emotional model for eating pathology'. *Psychiatry Research*, 245: 119–26.

Martinez, G., Cook-Darzens, S., Chaste, P., Mouren, M.C. & Doyen, C. (2014). 'Anorexia nervosa in the light of neurocognitive functioning: New theoretical and therapeutic perspectives'. *L'Encephale*, 40(2): 160–7.

Mayer, J.D. & Salovey, P. (1997). 'What is emotional intelligence?' In P. Salovey & D. Sluyter (eds.), *Emotional Development and Emotional Intelligence: Educational Implications*. Basic Books: New York, pp. 3–31.

McAdams, C.J. & Smith, W. (2015). 'Neural correlates of eating disorders: translational potential'. *Neuroscience and Neuroeconomics*. 4: 35–49.

McCann, J.B., Stein, A., Fairburn, C. & Dunger, D.B. (1994). 'Eating habits and attitudes of mothers of children with non-organic failure to thrive'. *Archives of Disease in Childhood*, 70: 234–6.

McDougall, J. (1978). *The Psychosoma and the Psychoanalytic Process. Plea for a Measure of Abnormality*. International Universities Press: New York.

McDougall, J. (1989). *Theaters of the Body: A Psychoanalytic Approach to Psychosomatic Illness*. Norton: New York.

Mendlewicz, L., Nef, F. & Simon, Y. (2001). 'Selective handling of information in patients suffering from restrictive anorexia in an emotional Stroop test and a word recognition test'. *Neuropsychobiology*, 44(2): 59–64.

Meyer, M., Zysset, S., Yves von Cramon, D. & Alter, K. (2005). 'Distinct fMRI responses to laughter, speech, and sounds along the human peri-sylvian cortex'. *Cognitive Brain Research*, 24: 291–306.

Micali, N., Crous-Bou, M., Treasure, J., & Lawson, E.A. (2016). 'Association between oxytocin receptor genotype, maternal care, and eating disorder behaviors in a community sample of women'. *European Eating Disorders Review*. DOI: 10.1002/erv.2486.

Miller, B.L., Seeley, W.W., Mychack, P., Rosen, H.J., Mena, I. & Boone, K. (2001). 'Neuroanatomy of the self. Evidence from patients with frontotemporal dementia'. *Neurology*, 57, 817–21.

Miller, N.E. (1969). 'Learning and visceral and glandular responses'. *Science*, 163: 434–445.

Miller, P. (1991). 'Understanding the eating-disordered patient: Engaging the concrete'. *Bulletin of the Menninger Clinic*, 55: 85–95.

Moncrieff-Boyd, J., Allen, K., Byrne, S. & Nunn, K. (2014). 'The Self-Disgust Scale Revised Version: validation and relationships with eating disorder symptomatology'. *Journal of Eating Disorders*, 2(Suppl 1). DOI: 10.1186/2050-2974-2-S1-O48.

Montague, P.R. & Lohrenz, T. (2007). 'To detect and correct: norm violations and their enforcement'. *Neuron*, 56: 14–18.

Murray, L. & Cooper, P.J. (1997). 'Effects of postnatal depression on infant development'. *Archives of Disease in Childhood*, 77: 99–101.

North, C., Gowers, S. & Byram, V. (1997). 'Family functioning and life events in the outcome of anorexia nervosa'. *British Journal of Psychiatry*, 171: 545–9.

Nunn, K., Frampton, I., Gordon, I. & Lask, B. (2008). 'The fault is not in her parents but in her insula—a neurobiological hypothesis of anorexia nervosa'. *European Eating Disorders Review*, 16,: 355–60.

Nunn, K., Frampton, I. & Lask, B. (2012). 'Anorexia nervosa—a noradrenergic dysregulation hypothesis'. *Medical Hypotheses*. 78: 580–4.

Nussbaum, M.P. (1992). 'Nutritional concerns'. In L. Bralow (ed.), *Textbook of Adolescent Medicine*. W. B. Saunders: Philadelphia, pp. 536–41.

Ornstein, R. (1997). *The Right Mind: Making Sense of the Hemispheres*. Harcourt Brace: New York.

Oskis, A., Clow, A., Thorn, L., Loveday, C. & Hucklebridge, F. (2012). 'Diurnal patterns of salivary cortisol and DHEA in adolescent anorexia nervosa'. *Strss*, 15(6): 601–7.

Padesky, C.A. (1994). 'Schema change processes in cognitive therapy'. *Clinical Psychology and Psychotherapy*, 1(5): 267–78.

Palazidou, E., Robinson, P. & Lishman, W.A. (1990). 'Neuroradiological and neuropsychological assessment in anorexia nervosa'. *Psychological Medicine*, 20: 521–7.

Pally, R. (1998). 'Bilaterality: Hemispheric specialisation and integration'. *International Journal of Psychoanalysis*, 79: 565–78.

Panksepp, J. (1998). *Affective Neuroscience: The Foundations of Human and Animal Emotions*, Oxford University Press: Oxford.

Parker, J.D.A., Taylor, G.J. & Bagby, R.M. (1993). 'Alexithymia and the recognition of facial expressions of emotion'. *Psychotherapy & Psychosomatics*, 59: 197–202.

Parker, J.D.A., Taylor, G.J., & Bagby, R.M. (1998). 'Alexithymia: Relationship with ego defense and coping styles'. *Comprehensive Psychiatry*, 39: 91–8.

Parker, J.D.A., Keightley, M.L., Smith, C.T. & Taylor, G.J. (1999). 'Interhemispheric transfer deficit in alexithymia: An experimental study'. *Psychosomatic Medicine*, 61: 464–8.

Pearlman, B. (1999). 'Dislocation within the early mother–child relationship and development of abstract emotional language'. Paper presented at European Council on Eating Disorders, Stockholm.

Perrin, F., Maquet, P., Peigneux, P., Ruby, P., Degueldre, C., Balteau, E., Del Fiore, G., Moonen, G., Luxen, A. & Laureys, S. (2005). 'Neural mechanisms involved in the detection of our first name: a combined ERPs and PET study'. *Neuropsychologia*, 43: 12–19.

Rapp, A.M., Leube, D.T., Erb, M., Grodd, W. & Kircher, T.T. (2004). 'Neural correlates of metaphor processing'. *Cognitive Brain Research*, 20: 395–402.

Rapport, M.D. (1993). 'Attention deficit hyperactivity disorder'. In T.H. Ollendick & M. Hersen (eds.), *Handbook of Child and Adolescent Assessment*. Allyn and Bacon: Toronto.

Rieger, E., Schotte, D.E., Touyz, S.W., Beaumont, P.J., Griffiths, R. & Russel, J. (1998). 'Attentional biases in eating disorders: A visual probe detection procedure'. *International Journal of Eating Disorders*, 23: 199–205.

Rizzuto, A.-M. (2001). 'Metaphors of bodily mind'. *Journal of the American Psychoanalytic Association*, 49, 535–68.

Rolls, E. T. (1995). 'A theory of emotion and consciousness, and its application to understanding the neural basis of emotion'. In M.S. Gazzaniga (ed.), *The Cognitive Neurosciences*. MIT Press: Cambridge, MA, pp. 1,091–106.

Rose, J. (2000). 'Symbols and their function in managing the anxiety of change: An intersubjective approach'. *International Journal of Psychoanalysis*, 81: 453–70.

Rose, M., Davis, J., Frampton, I. & Lask, B. (2011). 'The Ravello Profile: development of a global standard neuropsychological assessment for young people with anorexia nervosa' *Clinical Child Psychology and Psychiatry*, 16(2): 195–202.

Rouf, K., Fennell, M., Westbrook, D., Cooper, M. & Bennett-Levy, J. (2004). 'Devising effective behavioural experiments'. In J. Bennett-Levy, G. Butler, M. Fennell, A. Hackmann, M. Mueller & D. Westbrook (eds.), *Oxford Guide to Behavioural Experiments in Cognitive Therapy*. New York: Oxford University Press, pp. 21–58.

Rourke, B.P., Young, G.C. & Leenaars, A.A. (1989). 'A childhood learning disability that predisposes those afflicted to adolescent and adult depression and suicide risk'. *Journal of Learning Disabilities*, 22: 169–75.

Russell, A.R., Schmidt, U., Doherty, L., Young, V., Tchanturia, K. (2009). 'Aspects of social cognition in anorexia nervosa: Affective and cognitive theory of mind'. *Psychiatry Research*, 168(3): 181–5.

Rutter, M., Baily, A., Simonoff, E. & Pickles, A. (1997). 'Genetic influences and autism'. In D.J. Cohen & F.R. Volkmar (eds.), *Handbook of Autism and Pervasive Developmental Disorders* (2nd edn). Wiley: New York, pp. 370–87.

Salovey, P. & Mayer, J.D. (1990). 'Emotional intelligence'. *Imagination, Cognition & Personality*, 9: 185–211.

Salovey, P., Hsee, C.K. & Mayer, J.D. (1993). 'Emotional intelligence and the self-regulation of affect'. In D.M. Wegner & J.W. Pennebaker (eds.), *Handbook of Mental Control*. Prentice Hall: Englewood Cliffs, NJ, pp. 258–77.

Schaffer, C.E. (1993). 'The role of adult attachment in the experience and regulation of affect'. Doctoral dissertation, Yale University.

Scheidt, C.E., Waller, E., Schnock, C., Becker-Stoll, F., Zimmerman, P., Lucking, C.H. & Wirsching, M. (1999). 'Alexithymia and attachment representation in idiopathic spasmodic torticollis'. *Journal of Nervous Mental Diseases*, 187: 47–52.

Schmidt, G.L., DeBuse, C.J. & Seger, C.A. (2007). 'Right hemisphere metaphor processing? Characterizing the lateralization of semantic processes'. *Brain and Language*, 100: 127–141.

Schmidt, U., Oldershaw, A., Jichi, F., Sternheim, L., Startup, H., McIntosh, V., Jordan, J., Tchanturia, K., Wolff, G., Rooney, M., Landau, S. & Treasure, J. (2012). 'Out-patient psychological therapies for adults with anorexia nervosa: randomised controlled trial'. *British Journal of Psychiatry*, 201(5): 392–9. DOI: 10.1192/bjp.bp.112078.

Schore, A.N. (1994). *Affect Regulation and the Origin of the Self: The Neurobiology of Emotional Development*. Erlbaum: Hillsdale, NJ.

Schore, A.N. (1996). 'The experience-dependent maturation of a regulatory system in the orbital prefrontal cortex and the origin of developmental psychopathology'. *Developmental Psychopathology*, 8: 59–87.

Schore, A.N. (2005). 'A neuro-psychoanalytic viewpoint: Commentary on Paper by Steven H. Knoblauch'. *Psychoanalytic Dialogues*, 15(6): 829–54.

Schore, A.N. (2011). 'The right brain implicit self lies at the core of psychoanalysis'. *Psychoanalytic Dialogues*, 21(1): 75–100.

Schore, A.N. (2012). *The Science of the Art of Psychotherapy*. New York: W.W. Norton.

Schore, A.N. (2017). 'The right brain implicit self: a central mechanism of the psychotherapy change process'. In G. Craparo & C. Mucci (eds.), *Unrepressed Unconscious, Implicit Memory, and Clinical Work*. London: Karnac, Chapter Four.

Schutte, N.S., Malouff, J.M., Hall, L.E., Haggerty, D.J., Cooper, J.T., Golden, C.J. & Dornheim, L. (1998). 'Development and validation of a measure of emotional intelligence'. *Personality & Individual Differences*, 25: 167–77.

Seeley, W.W., Menon, V., Schatzberg, A.F., Keller, J., Glover, G.H., Kenna, H. et al. (2007). 'Dissociable intrinsic connectivity networks for salience processing and executive control'. *Journal of Neuroscience*, 27: 2,349–56.

Segal, H. (1957). 'Notes on symbol formation'. *International Journal of Psychoanalysis*, 38: 391–7.

Shenker, I.R. & Bunnell, D.W. (1992). 'Bulimia nervosa'. In L. Barlow (ed.), *Textbook of Adolescent Medicine*. W. B. Saunders: Philadelphia, pp. 542–46.

Shiv, B., Loewenstein, G., Bechara, A., Damasio, H. & Damasio, A.R. (2005). 'Investment behavior and the negative side of emotion'. *Psychological Science*, 16: 435–9.

Shuren, J.E. & Grafman, J. (2002). 'The neurology of reasoning'. *Archives of Neurology*, 59: 916–19.

Siegel, D.J. (1999). *The Developing Mind: How Relationships and the Brain Interact to Shape Who We Are*. Guilford Press: New York.

Sifneos, P. E. (1973). 'The prevalence of "alexithymic" characteristics in psychosomatic patients'. *Psychotherapy & Psychosomatics*, 22: 255–62.

Skarderud, F. (2007). 'Eating one's words, part 1: "Concretised metaphors" and reflective function in anorexia—an interview study'. *European Eating Disorders Review*, 15: 163–74.

Smeets, M.A. & Kosslyn S.M. (2001). 'Hemispheric differences in body image in anorexia nervosa'. *International Journal of Eating Disorders*, 29: 409–16.

Sohn, L. (1985). 'Narcissistic organisation, projective identification and the formation of the identificate'. *International Journal of Psychoanalysis*, 66: 201–14.

Solms, M. & Turnbull, O. (2003). *The Brain and the Inner World*. Karnac: London.

Sotillo, M., Carreti, L., Hinojosa, J.A., Tapiab, M., Mercadod, F., Lopez Martın, S. & Albert, J. (2005). 'Neural activity associated with metaphor comprehension: spatial analysis'. *Neuroscience Letters*, 373: 5–9.

Spezzano, C. (1993). *Affect in sychoanalysis: A Clinical Synthesis*. Analytic Press: Hillsdale NJ.

Steen, G.J. (2007). *Finding Metaphor in Grammar and Usage: A Methodological Analysis of Theory and Research.* John Benjamins: Amsterdam and Philadelphia.

Steiger, H., Jabalpurwala, S., Gauvin, L., Seguin, J.R. & Stotland, S. (1999). 'Hypersensitivity to social interactions in bulimic syndromes: relationship to binge eating'. *Journal of Consulting Clinical Psychology*, 67: 765–75.

Stein, A., Stein, J., Walters, A. & Fairburn, C. (1995). 'Eating habits and attitudes among mothers of children with feeding disorders'. *British Medical Journal*, 310: 228.

Stein, A., Woolley, H., Murray, L., Cooper, P., Cooper, S., Noble, F., Affonso, N. & Fairburn, C.G. (2001). 'Influence of psychiatric disorder on the controlling behaviour of mothers with 1-year-old infants'. *British Journal of Psychiatry*, 179: 157–62.

Steinberg, B.E. & Shaw, R.J. (1997). 'Bulimia as a disturbance of narcissism: Self-esteem and the capacity to self-soothe'. *Addictive Behaviours*, 22: 699–710.

Steinglass, J.E. & Walsh, B.T. (2006). 'Habit learning and anorexia nervosa: a' cognitive neuroscience hypothesis'. *International Journal of Eating Disorders*, 39 (4): 267–75.

Stern, D. (1985). *The Interpersonal World of the Infant: A View from Psychoanalysis and Developmental Psychology.* Basic Books: New York.

Stice, E. (2002). 'Risk and maintenance factors for eating pathology: a meta-analytic review'. *Psychological Bulletin*, 128: 825–48.

Strasburger, V.C. & Brown, R.T. (1998). *Adolescent Medicine: A Practical Guide* (2nd edn). Lippincott-Raven: Philadelphia.

Strathearn, L., Fonagy, P., Amico, J. & Montague, P.R. (2009). 'Adult attachment predicts maternal brain and oxytocin response to infant cues'. *Neuropsychopharmacology*, 34(13): 2655–66.

Striegel-Moore, R.H. (1993). 'Etiology of binge-eating: A developmental perspective'. In C.G. Fairburn & G. T. Wilson (eds.), *Binge-eating: Nature, Assessment, and Treatment.* Guilford Press: New York, pp 144–72.

Strother, E., Lemberg, R., Stanford, S.C., & Turberville, D. (2012). 'Eating disorders in men: underdiagnosed, undertreated and misunderstood'. *Eating Disorders*, 20(5): 346–55.

Stuss, D.T. & Alexander M.P. (1999). 'Affectively burnt in: one role of the right frontal lobe?' In E. Tulving (ed.), *Memory, Consciousness, and the Brain: The Tallinn Conference.* Psychology Press: Philadelphia, pp. 215–227.

Szmukler, G.I., Andrewes, D., Kingston, K., Chen, L., Stargatt, R. & Stanley, R. (1992). 'Neuropsychological impairment in anorexia nervosa: before and after refeeding'. *Journal of Clinical & Experimental Neuropsychology*, 14: 347–52.

Taylor, G.J. (1987). *Psychosomatic Medicine and Contemporary Psychoanalysis.* International Universities Press: Madison, CT.

Taylor, G.J. (2000). 'Recent development in alexithymia theory and research'. *Canadian Journal of Psychiatry*, 45: 134–42.

Taylor, G.J. & Bagby, R.M. (1988). 'Measurement of alexithymia: recommendations for clinical practice and future research'. *Psychiatric Clinics of North America*, 11(3): 351–66.

Taylor, G.J., & Bagby, R.M. (2000). 'Overview of the alexithymia construct'. In R. Bar-On and J.D.A. Parker (eds.), *Handbook of Emotional Intelligence.* Jossey-Bass: San Francisco.

Taylor, G.J., Bagby, R.M. & Parker, J.D.A. (1997). *Disorders of Affect Regulation: Alexithymia in Medical and Psychiatric Illness.* Cambridge University Press: Cambridge.

Taylor, G.J., Parker, J.D.A. & Bagby, R.M. (1999). 'Emotional intelligence and the emotional brain: Points of convergence and implications for psychoanalysis'. *Journal of the American Academy of Psychoanalysis*, 27: 339–54.

Tchanturia, K., Doris, E., Mountford, V. & Fleming, C. (2015). 'Cognitive Remediation and Emotion Skills Training (CREST) for anorexia nervosa in individual format: self-reported outcomes'. *BMC Psychiatry*, 20: 15:53. DOI: 10.1186/s12888-015-0434-9.

Tchanturia, K., Giombini, L., Leppanen, J. & Kinnaird, E. (2017). 'Evidence for Cognitive Remediation Therapy in young people with anorexia nervosa: Systematic review and meta-analysis of the literature', *European Eating Disorders Review*, 25(4): 227–36.

Tchanturia, K., Morris, R., Surguladze, S. & Treasure, J. (2003). 'Perceptual and cognitive set shifting tasks in acute anorexia nervosa and following recovery'. *Eating & Weight Disorders*, 7(4): 312–16.

Teicher, M.H., Ito, Y., Glod, C.A., Schiffer, F. & Gelbard, H.A. (1996). 'Neurophysiological mechanisms of stress response in children'. In C.R. Pfeffer (ed.), *Severe Stress and Mental Disturbance in Children*. American Psychiatric Press: Washington, DC, pp. 59–84.

Thackwray, D.E., Smith, M.C., Bodfish, J. W. & Meyers, A.W. (1993). 'A comparison of behavioural and cognitive–behavioural interventions for bulimia nervosa'. *Journal of Consulting & Clinical Psychology*, 61: 639–45.

Toner, B.B., Garfinkel, P.E. & Garner, D.M. (1987). 'Cognitive style of patients with bulimic and diet-restricting anorexia nervosa'. *American Journal of Psychiatry*, 144: 510–12.

Treasure, J. & Schmidt, U. (2013). 'The cognitive-interpersonal maintenance model of anorexia nervosa revisited: a summary of the evidence for cognitive, socio-emotional and interpersonal predisposing and perpetuating factors'. *Journal of Eating Disorders*, 1:13. DOI: 10.1186/2050-2974-1-13.

Trevarthen, C. (1990). 'Signs before speech'. In T.A. Sebeok & J. Umiker-Sebeok (eds.), *The Semiotic Web*. Berlin: Mouton de Gruyter.

Turner, M. (1995). *The Literary Mind*. Oxford University Press: New York.

Uddin, L.Q. (2015). 'Salience processing and insular cortical function and dysfunction'. www.nature.com/nrn/journal/v16/n1/abs/nrn3857.html.

Van Lancker, D. & Cummings, J.L. (1999). Expletives: Neurolinguistic and neurobehavioral perspectives on swearing. *Brain Research. Brain Research Reviews*, 31(1): 83–104. DOI: 10.1016/S0165–0173(99)00060–0.

Vrticka, P., Andersson, F., Grandjean, D., Sander, D. & Vuilleumier, P. (2008). 'Individual attachment style modulates human amygdala and striatum activation during social appraisal'. *Public Library of Science*, 3: e2868.

Wade, T.D., Martin, N.G., Tiggerman, M., Abraham, S., Treloar, S. & Heath, A.C. (2000). 'Genetic and environmental risk factors shared between disordered eating, psychological and family variables'. *Personality & Individual Differences*, 28: 729–40.

Wagar, B.M. & Dixon, M. (2006). 'Affective guidance in the Iowa gambling tas'. *Cognitive & Behavioural Neuroscience*, 6: 277–90.

Waller, G., Watkins, H., Shuck, V. & McManus, F. (1996). 'Bulimic psychopathology and attentional biases to ego threats among non eating-disordered women'. *International Journal of Eating. Disorders*, 20: 169–76.

Waller, G., Cordery, H., Corstorphine, E., Hinrichsen, H., Lawson, R., Mountford, V. & Russell, K. (2007). *Cognitive Behaviour Therapy for the Eating Disorders: A Comprehensive Treatment Guide*. Cambridge University Press: Cambridge.

Wallin, U., Kronovall, P. & Majewski, M.L. (2000). 'Body awareness therapy in teenage anorexia nervosa: outcome after two years'. *European Eating Disorders Review*, 8: 19–30.

Walsh, B.T., Fairburn, C.G., Mickley, D., Sysko, R. & Parides, M.K. (2004). 'Treatment of bulimia nervosa in a primary care setting'. *American Journal of Psychiatry*, 161: 556–61.

Walsh, B.T., Hadigan, C.M., Devlin, M.J., Gladis, M. & Roose, S.P. (1991). 'Long-term outcome of antidepressant treatment for bulimia nervosa'. *Journal of Psychiatry*, 148: 1,206–12.

Walsh, B.T., Wilson, G.T., Loeb, K.L., Devlin, M.J., Pike, K.M., Roose, S.P., Fleiss, J. & Waternaux, C. (1997). 'Medication and psychotherapy in the treatment of bulimia nervosa'. *American Journal of Psychiatry*, 154: 523–31.

Ward, A., Troop, N., Todd, G. & Treasure, J.L. (1996). 'To change or not to change–'how' is the question. *British Journal of Medical Psychology*, 69: 139–46.

Watt, D.F. (1990). 'Higher cortical functions and the ego: Explorations of the boundary between behavioral neurology, neuropsychology, and psychoanalysis. *Psychoanalytic Psychology*, 7: 487–527.

Weltzin, T.E. (2005). 'Eating disorders in men: Update'. *Journal of Men's Health & Gender*, 2: 186–93.

Werner, H., & Kaplan, B. (1963). *Symbol Formation*. Wiley: New York.

Williams, G. (1997). *Internal Landscapes and Foreign Bodies: Eating Disorders and Other Pathologies*. Tavistock Clinic Series: London.

Wilson, G.T., Fairburn, C.C., Agras, W.S., Walsh, B.T. & Kraemer, H. (2002). 'Cognitive-behavioral therapy for bulimia nervosa: time course and mechanisms of change'. *Journal of Consulting and Clinical Psychology*, 70: 267–74.

Winner, E. & Gardner, H. (1977). 'The comprehension of metaphor in brain-damaged patients'. *Brain*, 100: 717–729.

Winnicott, D.W. (1960). 'The theory of the parent–infant relationship'. In *The Maturational Processes and the Facilitating Environment*. International Universities Press: New York, pp. 37–55.

Winnicott, D.W. (1967). 'Mirror role of mother and family in child development'. In *Playing and Reality*. Tavistock Clinic: London, pp. 111–18.

Winnicott, D.W. (1971). *Playing and Reality*. Routledge & Kegan Paul: London.

Winnicott, D.W. (1975). *Collected Papers. Through Paediatrics to Psychoanalysis*. Tavistock Clinic: London.

Witt, E.D., Ryan, C. & George, L.K. (1985). 'Learning deficits in adolescents with anorexia nervosa'. *Journal of Nervous and Mental Diseases*, 173: 182–4.

Wittling, W. & Roschmann, R. (1993). 'Emotion-related hemisphere asymmetry: Subjective emotional responses to laterally presented films'. *Cortex, 29*, 431–48.

Woodside, D.B. (1995). 'A review of anorexia nervosa and bulimia nervosa'. *Current Problems in Pediatrics*, 25: 67–89.

Wright, K. (1991). *Vision and Separation: Between Mother and Baby*. Jason Aronson: Northvale, New York.

Yovell, Y. (2000). 'From hysteria to post-traumatic stress disorder: Psychoanalysis and the neurobiology of traumatic memories'. *Journal of Neuropsychoanalysis*, 2: 171–81.

Zeitlin, S.B., Lane, R.D., O'Leary, D.S. & Schrift, M.J. (1989), 'Interhemispheric transfer deficit and alexithymia'. *American Journal of Psychiatry*, 146: 1,434–39.

Bibliography

This bibliography is a resource for those readers wanting an up-to-date (at the time of publication) guide to the evidence based research in the field of eating disorders.

Agras, S., Hammer, L. & McNicholas, F. (1999). 'A prospective study of the influence of eating-disordered mothers on their children'. *International Journal of Eating Disorders*, 25(3): 253–62.

Agras, W.S., Crow, S.J., Halmi, K.A., Mitchell, J.E., Wilson, G.T. & Kraemer, H.C. (2000). 'Outcome predictors for the cognitive behavior treatment of bulimia nervosa: Data from a multisite study'. *American Journal of Psychiatry*, 157(8): 1,302–1,308.

Agras, W.S., Walsh, B.T., Fairburn, C.G., Wilson, G.T. & Kraemer, H.C. (2000a). 'A multi-centre comparison of cognitive–behavioural therapy and interpersonal psychotherapy for bulimia nervosa'. *Archives of General Psychiatry*, 54: 459–465.

Agras, W.S., Schneider, J.A., Arnow, B., Raeburn, S.D. & Telch, C.F. (1989). 'Cognitive–behavioural and response-prevention treatments for bulimia nervosa'. *Journal of Consulting & Clinical Psychology*, 57: 215–221.

Agras, W.S., Telch, C.F., Arnow, B., Eldredge, K.L., Detzer, M.J., Henderson, J. & Marnell, M. (1995). 'Does interpersonal therapy help patients with binge eating disorder who fail to respond to cognitive–behavioural therapy?' *Journal of Consulting & Clinical Psychology*, 63: 356–360.

Beglin, S.J. & Fairburn, C.G. (1992). 'What is meant by the term "binge"?' *American Journal of Psychiatry*, 149(1): 123–4.

Bemis, K. (1987). 'The present status of operant conditioning for the treatment of anorexia nervosa'. *Behavior Modification*, 11: 432–64.

Berkman, N.D., Bulik, C.M., Brownley, K.A., Lohr, K.N., Sedway, J.A., Rooks, A. & Gartlehner, G. (2006). *Management of Eating Disorders. Evidence Report (MEDE)*. Prepared by the RTI International-University of North Carolina Evidence-Based Practice Center.

Braun, D.L., Sunday, S.R. & Halmi, K.A. (1994). 'Psychiatric co-morbidity in patients with eating disorders'. *Psychological Medicine*, 24: 859–67.

Brewerton, T.D.1., Lesem, M.D., Kennedy, A. & Garvey, W.T. (2000). 'Reduced plasma leptin concentrations in bulimia nervosa'. *Psychoneuroendocrinology*, 25(7): 649–58.

Bruch, H. (1962). 'Perceptual and conceptual disturbances in anorexia nervosa'. *Psychosomatic Medicine*, 24: 187–94.

Bulik, C.M., Sullivan, P.F., Wade, T. & Kendler, K.S. (2000). 'Twin studies of eating disorders: a review'. *International Journal of Eating Disorders*, 27: 1–20.

Bunnell, D.R., Shenker, I.R., Nussbaum, M.D., Jacobson, M.S. & Cooper, P. (1990). 'Subclinical versus formal eating disorders: Differentiating psychological features'. *International Journal of Eating Disorders*, 9: 357–362.

Carter, J. & Fairburn, C.C. (1998). 'Cognitive-behavioral self-help for binge eating disorder: a controlled effectiveness study'. *Journal of Consulting & Clinical Psychology*, 66: 616–23.

Carter, J., Olmsted, M., Kaplan, A.S., McCabe, R.E., Mills, J.S. & Aime, A. (2003). 'Self-help for bulimia nervosa: A randomised controlled trial'. *American Journal of Psychiatry*, 160: 973–978.

Channon, S., de Silva, P., Hemsley, D. & Perkins, R. (1989). 'A controlled trial of cognitive behavioural and behavioural treatment of anorexia nervosa'. *Behavioural Research & Therapy*, 27: 529–535.

Chen, E., Touyz, S.W., Beumont, P.J., Fairburn, C.G., Griffiths, R., Butow, P., Russell, J., Schotte, D. E., Gertler, R. & Basten, C. (2003). 'Comparison of group and individual cognitive–behavioral therapy for patients with bulimia nervosa'. *International Journal of Eating Disorders*, 33: 241–254.

Clinton, D.N. & Glant, R. (1992). 'The eating disorders spectrum of DSM-IIIR'. *Journal of Nervous & Mental Disease*, 180: 244–50.

Cochrane Review (2007). *Psychotherapy for Bulimia Nervosa and Bingeing and the Management of Eating Disorders Report*. RTI International–University of North Carolina Evidence-based Practice Center (EPC).

Collings, S. & King, M. (1994). 'Ten-year follow-up of 50 patients with bulimia nervosa'. *British Journal of Psychiatry*, 164(1): 80–7.

Cooper, P.J., Coker, S. & Fleming, C. (1996). 'An evaluation of the efficacy of supervised cognitive behavioural self-help bulimia nervosa'. *Journal of Psychosomatics Research.*, 40(3): 281–7.

Cooper, Z. & Fairburn, C.G. (1987). 'The eating disorder examination: A semi-structured interview for the assessment of the specific psychopathology of eating disorders'. *International Journal of Eating Disorders*, 6(1): 1–8.

Cooper, Z. & Fairburn, C.G. (2011). 'The evolution of "enhanced" cognitive behaviour therapy for eating disorders: Learning from treatment nonresponse'. *Cognitive and Behavioral Practice*. 18(3): 394–402.

Crisp, A.H., Norton, K., Gowers, S., Halek, C., Bowyer, C., Yeldham, D., Levett, G. & Bhat, A. (1991). 'A controlled study of the effect of therapies aimed at adolescent and family psychopathology in anorexia nervosa'. *British Journal of Psychiatry*, 59: 325–333.

Crow, S., Praus, B. & Thuras, P. (1999). 'Mortality from eating disorders – A 5–10-year record linkage study'. *International Journal of Eating Disorders*, 26: 97–101.

Dare, C. & Crowther, C. (1995). 'Living dangerously: Psychoanalytic psychotherapy of anorexia nervosa'. In G. Szmukler, C. Dare & J. Treasure (eds.), *Eating Disorders: Handbook of Theory, Treatment and Research*. Wileyons: Chichester.

Dare, C., Eisler, I., Russell, G., Treasure, J. & Dodge, L. (2001). 'Psychological therapies for adults with anorexia nervosa: randomised controlled trial of out-patient treatments'. *British Journal of Psychiatry*, 178: 216–21.

Dingemans, A.E., Bruna, M.J. & van Furth, E.F. (2002). 'Binge eating disorder: a review'. *International Journal of Obesity*, 26: 299–307.

Eisler, I., Dare, C., Hodes, M., Russell, G., Dodge, E. & Le Grange, D. (2000). 'Family therapy for adolescent anorexia nervosa: The results of a controlled comparison of two family interventions'. *Journal of Child Psychology & Psychiatry and Allied Disciplines*, 41: 727–36.

Eisler, I., Le Grange, D. & Asen, E. (2003). 'Family interventions'. In J. Treasure, U. Schmidt & E. Van Furth (eds.), *Handbook of Eating Disorders*. Wiley: Chichester.

Eldredge, K.L., Agras, W.S., Arnow, B., Telch, C.F., Bell, S., Castonguay, L. & Marnell, M. (1997). 'The effects of extending cognitive–behavioural therapy for binge eating disorder among initial treatment non-responders'. *International Journal of Eating Disorders*, 21: 347–52.

Fairburn, C.G. & Beglin, S.J. (1990). 'Studies of the epidemiology of bulimia nervosa'. *American Journal of Psychiatry*, 147(4): 401–8.

Fairburn, C.G. & Cooper, Z. (1993). 'The Eating Disorder Examination (twelfth edn)'. In C.G. Fairburn & G.T. Wilson (eds.), *Binge Eating: Nature, Assessment and Treatment*. Guilford Press: New York, pp. 317–60.

Fairburn, C.G. & Harrison, P.J. (2003). 'Eating disorders'. *The Lancet*, 361(9355): 407–16.

Fairburn, C.G., Cooper, Z., Doll, H.A., Norman P. & O'Connor M. (2000). 'The natural course of bulimia nervosa and binge eating disorder in young women'. *Archives of General Psychiatry*, 57: 659–65.

Freeman, C., Barry, F., Dunkeld-Turnbull, J. & Henderson (1988). 'Controlled trial of psychotherapy for bulimia nervosa'. *British Medical Journal*, 296: 521–25.

Garner, D.M., Rockert, W., Davis, R., Garner, M.V., Olmsted, M. & Eagle, M. (1993). 'Comparison of cognitive–behavioural and supportive–expressive therapy for bulimia nervosa'. *American Journal of Psychiatry*, 150: 37–46.

Geist, R.A., Heineman, M., Stephens, D., Davis, R. & Katzman, D.K. (2000). 'Comparison of family therapy and family group psychoeducation in adolescents with anorexia nervosa'. *Canadian Journal of Psychiatry – Revue Canadienne de Psychiatrie*, 45: 173–8.

Geller, J., Kim, A.U., Williams, D. & Srikameswaran, S. (2001). 'Clinician stance in the treatment of chronic eating disorders'. *European Eating Disorders Review*, 6: 365–73.

Geracioti, T.D. & Liddle, R.A. (1998). 'Impaired cholecystokinin secretion in bulimia nervosa'. *New England Journal of Medicine*, 319(11): 683–8.

Godart, N., Berthoz, S., Rein, Z., Perdereau, F., Lang, F., Venisse, J.L., Halfon, O., Bizouard, P., Loas, G., Corcos, M., Jeammet, P., Flament, M. & Curt, F. (2006). 'Does the frequency of anxiety and depressive disorders differ between diagnostic subtypes of anorexia nervosa and bulimia?' *International Journal of Eating Disorders*, 39(8): 772–8.

Goldbloom, D.S. & Kennedy, S.H. (1995). Medical complications of anorexia nervosa. In K.D. Brownell and C.G. Fairburn (eds.), *Eating Disorders and Obesity: A Comprehensive Handbook*. Guilford Press: New York.

Golden, N.H., Ashtari, M., Kohn, M.R., Patel, M., Jacobson, M.S., Fletcher, A. & Shenker, I.R. (1996). 'Reversibility of cerebral ventricular enlargement in anorexia nervosa, demonstrated by quantitative magnetic resonance imaging'. *Journal of Pediatrics*, 128: 296–301.

Goldstein, D.J., Wilson, M.G., Thomson, V.L., Potvin, J.H. & Rampey, A.H. (1995). 'Long-term fluoxetine treatment of bulimia nervosa'. *British Journal of Psychiatry*, 166: 660–6.

Gorin, A.A. (2001). 'A controlled trial of cognitive-behavioural therapy with and without spousal involvement for binge eating disorder'. *Dissertation Abstracts International: Section B: the Sciences & Engineering*, 61.

Griffiths, R.A., Hadzi-Pavlovic, D. & Channon-Little, L. (1994). 'A controlled evaluation of hypnobehavioural treatment for bulimia nervosa: Immediate pre- post treatment effects'. *European Eating Disorders Review*, 2: 202–20.

Haas, H.L., Clopton, J.R. (2003). 'Comparing clinical and research treatments for eating disorders'. *International Journal of Eating Disorders*, 33: 412–20.

Hall, A. & Crisp, A.H. (1987). 'Brief psychotherapy in the treatment of anorexia nervosa: outcome at one year'. *British Journal of Psychiatry*, 151: 185–91.

Hall, A. & Hay, P.J. (1991). 'Eating disorder patient referrals from a population region 1977–1986'. *Psychological Medicine*, 21: 697–701.

Happé, F.G.E. (1994). 'An advanced test of theory of mind: Understanding of story characters' thoughts and feelings by able autistic, mentally handicapped and normal children and adults'. *Journal of Autism and Developmental Disorders*, 24: 1–24.

Hawkins, R., & Clement, P. (1984). 'Binge-eating: Measurement problems and a conceptual model'. In R. Hawkins, W. Fremouw & P. Clement (eds.), *The Binge–Purge Syndrome: Diagnosis, Treatment and Research*. Springer-Verlag: New York, pp. 229–251.

Hay, P. (1998). 'The epidemiology of eating disorder behaviors: An Australian community-based survey'. *International Journal of Eating Disorders*, 23: 371–82.

Herzog, T. & Hartmann, A. (1997). 'Psychoanalytically oriented treatment of anorexia nervosa. Methodology-related critical review of the literature using meta-analysis methods'. *Psychotherapy & Psychosomatic Medical Psychology*, 47(9–10): 299–315.

Howlett, M., McClelland, L. & Crisp, A.H. (1995). 'The cost of the illness that defies'. *Postgraduate Medical Journal*, 71: 36–9.

Hsu, L.K., Rand, W., Sullivan, S., Liu, D.W., Mulliken, B., McDonagh, B. & Kaye, W.H. (2001). 'Cognitive therapy, nutritional therapy and their combination in the treatment of bulimia nervosa'. *Psychological Medicine*, 31: 871–879.

Jacobs-Pilipski, M.J., Wilfley, D.E., Crow, S.J., Walsh, B.T., Lilenfeld, L.R., Smith, R., West, D., Berkowitz, R.I., Hudson, J.I. & Fairburn, C.G. (2007). 'Placebo response in binge eating disorder'. *International Journal of Eating Disorders*, 40: 204–11.

Jansen, A., Van den Hout, M.A., De Loof, C., Zandbergen, J. & Griez, E. (1989). 'A case of bulimia successfully treated by cue exposure'. *Journal of Behaviour Therapy & Experimental Psychiatry*, 20(4): 327–32.

Jimerson, D.C. (2002). 'Leptin and the neurobiology of eating disorders'. *Journal of Laboratory & Clinical Medicine*. 139(2): 70–71.

Johnson, W.G., Jarrell, M.P., Chupurdia, K.M. & Williamson, D.A. (1994). 'Repeated binge/purge cycles in bulimia nervosa: Role of glucose and insulin'. *International Journal of Eating Disorders*, 15(4): 331–41.

Kanerva, R., Rissanen, A. & Sarna, S. (1994). 'Fluoxetine in the treatment of anxiety, depressive symptoms and eating-related symptoms in bulimia nervosa'. *Journal of Psychiatry*, 49: 237–242.

Kaplan, A.S. (2002). 'Psychological treatments for anorexia nervosa: A review of published studies and promising new directions'. *Canadian Journal of Psychiatry*, 47: 235–242.

Kaye, W.H., Nagata, T., Weltzin, T.E., Hsu, L.K., Sokol, M.S., McConaha, C., Plotnicov, K.H., Weise, J. & Deep, D. (2001). 'Double-blind placebo-controlled administration of fluoxetine in restricting and restricting-purging-type anorexia nervosa'. *Biological Psychiatry*, 49: 644–52.

Keel, P.K., Mitchell, J.E., Miller, K.B., Davis, T.L. & Crow, S.J. (1999). 'Long-term outcome of bulimia nervosa'. *Archives of General Psychiatry*, 56(1): 63–9.

Kinzl, J.F., Traweger, C., Trefalt, E., Mangweth, B. & Biebl, W. (1999a). Binge eating disorder in females: A population-based investigation'. *International Journal of Eating Disorders*, 25: 287–92.

Kirkley, B.G., Schneider, J.A. & Agras, W.S. (1985). 'Comparison of two group treatments for bulimia'. *Journal of Consulting Clinical Psychology*, 53(1): 43–8.

Kohn, M.R., Ashtari, M., Golden, N.H., Schebendach, J., Patel, M., Jacobson, M.S. & Shenker, I.R. (1997). 'Structural brain changes and malnutrition in anorexia nervosa'. *Annals of the New York Academy of Science*, 817: 398–9.

Krieg, J.C., Pirke, K.M., Lauer, C. & Backmund, H. (1988). 'Endocrine, metabolic and cranial computed tomographic findings in anorexia nervosa'. *Biological Psychiatry*, 23: 377–87.

Lacey, J.H. & Smith, G. (1987). 'Bulimia nervosa. The impact of pregnancy on mother and baby'. *British Journal of Psychiatry*, 150: 777–81.

Lageix, P. & Steiger, H. (1997). 'Eating disorders and borderline personality disorder'. *Santé mentale au Québec*, –XXII(1): 127–42.

Lambe, E.K., Katzman, D.K., Mikulis, D.J., Kennedy, S.H. & Zipursky, R.B. (1997). 'Cerebral gray matter volume deficits after weight recovery from anorexia nervosa'. *Archives of General Psychiatry*, 54: 537–42.

Lee, N.F. & Rush, A.J. (1986). 'Cognitive-behavioural group therapy for bulimia'. *International Journal of Eating Disorders*, 5: 599–615.

Le Grange, D., Eisler, I., Dare, C. & Russell, G. (1992). 'Evaluation of family treatments in adolescent anorexia nervosa: A pilot study'. *International Journal of Eating Disorders*, 12: 347–357.

Leibowitz, S.F. & Alexander, J.T. (1998). 'Hypothalamic serotonin in control of eating behaviour, meal size and body weight'. *Biological Psychiatry*, 44: 851–64.

Leitenberg, H., Rosen, J.C., Gross, J., Nudelman, S. & Vara, L.S. (1988). 'Exposure plus response prevention treatment of bulimia nervosa'. *Journal of Consulting & Clinical Psychology*, 56: 535–41.

Litt, I., Simmonds, B. & Haydel, F. (1994). 'Factors associated with eating disorder symptoms in a community sample of 6th and 7th grade girls'. *International Journal of Eating Disorders*, 15: 357–67.

Lock, J., Agras, W.S., Le Grange, D., Couturier, J., Safer, D., Bryson, S.W. (2013). 'Do end of treatment assessments predict outcome at follow-up in eating disorders?' *International Journal of Eating Disorders*. 46(8): 771–8.

Loeb, K.L., Wilson, G.T., Gilbert, J.S. & Labouvie, E. (2000). 'Guided and unguided self-help for binge eating'. *Behaviour Research & Therapy*, 38: 259–72.

Lucas, A.R., Melton, L.J. III, Crowson, C.S. & O'Fallon, W.M. (1999). 'Long-term fracture risk among women with anorexia nervosa: A population-based cohort study'. *Mayo Clinic Proceedings*, 74: 972–7.

McCann, U.D. & Agras, W.S. (1990). 'Successful treatment of non-purging bulimia nervosa with desipramine: A double-blind, placebo-controlled study'. *American Journal of Psychiatry*, 147: 1,509–13.

McIntosh, V.V., Jordan, J., Carter, F.A., Luty, S.E., McKenzie, J.M., Bulik, C.M., Frampton, C.M.A. & Joyce, P.R. (2005). 'Three psychotherapies for anorexia nervosa: A randomized controlled trial'. *American Journal of Psychiatry*, 162: 741–7.

Mitchell, J.E. (2001a). 'Efficacy of citalopram in anorexia nervosa: a pilot study'. *European Neuropsychopharmacology*, 12: 453–59.

Mitchell, J.E., De Zwaan, M. & Roerig, J.L. (2003). 'Drug therapy for patients with eating disorders'. *Current Drug Targets CNS Neurological Disorders*, 2(1): 17–29.

Mitchell, J.E., Pomeroy, C. & Adson, D. (1997). 'Managing medical complications'. In D. Garner & P. Garfinkel (eds.), *Handbook of Treatment for Eating Disorders* (2nd edn). Guilford Press: New York, pp. 383–93.

Mitchell, J.E., Pyle, R.L., Eckert, E.D., Hatsukami, D., Pomeroy, C. & Zimmerman, R. (1990). 'A comparison study of antidepressants and structured intensive group psychotherapy in the treatment of bulimia nervosa'. *Archives of General Psychiatry*, 47: 149–57.

Mitrany, E. (1992). 'Atypical eating disorders'. *Journal of Adolescent Health*, 13(5): 400–2.

Mond, M. (2013). 'Classification of bulimic-type eating disorders: from DSM-IV to DSM-5'. *Journal of Eating Disorders*, 1: 33. DOI: 10.1186/2050-2974-1-33.

Monteleone, P., Di Lieto, A., Tortorella, A., Longobardi, N. & Maj, M. (2000). 'Circulating leptin in patients with anorexia nervosa, bulimia nervosa or binge-eating disorder: relationship to body weight, eating patterns, psychopathology and endocrine changes'. *Psychiatry Research*, 94: 121–29.

Morgan, J.F., Lacey, J.H. & Sedgwick, P.M. (1999). 'Impact of pregnancy on bulimia nervosa'. *British Journal of Psychiatry*, 174: 135–40.

Mumford, D.B. & Whitehouse, A.M. (1998). 'Increased prevalence of bulimia nervosa among Asian schoolgirls'. *British Medical Journal*, 297: 718–719.

Mussell, M.P., Binford, R.B. & Fulkerson, J.A. (2000). 'Eating disorders: Summary of risk factors, prevention programming, and prevention research'. *Counselling Psychologist*, 28: 764–796.

National Institute for Clinical Excellence (NICE) Report into Eating Disorders (2004). The British Psychological Society and Gaskell National Institute for Clinical Excellence.

Nauta, H., Hospers, H., Kok, G. & Jansen, A. (2000). 'A comparison between a cognitive and a behavioral treatment for obese binge eaters and obese non-binge eaters'. *Behavior Therapy*, 31: 441–61.

Ordman, A.M. & Kirschenbaum, D.S. (1985). 'Cognitive–behavioral therapy for bulimia: An initial outcome study'. *Journal of Consulting Clinical Psychology*, 53(3): 305–13.

Palmer, R.L., Birchall, H., Damani, S. & Gatward, N. (2003). 'A dialectical behavior therapy program for people with an eating disorder and borderline personality disorder'. *International Journal of Eating Disorders*, 15: 430–8.

Pawluck, D.E. & Gorey, K.M. (1998). 'Secular trends in the incidence of anorexia nervosa: integrative review of population-based studies'. *International Journal of Eating Disorders*, 23(4): 347–52.

Pike, K.M., Walsh, B.T. & Vitousek, K. (2003). 'Cognitive behavior therapy in the post hospitalization treatment of anorexia nervosa'. *American Journal of Psychiatry*, 160: 2,046–49.

Pope, H.G. Jr. & Hudson, J.I. (1982). 'Treatment of bulimia nervosa with antidepressants'. *Psychopharmacology*, 78, 176–9.

Pope, H.G., Hudson, J.I., Jonas, J.M. & Yurgelum-Todd, D. (1983). 'Bulimia treated with imipramine: A placebo-controlled, double-blind study'. *American Journal of Psychiatry*, 140, 554–8.

Raymond, L. & Phillips, J. (1989). 'The impact of pregnancy on anorexia nervosa and bulimia'. *International Journal of Eating Disorders*, 8(3): 285–95.

Reeves, R.S., McPherson, R.S., Nichaman, M.Z., Harrist, R.B., Foreyt, J.P. & Goodrick, G.K. (2001). 'Nutrient intake of obese female binge eaters'. *Journal of the American Dietetic Association*, 101: 209–15.

Ricca, V., Mannucci, E., Mezzani, B., Di Bernardo, M., Zucchi, T., Paionni, A., Placidi, G.P., Rotella, C.M. & Faravelli, C. (2001). 'Psychopathological and clinical features of outpatients with an eating disorder not otherwise specified'. *Eating and Weight Disorders*, 6: 157–65.

Robin, A.L., Siegel, P.T., Moye, A.W., Gilroy, M., Dennis, A.B. & Sikand, A. (1999). 'A controlled comparison of family versus individual therapy for adolescents with anorexia nervosa'. *American Academy of Child & Adolescent Psychiatry*, 38: 1,482–9.

Rosen, J. C. & Leitenberg, H. (1982). 'Bulimia nervosa: treatment with exposure and response prevention'. *Behaviour Therapy*, 13: 117–24.

Rosen, J. C., Leitenberg, H., Fisher, C. & Khazam, C. (1986). 'Binge-eating episodes in bulimia nervosa: The amount and type of food consumed'. *International Journal of Eating Disorders*, 5(2): 255–67.

Rosenvinge, J.H., Martinussen, M. & Ostensen, E. (2000). 'The co-morbidity of eating disorders and personality disorders: A meta-analytic review of studies published between 1983 and 1998'. *Eating & Weight Disorders*, 5(2): 52–61.

Rossiter, E.M. & Agras, W.S. (1990). 'An empirical test of DSM III-R definition of binge'. *International Journal of Eating Disorders*, 9: 513–18.

Rossiter, E.M., Agras, W.S., Telch, C.F. & Bruce, B. (1992). 'The eating patterns of non-purging bulimic subjects'. *International Journal of Eating Disorders*, 11: 111–20.

Russell, G.F., Szmukler, G.I., Dare, C. & Eisler, I. (1987). 'An evaluation of family therapy in anorexia nervosa and bulimia nervosa'. *Archives of General Psychiatry*, 44: 1,047–56.

Russell, G. (1979). 'Bulimia nervosa: an ominous variant of anorexia'. *Psychological Medicine*, 9: 429–48.

Safer, D.L., Telch, C.F. & Agras, W.S. (2001). 'Dialectical behaviour therapy for bulimia nervosa'. *American Journal of Psychiatry*, 158: 632–34.

Schmidt, U. & Marks, I. (1989). 'Exposure and prevention of binges versus exposure plus prevention of vomiting. A crossover study'. *Journal of Nervous Diseases*, 177: 259–66.

Schmidt, U. & Treasure, J. (1996). *Clinician's Guide to Getting Better Bit(e) by Bit(e). A Survival Kit for Sufferers of Bulimia Nervosa and Binge Eating Disorders.* Psychology Press: Hove.

Schmidt, U., Jiwany, A. & Treasure, J. (1993). 'A controlled study of alexithymia in eating disorders'. *Comprehensive Psychiatry*, 34: 54–8.

Schmidt, U., Tiller, J., Blanchard, M., Andrews, B. & Treasure, J. (1997). 'Is there a specific trauma precipitating anorexia nervosa?' *Psychological Medicine*, 27: 523–30.

Serfaty, M.A., Turkington, D., Heap, M., Ledsham, L. & Jolley, E. (1999). 'Cognitive therapy versus dietary counselling in the outpatient treatment of anorexia nervosa: Effects of the treatment phase'. *European Eating Disorders Review*, 7: 334–50.

Shoebridge, P. & Gowers, S.G. (2000). 'Parental high concern and adolescent-onset anorexia nervosa. A case-control study to investigate direction of causality'. *British Journal of Psychiatry*, 176: 132–7.

Sinha, R. & O'Malley, S. (2000). Alcohol and eating disorders: implications for alcohol treatment and health services research. *Alcoholism: Clinical & Experimental Research*, 24(8): 1,312–19.

Smith, K.A., Fairburn, C.G. & Cowen, P.J. (1999). 'Symptomatic relapse in bulimia nervosa following acute tryptophan depletion'. *Archives of General Psychiatry*, 56: 171–6.

Stein, A. & Fairburn, C.G. (1989). 'The children of mothers with bulimia nervosa'. *British Medical Journal*, 299: 777–8.

Stein, A., Woolley, H., Cooper, S.D. & Fairburn, C.G. (1994). 'An observational study of mothers with eating disorders and their infants'. *Journal of Child Psychology & Psychiatry*, 35(4): 733–48.

Steinhausen, H. (2002). 'The outcome of anorexia nervosa in the 20th century'. *American Journal of Psychiatry*, 159: 1,284–93.

Steinhausen, H., Winkler, C. & Meier, M. (1997). 'Eating disorders in adolescence in a Swiss epidemiological study'. *International Journal of Eating Disorders*, 22: 147–51.

Stice, E. & Agras, W.S. (1998). 'Predicting onset and cessation of bulimic behaviors during adolescence: A longitudinal grouping analysis'. *Behavior Therapy*, 29: 257–76.

Stice, E., Hayward, C., Cameron, R., Killen, J.D. & Taylor, C.B. (2000). 'Body-image and eating disturbances predict onset of depression in female adolescents: a longitudinal study'. *Journal of Abnormal Psychology*, 109: 438–44.

Striegel-Moore, R.H., Silberstein, L.R. & Rodin, J. (1986). 'Toward an understanding of risk factors for bulimia'. *American Psychologist*, 41(3): 246–63.

Striegel-Moore R.H., Wilfley D.E., Pike K.M., Dohm, F. & Fairburn, C.G. (2000). 'Recurrent binge eating in black American women'. *Archives of Family Medicine*, 9(1): 83–7.

Strober, M., Freeman, R. & Morrel, W. (1997). 'The long-term course of severe anorexia nervosa in adolescents: survival analysis of recovery, relapse and outcome predictors over 10–15 years in a prospective study'. *International Journal of Eating Disorders*, 22: 339–60.

Sundgot-Borgen, J., Rosenvinge, J.H., Bahr, R. & Schneider, L.S. (2002). 'The effect of exercise, cognitive therapy and nutritional counseling in treating bulimia nervosa'. *Medicine & Science in Sports & Exercise*, 34: 190–5.

Swayze, V.W., Andersen, A., Arndt, S., Rajarethinam, R., Fleming, F., Sato, Y. & Andreasen, N.C. (1996). 'Reversibility of brain tissue loss in anorexia nervosa assessed with a computerized Talairach 3-D proportional grid'. *Psychological Medicine*, 26: 381–90.

Swinbourne, J.M. & Touyz, S.W. (2007). 'The co-morbidity of eating disorders and anxiety disorders: a review'. *European Eating Disorders Review*, 15(4): 253–74.

Tanaka, M., Naruo, T. & Tetsuro, M. (2002). 'Increased fasting plasma ghrelin levels in patients with bulimia nervosa'. *European Journal of Endocrinology*, 146: R1–R3.

Taylor, A.V., Peveler, R.C., Hibbert, G.A. & Fairburn, C.G. (1993). 'Eating disorders among women receiving treatment for an alcohol problem'. *International Journal of Eating Disorders*, 14: 147–51.

Tchanturia, K. (2005). 'Cognitive remediation therapy as an intervention for acute anorexia nervosa; a case report'. *European Revue of Eating Disorder*, 13: 311–16.

Tchanturia, K., Liao, P.C., Uher, R., Lawrence, N., Treasure, J. & Campbell, I.C. (2007). 'An investigation of decision making in anorexia nervosa using the Iowa Gambling Task and skin conductance measurements'. *Journal of the International Neuropsychological Society*, 13(4): 635–41.

Tchanturia, K., Serpell, L., Troop, N. & Treasure, J. (2001). 'Perceptual illusions in eating disorders: rigid and fluctuating styles'. *Journal of Behavior Therapy & Experimental Psychiatry*, 32: 107–15.

Telch, C.F., Agras, W.S. & Linehan, M.M. (2000). 'Group dialectical behavior therapy for binge-eating disorder: A preliminary, uncontrolled trial'. *Behavior Therapy*, 31: 569–82.

Telch, C.F., Agras, W.S. & Linehan, M.M. (2001). 'Dialectical behaviour therapy for binge eating disorder'. *Journal of Consulting & Clinical Psychology*, 69: 1,061–65.

Telch, C.F., Agras, W.S., Rossiter, E.M., Wilfley, D. & Kenardy J. (1990). 'Group cognitive behavioural treatment for the non-purging bulimic: an initial evaluation'. *Journal of Consulting & Clinical Psychology*, 58(5): 629–35.

Tozzi, F., Sullivan, P., Fear, J., McKenzie, J., & Bulik, C. (2003). 'Causes and recovery in anorexia nervosa: the patient's perspective'. *International Journal of Eating Disorders*, 33: 143–54.

Treasure, J.L. & Ward, A. (1997). 'A practical guide to the use of motivational interviewing in anorexia nervosa'. *European Eating Disorders Review*, 5: 102–14.

Treasure, J.L., Schmidt, U., Troop, N., Tiller, J., Todd, G. & Turnbull, S. (1996). 'Sequential treatment for bulimia nervosa incorporating a self-care manual'. *British Journal of Psychiatry*, 168: 84–98.

Treasure, J.L., Schmidt, U., Troop, N., Tiller, J., Todd, G., Keilen, M. & Dodge, E. (1994). 'First step in managing bulimia nervosa: controlled trial of a therapeutic manual'. *British Medical Journal*, 308: 686–9.

Treasure, J.L., Todd, G., Brolly, M., Tiller, J., Nehmed, A. & Denman, F. (1995). 'A pilot study of a randomised trial of cognitive analytical therapy vs educational behavioural therapy for adult anorexia nervosa'. *Behavioural Research & Therapy*, 33: 363–7.

Turner, H. & Bryant-Waugh, R. (2004). 'Eating disorder not otherwise specified (EDNOS): profiles of clients presenting at a community eating disorders service'. *European Eating Disorders Review*, 12: 18–26.

Vandereycken, W. & Pierloot, R. (1983). Drop-out during in-patient treatment of anorexia nervosa. *British Journal of Medical Psychology*, 56: 145–56.

Vitousek, K.M., Watson, S. & Wilson, G.T. (1998). 'Enhancing motivation for change in treatment resistant eating disorders'. *Clinical Psychology Review*, 18: 391–420.

Vogeltanz-Holm, N., Wonderlich, S.A. & Lewis, B. (2000). 'Longitudinal predictors of binge eating, intense dieting and weight concerns in a national sample of women'. *Behaviour Therapy*, 31: 221–35.

Ward, A., Tiller, J., Treasure, J. & Russell, G. (2000). 'Eating disorders: psyche or soma?' *International Journal of Eating Disorders*, 27: 279–87.

Waugh, E. & Bulik, C. M. (1999). 'Offspring of women with eating disorders'. *International Journal of Eating Disorders*, 25: 123–33.

Welch, S.L., Doll, H.A. & Fairburn, C.G. (1997). 'Life events and the onset of bulimia nervosa: a controlled study'. *Psychological Medicine*, 27: 515–22.

Weltzin, T.E., Fernstrom, M.H., Fernstrom, J.D., Neuberger, S.K. & Kaye, W.H. (1995). 'Acute tryptophan depletion and increased food intake and irritability in bulimia nervosa'. *American Journal of Psychiatry*, 152: 1,668–71.

Wilfley, D.E. (2002). 'Psychological treatment of binge eating disorder'. In C.G. Fairburn & K.D. Brownell (eds.), *Eating Disorders and Obesity: A Comprehensive Handbook* (2nd edn). Guilford Press: New York, pp. 350–53.

Wilfley, D.E., Agras, W.S., Telch, C.F., Rossiter, E.M., Schneider, J.A., Cole, A.G., Sifford, L.A. & Raeburn, S.D. (1993). 'Group cognitive behavioral and group interpersonal psychotherapy for the nonpurging bulimic individual: a controlled comparison'. *Journal of Consulting and Clinical Psychology*, 61: 296–305.

Wilson, G.T., Eldredge, K.L., Smith, D. & Niles, B. (1991). 'Cognitive-behavioral treatment with and without response prevention for bulimia'. *Behaviour Research and Therapy*, 29: 575–83.

Wilson, G.T., Rossiter, E., Kleifield, E.I. & Lindholm, L. (1986). 'Cognitive–behavioral treatment of bulimia nervosa: a controlled comparison'. *Behaviour Research and Therapy*, 24: 277–88.

Wiseman, M.A. & Matt, G.E. (2002). 'A randomized comparison of group cognitive-behavioral therapy and group interpersonal psychotherapy for the treatment of overweight individuals with binge-eating disorder'. *Archives of General Psychiatry*, 25: 713–21.

Wiser, S. & Telch, C. (1999). 'Dialectical behavior therapy for binge-eating disorder'. *Journal of Clinical Psychology*, 55: 755–68.

Wolf, E.M. & Crowther, J.H. (1992). 'An evaluation of behavioral and cognitive-behavioral group interventions for the treatment of bulimia nervosa in women'. *International Journal of Eating Disorders*, 11: 3–15.

Wonderlich, S., Fullerton, D., Swift, W.J. & Klein, M.J. (1994). 'Five-year outcome from eating disorders: relevance of personality disorders'. *International Journal of Eating Disorders*, 15, 233–43.

Woodside, D.B. (2005). 'Commentary: Treatment of anorexia nervosa: more questions than answers'. *International Journal of Eating Disorders*, 37: S41–S42.

Woodside, D.B., Shekter-Wolfson, L., Brandes, J. & Lackstrom, J.B. (1993). *Eating Disorders and Marriage: The Couple in Focus*. Brunner/Mazel: New York.

Woodside, D.B., Shekter-Wolfson, L., Garfinkel, P.E., Olmsted, M.P. (1995). 'Family interactions in bulimia nervosa I: Study design, comparisons to established population norms, and changes over the course of an intensive day hospital treatment program'. *International Journal of Eating Disorders*, 17(2): 105–15.

Yates, A.J. & Sambrailo, F. (1984). 'Bulimia nervosa: a descriptive and therapeutic study'. *Behaviour Research & Therapy*, 22: 503–17.

Index